D0891880

Pawnee Passage: 1870–1875

The Civilization of the American Indian Series

Pawnee Passage: 1870–1875

By Martha Royce Blaine

University of Oklahoma Press : Norman and London

By Martha Royce Blaine

The Ioway Indians (Norman, 1979)
The Pawnees: A Critical Bibliography (Bloomington, Indiana, 1981)
Pawnee Passage: 1870–1875 (Norman, 1990)

Publication of this volume has been made possible in part through the generous support of Edith Gaylord Harper.

Library of Congress Cataloging-in-Publication Data
Blaine, Martha Royce, 1923–
    Pawnee Passage, 1870–1875 / by Martha Royce Blaine. — 1st ed.
        p.   cm. — (The Civilization of the American Indian
    series ; v. 202)
        Includes bibliographical references and index.
        ISBN 0–8061–2300–1 (alk. paper)
        1. Pawnee Indians—History—19th century.   2. Pawnee
    Indians—Government relations.   3. Pawnee Indians—Social
    conditions.   4. Nebraska—History—19th century.
    I. Title.   II. Series.
    E99.P3B57   1990
    973'.04975—dc20   90–50228

Pawnee Passage: 1870–1875 is Volume 202 in The Civilization of the American Indian Series.

For Garland James Blaine,
Tirawahut we-si-ta-wa,
From the Heavens Two Eagles Come Flying,
Who told me much of what is written here about his people,
And for my kinsmen and friends, the Pawnee people.

Contents

Illustrations

Maps

Tables

Preface

The Pawnees lived for centuries on the central Nebraska and Kansas plains in large earthlodge villages located along water courses, surrounded by their fields of corn, beans, squash, and other plants. They had highly organized and interrelated religious, economic, political, and social systems. This book is an effort to widen the view of the Pawnees during the years 1870–75, by adding to existing evidence in archives and to other printed sources original selections from Pawnee oral history containing views of events of that time. It is hoped that the inclusion of primary source material supplied by Pawnee speakers and descendants of people who lived during those years will add a dimension and understanding of those times that will enrich, broaden, and sometimes modify the perspectives expressed in documentary and published sources.

During the period that marked the end of the Pawnee years in Nebraska, the tribe lived on a reservation, a small part of the vast country they had once claimed and used. The Pawnees called these last days the *we-tuks* years, the frightful years, when life under U.S. government control was constrained and difficult, and hunger and outsiders' hostility and clamor to remove the Pawnees and take over their lands filled their days. It was also a time when the tribe tried to adhere to its beliefs about how their world should be and to follow the traditions that had made the Pawnees a successful people.

My husband, the late Garland J. Blaine, whose grandparents were a helpful source for the musicologist, Frances Densmore, and the anthropologist, Gene Weltfish, carried a sense of responsibility to preserve and add to existing knowledge, and in some cases to correct misinformation, about Pawnee beliefs and experiences. Over the years many sought him out for his obvious depth of information and language ability. This book, conveying his words, will add to the knowledge he has already shared.

This work is not intended to be a Pawnee culture study. There is sufficient cultural background given for each topic discussed to aid the reader in understanding the situation from the Pawnee standpoint as U.S. government officials, operating under Indian Office policy and rules, endeavored to change and control the Pawnee way of life. There are several sources for those wishing to learn about Pawnee culture, although none of them are complete. The book's bibliography contains work by Gene Weltfish, John B. Dunbar, James R. Murie, George B. Grinnell, and others. Blaine's *Critical Bibliography of the Pawnees* gives sources for both culture and history.

There are some who may object to the use of *Sioux* rather than *Lakota, Dakota,* or other linguistically correct terms for that people and their language. I preferred the term *Sioux* because the documents used here contained the term, and the Pawnees now call them that, rather than the opprobrious term formerly used when the two groups were implacable enemies in the last century.

The same is true for the band name, *Skiri,* which is linguistically correct while *Skidi* is not, because the Pawnee language has no *d* sound. This usage grew as nonspeakers heard and wrote down Pawnee names in the past. Hence, the documents and printed sources used in this work never contain the word *Skiri,* but instead *Skidi* is used. The Skidis call themselves by that name now, so I, as a relative by marriage, use that term also.

It is acknowledged by the author that in the Pawnee accounts in the text, the Pawnee language is not always written according to linguistic standards. The Pawnee names and words written by Garland J. Blaine and others were written down as they sounded to them.

MARTHA ROYCE BLAINE

Oklahoma City and Pawnee, Oklahoma

Acknowledgments

My husband, Garland James Blaine, is silent now. But in the years before his death in 1979, he talked and I wrote down or tape recorded many accounts of his family, his Pitahawirata Band, and his narrative of Pawnee history and ways of life. He was reared by his grandparents, Wichita and Effie Blaine, who were born in Nebraska and spoke no English, nor did he until he was twelve. He learned the ways of his people and how to become a chief as were his people before him in his mother's (Skidi) and father's (Pitahawirata) bands. To him must be offered the greatest gratitude because without his insight and extensive knowledge, there would not be a widened view of Pawnee history and culture contained in his words in this book.

Pawnee relatives and friends from other bands also contributed accounts of the Chaui, Kitkahahki, and Skidi past, told by their parents and grandparents. Appreciation for the time they spent with Garland and me over the years is offered here.

For many years encouragement came from my friends, Waldo R. and Mildred Mott Wedel, Angie Debo, and Rella Looney, head archivist and my predecessor at the Indian Archives and Manuscripts Division of the Oklahoma Historical Society, as well as other staff members there. It also came from my three children, Ann, Deirdre, and Michael.

Thanks are also due to Christie K. Stanley, Manuscripts Department, Kansas State Historical Society; John R. Lovett, Photographic Archives, Western History Collection, University of Oklahoma; and the Nebraska State Historical Society staff. Dr. Ralph E. Venk, president of the American Society of Photographers, photographed objects from my collection and made copies of photographs from the Hastings Nebraska Museum. From his extensive research collection of names of early Indian and Oklahoma Territory professional photographers, Chester Cowen identified Pawnee and other nearby town photographic sources for me.

To all of the above, I say with appreciation, this work would not have been completed without your help. *Ra wa.*

M. R. B.

Pawnee Passage: 1870–1875

✝✝✝

1

Surrounded by Strangers

The Difficult Time

The Pawnees always said that they were anxious to be at peace with the whites because they were at war with so many different Indian tribes they would have no place to go if they were at war with the whites.
—Capt. Luther H. North

It was inevitable. As more and more white settlers moved wagon-loads of belongings, families, and animals into the rich lands of Nebraska to establish farms and communities, the U.S. political entity, first called a territory, would in a short time become a state. At this point, protest against the presence of the Indian tribes began, first as talk, then in the form of petitions, and eventually as strong resolutions drawn by the Nebraska legislature demanding the confinement, and finally the removal, of the native population from Nebraska. The state's resident Indian tribes were the Pawnees, Santees, Poncas, Otoes, Missourias, Ioways, Omahas, and Winnebagoes.

Pressure for removal began as early as February 12, 1867. At that time the territorial legislature memorialized the U.S. Congress, declaring that the small Otoe and Missouria tribes should be removed. Their reservation, which lay in the southern part of the fertile lands of Gage County, had been created in 1854, after the tribes' cession of a larger area. The memorial claimed that the tribes were not cultivating the land and that there was not enough game to maintain them. Therefore, it reasoned, the Indi-

3

Pawnee Indian earthlodge, 1886. Photo by W. S. Prettyman. Pawnee extended family groups lived in earthlodge villages surrounded by their fields of corns, beans and other crops. These structures were supported by large inner pillars. They were built with a framework of saplings covered with sod slabs. Entryways projected from the front and usually faced east. When the Pawnees left Nebraska, they built some earthlodges on their Indian Territory reservation. Courtesy of Archives and Manuscripts Division of the Oklahoma Historical Society.

ans should leave and be placed with some other tribe whose "reservation lies further in the interior" (not in Nebraska Territory).[1]

There were, however, dissenters who objected to Indian removal. In June 1869, Charles Little and James B. Chase, of Fremont, Nebraska, representing the state's General Congregationalist Association of Nebraska, sent a letter to Pres. Ulysses S. Grant, asking him to disregard all requests or arguments for Indian removal from the state based on "selfish territorial or financial or political reasons." The two men said they supported Grant in his new program for "civilizing" the Indians (provided it also had support of the military). They promised their churches' cooperation to evangelize and "civilize" the nation's wards.[2] Perhaps more than interest in the Indians' welfare was evident here, when it became known that the President sought religious groups' cooperation in his efforts to rectify Indian Service abuses.

But few such voices were heard. David Butler, first governor of Nebraska in the late 1860s and early 1870s, reflected negative attitudes at local and state levels in his messages to the state legislature, and in other public comments regarding the state's Indians as he asked for consideration of Indian removal.

On March 2, 1870, the legislature claimed in a memorial that the land the Indians lived on was valuable and could not be developed or improved as long as the Indians occupied it. Such land should be allowed to pass into the hands of enterprising and industrious citizens. "We deny the so-called original rights of the aborigine to the soil," the writers stated. The memorial encouraged the state's U.S. congressional representatives to make efforts to abolish Indian title to the public domain and to see to the removal of all reservation Indians. It said that the tribes should be taken to "more congenial and advantageous localities where their presence will not retard settlement by the whites."[3]

Supt. Samuel Janney of the Northern Superintendency that had jurisdiction over the Pawnee and other regional agencies under the Commissioner of Indian Affairs in Washington watched all this activity with interest, reporting to Com. of Indian Affairs Ely Parker that "the politicians in Nebraska do not favor Presidential policy which has deprived them of large profits formerly obtained from the Indian agencies and from contracts for building and [Indian] subsistence."[4]

In 1872, there was a strong anti-Indian response among Nebraskans against the proposed removal to Nebraska of the Wisconsin Winnebagoes. Supt. Barclay White, who had replaced Janney, reported that such widespread agitation was injurious to Indians who were already residents of the state, because public opinion would form against all of them. This was true and on February 26, 1873, another legislative memorial urging Indian removal was sent to Washington.

At this point, the Pawnees had become a center of attention. It was known that certain tribes, including the Pawnees, had the right by treaty to journey to hunt on the Republican River in southwestern Nebraska. Although the Indians were always escorted by white men, it was claimed that as the tribe passed through the state for two hundred miles, they were "lawless in their conduct and indecent in their dress." The Pawnees were a nuisance to the settlements they passed, where they went from door to door begging and frightening the inhabitants. Such behavior would discourage the growth of the state and would lead to war and bloodshed between "these lawless bands of Indians" and the discomfited settlers.[5]

At this time several new counties were being formed and promoted by the state's Board of Immigration. The Pawnees en route to their Republican River hunting ground were mentioned as a menace because they passed through newly formed Frontier and Red Willow counties.[6]

Gov. Robert Wilkinson Furnas, who had once been an Omaha and Winnebago Indian agent, now complained to White that Indians who were off their reservations were detrimental to the state's development and should be confined to their reservations. He had received complaints of depredations committed by them at these times.[7] To this White replied firmly that he had received no complaints, and if there were any he would like to hear about them. Furnas answered that the complaints were against Indians going on their hunts and journeying across the state to get to their hunting grounds. White reminded Furnas that each tribe was accompanied by a white man who was in charge and insured that no trespass or depredations would occur. This had been done to prevent such criticism, he added.[8]

In August 1873, some state newspapers sounded the alarm, reporting that the Pawnees would be going on the warpath against the Sioux in retaliation for a Sioux massacre of a Pawnee hunting party near the Republican River earlier in the month. This report was printed in spite of the fact that the Pawnees' agent said that no apparent preparations for war were evident and that the Pawnee chiefs had said in council that they would not take any hostile action and would await the government's aid in obtaining reparation for their losses in horses, hides, meat, and hunting equipment.

In a continuing barrage, however, Furnas declared, "Our people do not recognize the legal authority of even the Indian Department to grant special orders or otherwise permit Indians to frequent or sojourn for any purpose in any organized or settled portion of this State. . . . Their presence within the borders of our state on legally designated reservations is detrimental to our interest, development and progress." As a final shot, he added that he was in direct communication with the President on the subject.[9]

The contrasting attitude of the Nebraska white population to conditions that were difficult for both Indians and settlers was illustrated in the events of 1873. Rocky mountain locusts, or grasshoppers, invaded the state in sky-blackening swarms, devastating all vegetation in their path, including crops planted by whites and Indians. In six western Nebraska counties insects devastated the crops. Soon a Nebraska Relief and Aid Society was organized, with Gen. Edward O. C. Ord elected chairman. A cash amount of $37,280 was raised, and $30,000 in goods donated. But the relief effort focused on the homesteaders. The railroad transported these items without cost. The War Department gave a large supply of clothing. Congress made an appropriation of $30,000 to purchase seed grain and extended time of payment to delinquent homesteaders. The state legislature passed an act authorizing issue of bonds so that $50,000 could be expended on more seed grain. Governor Furnas proclaimed that the state had an obligation to these settlers, who for the most part were Civil War veterans.[10] Pity and assistance were given to these non-Indian unfortunates who had fought for their country—but not to those Indians who had given their lands to them and now faced starvation on reservations also devastated by grasshoppers. No public outcry was heard for hungry Indians begging for food in the white settlements and indecently dressed because they did not have enough to wear.

The anti-Indian campaign continued in 1874 in a bill introduced in Congress that would allow white citizens to carry guns for protection against the Nebraska Indians. Newspapers continued their assertions that great danger existed for citizen life and property.[11] The hand of U.S. Sen. P. W. Hitchcock was evident from time to time, pressing for removal of the state's Indian population. In March 1874, he wrote to the commissioner of Indian Affairs. He wanted to know which tribes had consented to sell their land and for how much, as well as what appraisals had been made and what the average appraised value of such lands was.[12] The next year, he was a leading proponent of the bill supporting Pawnee removal and sale of their lands. At the same time, he also wanted to have the Otoes removed with the Pawnees, thus freeing more Nebraska land for settlement and development.[13]

Problems Off the Reservation and Intruders on It

In the early 1870s, Pawnee who left the reservation were liable to encounter hostility, such as that Governor Furnas alluded to. Agent Jacob Troth began to believe the time had come to confine the Pawnees to the reservation as the only way to prevent them from suffering injustice outside of it, particularly if they were accused unjustly of crimes. At this time, cases for crimes committed off the reservation were under the jurisdiction of the court of the county in which the offense had been committed. In Troth's experience with such county court proceedings, those involved in this system were often prejudiced and obtaining justice for Indians was "simply impossible."[14]

Antagonism against the Pawnees increased. One example involved U.S. Army Pawnee Scouts who guarded railroad crews from hostile Indian attacks during construction of the Union Pacific railway line. For this service, the company issued passes to the Pawnees to ride free on the tops of the railcars to such places as Fremont, Columbus, and Omaha to trade or visit. Riding the railroad cars to these places was a big event looked forward to by Pawnees, who were bored with the inactivity of reservation life.[15]

All went well until the mayor of Omaha complained to the Pawnee agent that large numbers of Indians were on the streets not wearing "decent" clothes, begging for food, and annoying the citizens. He claimed many of them were Pawnees. Upon hearing this news the agent sent two chiefs and two tribal soldiers to gather the Pawnees together and bring them and others at Council Bluffs back to the reservation. As a result of such complaints, Superintendent Janney reported to the commissioner of Indian Affairs that every effort would be made to keep the Pawnees on their reservation.[16] Public sensibility should be protected, and citizens guarded from face-to-face encounters with the hunger and poverty that the nation's Indian wards endured.

Problems for Pawnees away from the reservation continued. Several years after the Omaha incident, a petition was signed by several white settlers who complained about the Pawnees roaming along the Platte River near Prairie Grove. It was winter, and it is probable that they were hunting in places known for centuries as good areas for game. The agent responded that they were away without permission, and he would send two Pawnee soldiers after them.[17]

One such letter prompted the following response from Agent William Burgess, who knew that other tribes' members were frequently reported as Pawnees.

> Now when the Pawnees are guilty of any wrong act I wish to learn the facts, to detect and punish them, and will always aid in hunting out the guilty parties, but at the same time I wish to screen them from unjust and unfounded charges made at random with no regard to either principle or consequences. If the three Indians seen near your place were Pawnees, known as such by any positive signs or marks, I shall try to find out who they were and why they were there.[18]

He also explained that a party of Sioux had been in that neighborhood, leaving signs of their presence by appearance, camp sites, and final route north.

Not all Nebraskans complained about the Pawnees. William Stolley, of Grand Island, respected and treated them fairly, if his account is accurate. He made friends with them as they passed near Grand Island on their way to the semiannual hunt. While camping there, the local children and others would visit their tipis and attend their dances. Stolley treated the Indians who came to him for medical assistance with his cure-all, Epsom salts. Two Pawnees whom he referred to as Na-sarre-sarr-ricks and Lelu-la-scharr became his friends. Stolley was interested enough in the Pawnee language to compile an English-German-Pawnee vocabulary of some 150 words and phrases.[19]

Another individual who had high regard for the Pawnee people was the agency's trader, William H. Walton, a Quaker appointed by President Grant in 1870. He said he had made a good profit from his trade, which may account for his positive remarks. Walton stated that the tribe was "honest and reliable and while he allowed many of them to run accounts with him, he never lost a cent on a Pawnee account." He added that they were liberal with one another and shared what they had with the less fortunate members. According to a Nebraska writer who interviewed the aged gentlemen in 1934, he had only good things to say about their honesty, integrity, morals, and conduct.[20] How the Pawnees felt toward him was not reported.

While Pawnees were often unjustly accused of committing depredations in surrounding settlements, white citizens were intruding on the Pawnee reservation, causing Pawnee resentment. Governor Furnas, the newspapers, and others clamoring against the Indians neglected to mention this aspect of social inequity.

When settlements on the east side of the reservation sprang up, settlers often would not observe reservation boundary lines when they built their fences and placed their cattle to graze. In addition, Pawnee timber was continually taken by the wagonload, and Pawnee women and children threatened in their own fields.

So rampant were the intrusions that it was decided to resurvey the reservation and clearly mark the reservation borders in hopes that the settlers' excuses that they could not tell where the boundaries were would no longer provide justification for trespassing.[21] The intrusions on the Pawnee reservation continued until the state was finally successful in having the tribe removed.

The whiskey peddler was an intruder who plagued many Indian reservations. The Pawnees, in comparison with some other tribes, are rarely mentioned as having serious problems with whiskey misuse. The Pawnees have a story that gives some reasons for this. Wichita and Effie Blaine, born in the 1860s in Nebraska, recalled their parents telling them about men bringing whiskey when they came to talk with the chiefs. It may have occurred during treaty making times, they thought. At one such time, the chiefs went into the lodge dressed in their finery, but when they came out, they were disheveled, and some of them had ashes on them as if they had fallen in the firepit area. Everyone was surprised to see the chiefs look and act like that. Not all of the chiefs were there, however. Some were late arriving because they had to travel some distance. (This suggests a prereservation time, when the band villages were located at some distance from one another.) When one chief arrived and saw what was happening, he took his hunting belt or his whip and beat the drunken chiefs and talked in a loud voice about their disgrace. From that time forward, the chiefs never could be induced to drink at councils with the white men. There were "hard" lectures given after this initial episode, and the dangers were emphasized. The old chiefs had observed how drunkenness had affected other tribes downriver (the Platte and Missouri), and they did not want that to happen to their people.

Even so, the common man occasionally had access to whiskey, and Effie Blaine saw the following result. When she was a little girl in the Pitahawirata village near Genoa, she recalled seeing one man walking unsteadily down the village street and her kinfolks saying he was drunk. Her father, the chief, summoned the village soldiers (rekita), and they came with their whips and beat him in front of everyone. Once in awhile a man was given whiskey to drink by a trader, and then he would try to escape detection by going off to the place where the village ashes were dumped. You could always tell who such men were by the look of their clothes. They, too, were punished by the soldiers. Effie Blaine said, "We were taught that Tirawahut gave us a mind to think with. We are responsible for our thoughts. To drink and become drunk and not control one's thoughts was against Tirawahut's wishes for us."[22]

Once in awhile a whiskey peddler would appear on the reservation. In one instance, Agent Troth gathered enough evidence to take W. N. Harvey to Omaha for trial.[23] In his last annual report in 1875, Supt. Barclay White said of the Northern Superintendency tribes, "As a rule these Indians are honest and temperate in regard to strong drink, in these respects being probably above the average of the same number of white persons in the State where they reside."[24]

Non-Indian intrusion on the reservation to steal timber was one of the strongest sources of antagonism between the Pawnees and the settlers. For the Pawnees, wood was a necessity for cooking, heating, and building. Timbers needed for the large center support posts, roof, and side framing for the large Pawnee earthlodges came from trees that grew mainly along the Nebraska waterways, on Grand Island, and in other selected places. When the Pawnees were restricted to their reservation area near Genoa, the problems of obtaining wood became more acute as the supply steadily dwindled. Settlers needed wood, also, and although it was prohibited, they did not hesitate to take wagons onto the reservation and remove standing and fallen Pawnee timber, much to the anger of the chiefs and the distress of the tribe. A story long remembered tells of a settler called The Mean One. He lived close to the reservation cornfields, and he chased the women and children out of them when he could. Effie Blaine recalled,

One day, my father's sister's little girls went to the fields to work. On the way back later they picked up some sticks for firewood. This man came up to them and he had a long whip. He lashed out and hit the girls with it and they dropped the sticks and ran back to the mudlodge crying. It just happened that my mother's brother came in and said, "Why are you crying?" And they said that the Mean One had whipped them. "Oh," he said, "I always heard that he was a mean man, so I am going to go talk to him. I am going to ask him to not do that anymore." Now everyone knew that he, himself, was a quick tempered man. So when he went down there, they went with him, but kept a fair distance behind him as he angrily strode ahead.

He got to the place and called this man out of his house. In a mild voice he said, "My niece here, she is crying, and I want you to feel sorry for her. You should not have done that. You are a warrior, I mean a man, and these are only little girls." Then the man said, "They were gathering my wood." Uncle answered, "That is *not* your wood. This is our land, and these are little girls. How much wood could they carry anyway?"

So the man started cursing him and told him to get out of there. Uncle said, "Oh, I know these words. In the army I heard these words. (He was a u.s. Army Pawnee Scout.) They tell me that when a man calls you these things it is very bad. Now I came in a nice way to talk to you, but I see you are not going to listen. So, I'm going to tell you and then I am going to make you." So he grabbed him and took his whip away from him and began to lash him with it. It is said he hit him twenty times or more with what they called the blacksnake whip. The other relatives saw that he was very angry. They rushed in and held him and said, "Better stop now, you might kill him." He let go and left The Mean One on the ground.

Of course, The Mean One reported the whipping to the agent

and there was a council about it. The agent, Wi-ti-wah [William Burgess], asked Uncle, "Did you go there and whip him?" And he said, "Yes, and I am going back there in a few days and whip him again. If I don't do this, he might get in the habit of whipping our little girls, and I don't want him to get the habit." Wi-ti-wah said, "That was a bad thing you did. I understand why you did it, but it is not right." The white man says that from here on, you tell me what's wrong and I will take care of it. Uncle said, "Don't tell me, tell him! He is the one who did the offense. If he never offends again, then I will never have anything to talk to you about." Effie Blaine said his name was Two Chiefs, or Twice a Chief, Resaru Pitku.[25]

Even though it was necessary for all men to go on the winter hunt to procure food, in 1872 a large number of Pawnees decided to stay on the reservation to watch for intruders who wanted Pawnee timber.[26] In council, Lone Chief, a Skidi, said he would stay home and guard his people's timber or else the white people would take all that was left.

This was a year of extreme hunger, and every buffalo that could be found and killed was needed for survival. Yet wood for cooking and heating was also vital in the cold Nebraska winter. Besides, it was galling for the Pawnees to observe the impunity with which the whites boldly drove their wagons onto reservation land and stole their wood. Over two hundred wagonloads were counted at one time.

Agent Troth, well aware of the situation, forwarded Pawnee complaints to Superintendent White, who in turn wrote to the commissioner of Indian Affairs. White said there were at least a hundred cases of timber stealing that should be brought before a grand jury of the U.S. District Court, if such a procedure were approved. White commented, "I am not disposed to compromise with crime, but would respectfully ask, if it would be prudent to allow such of these offenders as desire to do so to pay for the timber they have taken." It was said that persons involved were of good community standing and were willing to pay for what they had taken.[27]

It might appear that White did not want to bring the local worthies to court or did not think a jury of their peers would convict or fine them. In December, White went to one locality and settled with sixty individuals and received $300. He planned to visit two other neighborhoods at Clarksville and Lone Tree and settle with the timber thieves there.[28]

He reported his success in collecting fines to the Pawnee leaders, who were pleased that over one hundred people had paid their debts to the tribe. They expressed their hope that the money be extended for their pressing needs, rather than being deposited in the U.S. Treasury to their credit, as they were told it would be. They wished to purchase immediately flour, beef, and other provisions "for themselves and the poor people in the villages whom they say are very needy," Agent Troth reported.[29] Nevertheless, the money went its bureaucratic way into the treasury.

This attempt to stop timber poaching by collecting fines did not stop the practice. Even the whites vandalized each other. One settler accused of stealing Pawnee timber told how his own neighbors drove up to his place with wagons and told him that their families had no wood and they would not allow them to suffer. They drew their guns and said they would take his wood by force if necessary, which they did. Thus, he was then forced to steal from the Pawnees, the man stated in his abili.[30] The intensity of the problem is further shown by the fact that although the Quaker agent was against violence and bloodshed, in December 1873, he sent Big Spotted Horse, a leading warrior, with a group of Pawnee soldiers to stop any timber stealing that should occur.[31]

In 1875, Pawnee destitution increased. A devastating grasshopper invasion and failure of the hunt left them without sufficient food for the winter. They requested that they be allowed to sell some of their fallen timber to buy food, but they were not allowed to do so.[32]

The last of the Pawnees were removed from the reservation and taken to Indian Territory late in the year.* Then settlers

---

*Indian Territory consisted of lands given to the Cherokees, Choctaws, Creeks, Chickasaws, and Seminoles by the United States in exchange for their original lands ceded east of the Mississippi River in the 1820–1830s. It lay south of Kansas, and it and Oklahoma Territory later became the state of Oklahoma. Many tribes from various parts of the United States were brought to Indian Territory and settled on reservations.

moved onto the reservation with their wagons. Now there would be no interference with their wood gathering.

Monetary Claims Against the Pawnees

Another source of bad feeling between the Pawnees and the settlers came with demands for Pawnee payment for numerous purported acts of destruction or theft while away from the reservation. Usually, claimants insisted that the closest tribe to their farm or dwelling was the one responsible for depredations. Over the years, records contain hundreds of such claims, some justifiable, and many others that were not. It could be quite profitable to present fictitious claims for damages in hopes that the government would pay. On many occasions, claims were attempts to make money by falsely alleging damage to fields or crops, or demanding payment for lost or stolen animals or for other destructive acts. This type of aggravation and harassment was another factor that created growing tension and dislike between the Pawnees and their neighbors.

An observer of this practice was Wilhelm A. Dinesen, a Dane of some status in his country who was interested in the American West. In 1872, he visited the Pawnee Agency. He lodged with Pawnee trader Lester Platt. Dinesen soon noticed that "every minute a farmer came to us and wished to file a complaint. He had lost a sheep, a calf, a pony, and in all probability he said a Pawnee had taken it, when he had not."[33]

The Pawnees found these accusations particularly irksome. Council minutes and correspondence reflect a certain pattern of Pawnee denial and agent disavowal of claims in the majority of cases. The following is a typical reply Agent Burgess made to Superintendent White regarding a claim.

> In our late Council I brought the claim of Wm. Hewitt to their notice. We examined the papers and documents on hand to endeavor to get some clue to the basis of the claim, but could find nothing, nor could we get any evidence or admission on the part of the Pawnees, that any such claim had even the shadow of foundation in either fact or justice. I also conferred with former Agent Troth who coincided in my view as he had never found anything to warrant a just claim. I therefore return the papers as requested.[34]

Earlier, a justifiable claim was made by Nathan Denman for cattle killed by the Pawnees. The chiefs judged it valid and ordered payment.[35]

In 1871, after returning from a hunt accompanied by the Poncas, the Pawnees were accused of stealing corn from a settler. The Pawnee chiefs stated that the Poncas were responsible and pointed out that the agent never received complaints when the Pawnees went alone. Eagle Chief declared that nearby whites told him that the Poncas stole the corn as well as some pumpkins. He showed his frustration by declaring, "The whites know we do not read or write so make many claims against us."[36]

Settlers' hay damage claims were also a source of annoyance. In January 1872, the Chaui and Pitahawirata bands paid a white claimant for hay he said they had scattered or broken down. Pitaresaru, the head chief, told the agent that fifteen blankets were given to the man, but after this transaction, some other white men said they should not have paid anything since the hay was rotten. Then, Pitaresaru continued, another man came and made a claim for the same hay, followed by others making claims for it.[37]

In June 1873, Peter Holm and William Matson presented a claim for damage by a Pawnee who, they said, set fire to the prairie and destroyed their hay. The chiefs, whose sagacity about the white man's values and legal system was increasing, said that the Pawnee must be identified or they would not pay. Another claimant wanted the Chaui Band to pay for cowhides stolen by members of that band. The chiefs indignantly stated that the hides were from drowned cattle and had been given to them as unusable.[38]

Frequently claims requested payment for stolen horses. The settlers found it easier to press claims on the nearby Pawnees than to try to obtain redress and payment from the distant and hostile Sioux, who were often the culprits. In the fall of 1873, King D. Fisher presented a claim for $700 for six horses supposedly stolen by the Pawnees. The Pawnees said they knew nothing about the theft and refused to pay.[39]

Some claims for Indian depredations were valid. Often such acts were the result of Indian need or negligence or, in some cases, possibly willful behavior for what was considered a good reason. The Pawnees resented being thought of as fair game. Conversely, their neighbors, who may have had legitimate claims, resented the Pawnees' refusal to pay when the settlers could not prove their assertions. The whole situation was used effectively by those favoring Indian confinement to reservations and by those fanning opposition to the Indians remaining within the state's boundaries.

The Pawnees and the Justice System

In the early 1870s, the Pawnees were embittered by the inequities in the Nebraska and U.S. judicial systems. For almost two years, several Pawnees were held in prison while the federal government and Nebraska court system decided who had jurisdiction and when and where the trial would be held.[40] Considering the prevailing bias, conscious or otherwise, of non-Indian citizens against Indians, it is not surprising that withholding the right of due process to the Indians did occur. The bill making Nebraska a state in 1867 stated that ". . . there be no denial of elective franchise or any other right to any person by reason of race or color, except Indians not taxed."[41]

The right to reasonable and responsible justice did not seem to exist in the Pawnee Yellow Sun murder case. On May 8, 1869, Edwin McMurtry (sometimes spelled McMurty), a citizen of Polk City, Butler County, was murdered on an island in the Platte River. The place had belonged to and was frequented by the Pawnees long before white settlers arrived. Now a great uproar among the citizenry ensued and on June 30, Superintendent Janney went to the Pawnee Agency, where he informed the chiefs that some Pawnees were accused of the murder and that they must be surrendered and tried by a U.S. court. Then, "He read a letter from Indian Commissioner Ely S. Parker warning the chiefs that whenever any Pawnees violated the laws of the United States, the government would hold the entire Pawnee nation accountable and that their treaty annuities would be withheld until they surrendered the guilty men."[42]

The chiefs were angered by this statement and others made by the superintendent. Pitaresaru replied that thirteen Pawnees had been recently killed by whites and that nothing had been done about it. He concluded by saying, "We are willing to say nothing about the men we have lost by the whites, if you say no more about the white man that has been killed." Janney refused to agree and told them to surrender the murderers or he would stop delivery of the annuity goods and funds held in Omaha.

Eventually, the chiefs gave in and stated that they would surrender Yellow Sun, Horse Driver, Little or Young Wolf, Great Traveler, Man Scared of Horses, Lucky Man, and Blue Hawk, all of whom were delivered to an Omaha jail. Only then did Janney send the annuity goods and money to the Pawnees.[43]

With the approval of the Indian commissioner, Troth and Janney began to plan for the prisoners' court defense and hired C. S. Chase as their attorney. Yellow Sun, a man of about sixty years, became the principal defendant. He was a Pawnee doctor and lived with his family on Grand Island, where he hunted and trapped with one or two other Pawnee families.[44] Now he was in Omaha in prison, and it was not until September that a hearing was held before the U.S. Circuit Court, and he and four of the group were indicted.[45] During this hearing, the attorneys for the prosecution made a plea for the children and widow of the deceased, who had brought suit against the Pawnees, asking for $25,000 as compensation for her husband's death.

In November 1869, Yellow Sun, Blue Hawk, Horse Driver, and Little Wolf were convicted of murder in the federal court. In January 1870, the question arose whether the federal or state court had jurisdiction in sentencing of the prisoners.[46] Punishment of death by hanging was expected and fears of mob violence were expressed if the prisoners were taken to a state court for sentencing. The agent and superintendent wanted the federal court to have precedence and hoped that the nation's President could be persuaded to commute the death sentence to life imprisonment for Yellow Sun and pardon the others. It was obvious that the evidence against all of them was only circumstantial. There was serious doubt whether Blue Hawk had had anything to do with the event, although he had given himself up as a representative of the Pitahawirata Band. The sheriff arresting him said that there were several Blue Hawks in the tribe, and he was not certain whether the one in jail was the right one. In addition, certain non-Indians in Lone Tree were willing to petition for his pardon.[47]

Earlier, the chiefs, on their own, had tried to determine if any of the accused Pawnees were guilty. Pawnees living on the island were brought to council, and each was asked to make a statement. Yellow Sun said that if he saw an Indian trying to shoot a white man, he would shoot him with an arrow.

There are varying accounts of the events that occurred, after Yellow Sun and the others were incarcerated. Some chiefs were taken to visit the prisoners in order to try to obtain the truth. They were said to have told the prisoners that the Pawnee children were suffering, the people were starving, and the tribe was not allowed to go on the hunt. If they knew the truth, they should tell it.

According to Agent Troth's account of this visit, Yellow Sun was not allowed to speak.[48] Troth thought that this was because he told different stories at different times, but this may not have been the reason. All the men continued to deny their guilt, even when they were told of the dire conditions of their families. What was really said among the Pawnees is unknown, for the Pawnee interpreter told Troth only what he wanted him to hear or what the chiefs told him to say.

Near the end of January 1870, Superintendent Janney reported to Commissioner Parker that the judge "will in passing sentence, allow all the time we may require before execution." Probably on January 26, Janney and Colonel Chase, the Pawnees' attorney, visited federal Judge Elmer S. Dundy, who had become reluctant to pass sentence because of the question of jurisdiction and wanted to go to Washington to determine whether the case was his court's responsibility. He told Janney and Chase what they already knew: in state courts the Pawnees would probably be tried and sentenced to execution. Janney reported, "We all think the ends of justice would be better promoted by keeping this case under the control of the United States government than by its transfer to a state court . . . and in this case where evidence is not conclusive, imprisonment is greatly desired." He also added that long imprisonment and labor rather than a quick death by hanging would help eradicate from the Indian mind the old vindictive policy of blood for blood.[49] Janney's cold-hearted suggestion to use the Pawnees as an object lesson without absolute proof of guilt indicates the strange and questionable standard of justice then prevalent toward the Indians.

In February 1870, two judges of the U.S. circuit and district courts discussed the case and decided to postpone the hearing until the next term in May. They were still uncertain of the jurisdiction, and Washington had given no direction. Janney again asked for a pardon for Blue Hawk, but Judge Dundy said the President was the only one who could pardon him without waiting for a sentence to be passed.[50] March came and Dundy decided that he could not go to Washington to get an answer as to procedure. He asked Janney if the Indian commissioner would have the U.S. attorney general give an opinion as to whether the case was under his jurisdiction or not.[51]

The May term arrived, with Judges Dillon and Dundy presiding. On May 4, Dillon delivered the opinion that his court had no jurisdiction in the Pawnee case. The reason given was that the crime had been committed on state, not federal, land. He allowed twenty days for the proper state officers to claim the prisoners. If this was not done, they would go free. Superintendent Janney and Colonel Chase now planned for the state trial that they assumed would be held. Governor Butler, whose anti-Indian views were well known, was a friend of Chase's, and it was hoped that Chase could influence the governor to ameliorate the Pawnees' situation.

Janney reported to the Indian commissioner that he did not know what action the state authorities would take because there was no conclusive evidence against any of the prisoners except, perhaps, Yellow Sun. It was not certain if the others would be tried or not.[52] The speculation was that the cost of the trial would be great and that anticipation of such an expense might influence the officials to avoid taking action. But Janney's prediction was wrong. On May 19, the Butler County sheriff came to discuss the matter. He was concerned that the Pawnees would be mobbed if he took them to Butler County, where there was no place he could put them where he could assure their safety. He sought permission to leave them in the Omaha prison. Arrangements were made to keep them there, where they had already been held for a year, in a cell described as "partly underground and ill ventilated."[53]

A Butler County grand jury met in August, and the four Pawnees were indicted. Their attorney applied for a change of venue, saying that prejudice against them in the county where the crime occurred would prevent a fair trial. The presiding judge granted the request and set the date of November 22, 1870, for a trial at Lincoln in Lancaster County.[54] On November 30, Janney informed the commissioner that the trial had been postponed because one of the principal witnesses for the prosecution could not attend. It was possible that a special term would be held in January 1871. Otherwise, the case would be held until the spring term. The Pawnees' attorneys, Colonel Chase and E. Wakely, resisted the motion and postponement to no avail,[55] and finally the trial was delayed until May 1871, two years after the crime.

Superintendent Janney, Agent Troth, the Pawnees' attorneys, some Pawnee chiefs, and an interpreter traveled to Lincoln. The Pawnee contingent waited for the trial to begin, only to be informed that the prosecuting attorney was not prepared to go to trial. Again there was a postponement. A special court term was scheduled for June to take up the case.

In discouragement, Janney wrote to the commissioner, "We have been so often baffled that I do not know what to calculate on."[56] However, there was a small consolation. The Pawnees' attorneys petitioned the judge to discharge the prisoners from jail awaiting the trial. This petition was heard and on June 12, 1871, a writ of habeas corpus was issued. The defendants were released on bail under custody of their chiefs, the agent, and the superintendent. The sureties for the chiefs were $5,000 and $1,000 for the agent and superintendent. The Pawnee chiefs promised to forfeit annuity if the prisoners should not appear at the next hearing. Troth reported, "Last night the prisoners under the charge of the agent and the chiefs went by night train, rejoicing greatly at their liberation after twenty-two months of imprisonment."[57] While the Pawnee chiefs were in Lincoln, the local newspapers reported their presence. "They were decked out with full Indian paraphernalia, necklaces of bear claws, scalps, feathers, buttons, medals and tomahawks and attracted much attention about town during the day."[58]

In the courtroom, Two Chiefs became increasingly irritated and suddenly arose and walked to the center of the court room. After the usual shaking of hands of those around, he turned to the astonished judge and said, "My father, you have lost one man. Fourteen of my men have recently been killed by white men. Let us call it even."[59] The government had taken no notice of the killings of the Indians, even when they were protested by the chiefs. Two Chiefs took this opportunity to remind the representatives of the U.S. government of the inequality of the form of justice now in progress. The incident he referred to happened when the Pawnees were returning from a tribal visit to the Wichitas and stopped at a farmhouse to ask for food and all were shot.

At last, the trial was held in Second Judicial District Court at Lincoln on October 23, 1871. On motion the case was ordered stricken from the docket, with the possibility of it being reinstated on motion. The Pawnee defendants were released from custody without bail. If no further evidence or testimony should be found implicating them in the crime, no more proceedings would be initiated against them.[60] Capt. Luther North later wrote that while they were in jail, Yellow Sun and Horse Driver had attempted suicide and Little Wolf had died there. Blue Hawk had escaped once, but Maj. Frank North had taken him back to Omaha. Those Pawnees who were released all died within a short time.[61]

Some years later, after the Pawnees had been removed to Indian Territory, Barclay White, who succeeded Samuel Janney as superintendent, visited the Pawnees. He wrote in his journal,

> I took the opportunity of a private interview with B. Bayhylle, a Pawnee interpreter, who had held that office during the trials of those Indians and with whom I had always been friendly and asked him the direct question, 'Baptiste, we have always been good friends. I believed those Pawnee Indians accused of the murder of McMurtire [sic] to be innocent of those charges and you know how I assisted in getting them released. I am not now in the Government's service, will you please tell me in confidence who was the murderer of McMurtrie?" "Yes," he replied, "after we removed to the Indian Territory there was much sickness and death

among us. One Pawnee who was never suspected of that murder, sickened and before death confessed it had been him who shot McMurtrie on the island in the Platte where his body was found." He said he, the Indian, was camped on that island, when he discovered McMurtrie trying to drive off and steal his ponies. Finding he could not stop him by any other means, he shot McMurtrie and left the body where it fell.[62]

The white man's pattern of declaring guilt by circumstantial evidence in the Yellow Sun case seemed illogical and unjust to the Pawnees. Among the Pawnees, accusations of serious wrongdoing were not made lightly. Only first-hand observations of events were acceptable as indicators of guilt. Second- or third-hand accounts would be considered erroneous or inaccurate, plain gossip. As an example, in a case of a paternity question, if a man was accused of fathering a child of an unmarried, or an unfaithful married, or a widowed woman, the Pawnee reply to the accuser of the man was, "Were you there when they did it? Did you lift the robe and look under? Did you see this man enter the woman?" The answer, of course, would always be "No," and the accuser knew that he or she was not believed and was considered a slanderous gossip. Such questions could be used in any situation where the speaker was describing an event or accusing another of negative behavior. The structure of the Pawnee language indicated when a speaker was telling of an event at which he was present or took part in, or of one that he had heard of from another, or of one that was even more remotely learned about. Validity of the event or its accuracy was thus judged.[63]

Unsubstantiated accusations of murder by Pawnees continued after the Yellow Sun case. In one instance, when Pawnees were accused, the evidence—a Sioux City flour sack and willow bark for smoking—left near the scene of the crime indicated another tribe was possibly guilty because those items were not Pawnee. On another occasion three "Germans" were killed north of Fort McPherson, and the Pawnees were blamed. Superintendent White investigated the matter and found no evidence against the Pawnees.[64]

When the Sioux warriors, Fat Badger, Whistler, and Hand Smeller, were killed out on the prairie, the Pawnees, their great

Pawnee chiefs and warriors stand beside a village earthlodge in Nebraska, ca. 1871. They are wearing bear claw necklaces; turbans; decorated fur headdresses; government issued blankets; buffalo robes (worn with fur inside) with painted designs on the skin side; yard goods shirts; peace medals; multiple earrings; eagle feathers; beaded necklaces and leggings; and facial painting. Two men carry pipe tomahawks. Courtesy of Nebraska State Historical Society.

enemies, were accused of the deed. But this time, the Lowell, Nebraska, newspaper defended their innocence and went so far as to accuse a John C. Ralston and "Wild Bill" Hickock, who apparently were not well thought of in the town. Capt. Luther North thought that Newton Moreland and his partner were guilty.[65] In any event the Pawnees were left alone and their fears that some of them might have to endure another long period of imprisonment were eliminated.

All evidence indicates that the Pawnees did not lift their hands in anger against the whites during these difficult years. Barclay White stated in 1874 that only two known murders had been committed by Indians in the state since 1871, and the accused were probably not Nebraska Indians.[66] Nevertheless, many settlers continued to believe their lives were in danger and made wild accusations against the Pawnees and other tribes in the state. These were bitter times for Indian people. Mistrust, hostility, and accusations against them continued. And the deaths of eighteen or more Pawnee tribesmen, murdered during these years by whites who went unpunished, increased their resentment and galled their spirit.[67]

After 1870 the Pawnees saw an intensification of efforts to harass and restrict their lives in Nebraska. The pressure and hostility from the non-Indian community consisted of false accusations and claims against the Pawnees for depredations on property as well as charges of murder. The Pawnee reservation was continually trespassed on by timber thieves and cattle grazers.

Confinement to the reservation prevented the Pawnees from journeying at will over their ancient lands to hunt; to visit ancestral graves near abandoned villages; to seek visions on high, grassy hills; and to take the Sacred Pipe to visit and adopt members of other tribes and thus establish and maintain bonds between the tribes. They could not pursue their enemies in response to attack. Moreover, white politicians fostered plans aimed at sooner or later removing the Pawnees from their homeland so as to acquire their valuable land.

†††
2
The Fields and Forests Feed Us

*Before we go on a hunt, before we plant, we make a feast
and old men sing, and God [Tirawahut] lets things grow.*
— *Pitaresaru, Pawnee Chief, 1872*

Part I

Despite the harassment and hostility often shown by the white
settlers around them, the Pawnees tried to continue their traditional life ways. They still grew and gathered food by the old
methods and followed sacred rituals associated with these activities, which they believed were imperative for their survival as
a tribe.

There are many Pawnee myths and origin legends that tell
that Sacred Beings gave certain foods to the Pawnees in the
"long ago time." In one, the North Wind, called Ready to Give
or Wind of Fortune, begot a child by a young Pawnee woman.
One day when the child had grown, he wandered into the forest
and his father came through the trees and visited him. During
this and other visits, North Wind taught his son to hunt first the
rabbit, then larger game, until at last he gave him the buffalo to
hunt. Then he directed his son to search in the sand along the
river and find the place where the rats (voles) had hidden caches
of ground beans. These, too, were to be food for his Pawnee
people. Another day, North Wind took his son to the places
where artichokes could be found and said that these were to be

food also. When the spring came, his father returned and gave the boy white corn for his mother, red corn for his sister, and black (blue) corn for his grandmother. He then instructed him how to teach them to plant and care for the growing seedlings. Finally, North Wind told his son how to make a Sacred Bundle and how to care for and use it.[1]

In this tale and others, the Sacred Beings such as the Sun, the Moon, and the Evening Star introduced or gave certain plant and animal foods to the Pawnees. Most frequently mentioned is corn, considered sacred and called *Atira*, or Mother. The Gods gave the Pawnees the right and responsibility for the planting, caring for, and harvesting of the corn. A description of this was given by Effie Blaine:

> We women felt greatly honored by a custom of the old men when we went planting. An old man would sit on top of a mud-lodge at this time and talk to us. He would say, "Dear ladies, you are disfiguring your bodies with mud today, because the Heavens have endowed you with the wonderful bows and arrows."[*] Then he continued his speech: "It is Heaven that endowed you with this wonderful power through which you continue to nourish me. When you have planted the seeds and the corn grows, that is how you provide me with nourishment, dear ladies."
>
> The first thing the women did when they went planting was to clear the ground of grass and weeds. When I was a little girl I would be awakened very early in the morning and before sunrise my mother and I would be in the fields. My mother took along a pot of porridge for me. She would make mounds of earth, and dig a hole in the top of each one for the seeds. She put seven grains of corn in each mound and she would make sure that the individual grains were well spaced. Then she covered them over with earth and smoothed out the mound. The different varieties were planted in separate rows; there was a row of blue corn, another of speckled corn, then a row of red beans, then yellow beans, then another row of flint corn, then a row of stubby-eared corn, a row of yellow flint corn, and of white corn. That's all of this type of seed.

* In the Pawnee text the words *tiraktara wuxwaruksti* are translated by Welt-fish as "bows and arrows" but should read "stalks of corn," according to Garland J. Blaine.

Pawnee women and children in Nebraska. Women's responsibilities included planting, caring for, and harvesting the field crops; drying and storing corn, beans, and other foods; gathering various plants, berries, and roots; carrying wood for fuel; and preparing hides for clothing and shelter. They also played the largest role in construction of the earthlodges and were in charge of pack horses and setting up camp on the hunt. Courtesy of National Anthropological Archives, Smithsonian Institution.

The pumpkin field was off to one side. The different varieties of pumpkin were also planted in separate patches. There was a patch of green-squash-with-curved-neck, one of big-yellow-pumpkins-with grooves, another of green-squash-with-tapering-ends, and another of small pumpkins. These are all the pumpkin varieties.

The next planting to be done is for the daughter-in-law. The women and girl relatives of the boy are invited to participate. Someone is sent to get the seeds from the daughter-in-law's home. When the seeds are brought she leads them to her field. There would be about twenty-five young women and two old women in the party. The young women would line up at one end of the field

and the two old women at the other end. The field would be about
the length of this street (half a block) by the distance from here to
the Pawnee Post Office (a block and a half). The young women
who were lined up at one end of the field would begin to make the
mounds for planting, while the two old women who sat at the other
end would sing old men's (priests) songs. I remember the song:

> "You are hoeing around
> In the great ground
> In the lucky [blessed] * ground."

After the mounds are finished, the seeds are planted. After the
planting the daughter-in-law would give a feast of dry meat and
corn [cooked together] for the women who had planted her fields.

When the plants come up and the weeds begin to sprout the
field is weeded and cultivated. When the first shoot comes up an
old woman goes there to perform a rite of thanksgiving over the
plant. She rubs the plant with her hands in blessing, saying, "Oh
big bow" [corn stalk]. Then directly she rubs a baby with her
hands in a similar fashion, passing on the blessing from the plant
to the child. Everyone is happy at the sight of the first plant.
There is an ancient legend that states that when the plants fail to
come up, we will all cease to exist. That is why everyone is happy
when the plants come up, for upon it depends our very lives. Even
now I am happy when I see the plants come up because it reminds
me of the ancient legend.

When the stalks are about waist high the women cultivate the
fields. In the morning when the plants were wet with dew, how
wet the women would get at their work. They would pile the earth
up around the corn hills and smooth them and her left side would
get all muddy as she rubbed against the wet earth. No one would
presume to mention the fact that the woman was all smeared with
mud as she had muddied herself in a good cause. Her face and
hands would be all muddy and, that is what the old man meant
when he said in his speech, "You disfigure yourself for my sake."
He said too, "While the hoe is still muddy, you will be eating
corn." After our work we all went to a nearby stream to swim: the

---

* This word has a deeper meaning than "lucky," according to Blaine. It con-
notes aspects of the sacred nature of the earth and the blessings therefrom. The
brackets are the author's.

surface of the water would be dotted with heads. We girls would sit splashing our feet in the water; we would have a contest as to who could make the loudest splash. Then we would wash the hoes and carry them home. We would cultivate not only our own fields, but also that of the daughter-in-law. We would also roast her corn as well as our own.

There would come a time when someone would call out, "The corn is ripe" and she would bring in an ear to show us. "The stalks are laden with ears and near the bottom are many suckers," they would say if there were a good crop. "We will set such and such a day for the roasting." The daughter-in-law's corn is always roasted first. "Now, daughter-in-law," they would announce, "we are going to roast for you."

This is the way they used to roast the corn: They carried on their back a bag made of scraped hide into which they would toss the ears of corn as they gathered them. Then they would dump them into one big heap. The pile would be so high that it looked as if wagons had been used to do the hauling instead of the simple carrying bags. The next step was to build a long narrow ditch with mud embankments along each side against which to lean the corn.* They would build a big fire and throw the ears into it. One would have to stick one's hand in and out of the flame repeatedly to turn the ears over, but one would never burn oneself. When the wood has burned down the naked ears are roasted in the coals. The corn would be left to roast all night as this gives it a delicious flavor. Early the next morning, whatever shucks remained on the corn would be removed and they would proceed to cut the kernels from the cobs. For this purpose they would in most cases use a clam shell. Kernels from small-grained ears were removed with a knife. Large hide covers were then spread out upon the ground and pegged down tight so that they would be very smooth and upon these the kernels were spread out to dry. The blue corn was separated into three groups by size, the smallest, the medium, and the largest. When the kernels were dry they were winnowed and put into sacks made of tanned hide. After each sack was full they would beat upon it with a long stick to make sure that the grains

---

* According to Garland J. Blaine, ditch dimensions used in Indian Territory by a Pawnee family averaged about six feet long by one and a half feet wide and three-quarters foot deep. Earth embankments were built along the two long sides. The corn was arranged along the sides and the fire burned in the bottom.

settled compactly into the bag. Then they would place a lid inside the bag and pull the drawstring. After we had filled them all there would be a big pile of bags. Those that were for the daughter-in-law were carried to her home. The white flint corn is simply dried without roasting.

The beans in their pods would be spread out upon a hide which was pegged to the ground and when they were dry would be beaten with a stick to release them from the pods. When she had finished she would winnow the beans in a manner similar to the way in which she had handled the corn. She would also pack the beans in bags in the same way.

Then they would get to work on the pumpkins. Each woman would take a pumpkin from the pile and sit down with it. The first step was to peel the pumpkins. Then it is decided that braided pumpkin mats are to be made, the pumpkins are cut spirally into strips from top to bottom. Other pumpkins are cut into rings and hung on a cross pole to dry. After the whole pumpkin has been stripped there is left a disc at the bottom which is known as "Sitting-one." The pumpkin is then left to dry for about a day when it is in the proper stage for braiding and for the stringing of the bottom discs. After they are braided, the pumpkin mats are left out in the sun to dry.[2]

An entire order of Sacred Bundles existed with ceremonies in which the people sought success in hunting, planting, growing, and harvesting. In 1872 the Pawnee chief, Pitaresaru, attempted to explain the Pawnee way to the Indian agent. He said that God gave the Pawnees corn, pumpkins, and other things. "Before we go on a hunt, before we plant, we make a feast and old men sing and God [Tirawahut] lets things grow. When corn gets so high, we have a ceremony, and ask God to give us it to live and to get Buffalo. We offer our food to God before eating.* I like this way and don't want to lose it."[3]

Cultivating the soil and raising successive generations of Mother Corn, beans, pumpkins, and squashes in the manner described by Effie Blaine and ordained by the Sacred Beings would

---

* The food blessing ceremony is still performed during certain events among the Pawnees in Oklahoma today. Sam Young, a Chaui chief by blood, who was authorized to perform the ceremony, died in 1985, but others now perform it.

continue through time according to Pawnee belief. But just where the sites of the first Pawnee gardening efforts were may never be found because there is yet no historical or archaeological evidence showing locations of the ancestral gardeners. *

When the Pawnee ancestors first entered the Central Plains is unknown. The earliest prehistoric regional sites show corn and bean cultivation associated with human occupation of small villages are along the Missouri River near Kansas City. These sites are dated in the second or third centuries A.D., and are designated part of the Hopewellian Phase.[4] These early gardeners lived in settled villages near rivers or streams, occupying round or square houses that show evidence of interior roof and wall supporting posts.

The Lower Loup Phase is associated with Pawnee prehistory in Nebraska.[5] Along the Loup River were village site remains with agricultural components dating around 1500 A.D.[6] This same area's inhabitants were called "the Pawnees" by the eighteenth-century Europeans who first visited and described them. Before the Lower Loup people, other cultures that left signs of horticulture occupied adjacent regions of the Central and Northern Plains. One group belonging to the Upper Republican Phase may possibly have been ancestral to the Lower Loup Phase peoples. But, except for a cord-roughened pottery that is found in the early level of some Lower Loup village sites and more numerously in the pre-1500 Upper Republican sites, no direct relationship can yet be proven to link the two phases. Both peoples were maize and bean growers. The direct ancestors of the Pawnees, the Lower Loup people, were good farmers, and their large underground storage pits attest to agricultural surpluses.[7]

* The first signs of New World maize agriculture have been found in Central America and Mexico, and date to several thousand years ago. Eventually the ideas and seeds were carried northward over the centuries into the southwestern part of present United States, and up the Mississippi River Valley and across this river from the southeastern Indian cultures. Some of their seed types appear to have originated in the Circum-Caribbean area. Maize was cultivated at the American Bottom sites east of the Mississippi River, opposite the present site of St. Louis, around 800 A.D. (See Driver, *INDIANS OF NORTH AMERICA*, 38–41., Holder, *The Hoe and the Horse*; viii, Barreis and Porter, eds., *AMERICAN BOTTOM ARCHEOLOGY*.)

The Importance of Food

The importance of producing and procuring food at first hand is only occasionally experienced by a few in present so-called western cultures. It is not usually a direct, hand-to-mouth effort but an event where currency, grocery shelves, and fast food restaurants intervene, and blur the memories of ancestors who hunted and of necessity grew their own sustenance. Today, it is not easy to understand the importance of food to the Indians of a century or more ago. John Dunbar, a missionary who had first-hand knowledge of the Pawnees, said there was a Pawnee proverb, "Even the dogs, it is well for them to eat in peace." This saying seemed to indicate, that to the Pawnees eating was an act that deserved deferential respect. "The question (of) what he should eat was as potent as any other that influenced his life. It demanded ever his serious thought, provoked his ingenuity, taxed his energy, and largely controlled his movements during the entire year. . . . [T]he ability and readiness to eat whenever occasion offered was in their estimation an exponent of health, and if an invalid failed to take food, all hope of recovery was immediately relinquished."[8]

When food was plentiful, feasting was the rule as visitors to nineteenth-century villages reported.[9] Not only one, but consecutive invitations were issued to a guest, and at each lodge one was expected to partake of food with obvious interest and pleasure. Food was a blessing to be enthusiastically and yet reverently consumed. To feed a man and to pray for him and to have him in turn pray for you was the greatest thing a man could do in the eyes of Tirawahut, for in so doing a man might receive a blessing in some form himself.[10]

Although basic foods were meat, corn, squash, and beans, there were many other plants, such as edible roots, available near the village in the forests, along stream banks, or in the open fields. The search for food was a constant effort, particularly among the women. It meant "hundreds of hard days" spent digging Indian potatoes after the ground thawed. The women and girls would leave the village at daybreak carrying hoes or adzes on their shoulders. They would work until sunset, digging the wild potatoes that grew in great numbers along the Loup River, as well as other places. During hard times, many women had to spend more than half their time obtaining food for themselves and their children. If they worked in their corn fields one day, the next day they must dig roots or go hungry. Dunbar observed that in the afternoon the women could be seen wandering along a bluff searching for a root that resembled a turnip.[11] As each plant, berry, and nut came into season, it was gathered, prepared, eaten, or processed for future use. Combinations of food were prepared and cooked together—for example, corn, beans, and meat; corn and pumpkin; or berries, ground with fat and made into small cakes. Corn was also eaten as roasting ears or as mush or gruel. Tables 1, 2, 3, and 4 list the gathered and cultivated foods of the Pawnees.

Table 1
Foods Gathered by the Pawnees

Nuts	Hackberry, walnut, hickory.
Fruits	Wild strawberry, buffalo berry, prickly pear, western choke cherry, wild plum, sand cherry, wild black raspberry, elderberry, bear berry, black haw, wild grape, choke cherry, prairie rose haws, ground plum, Kentucky coffee tree beans.
Tubers, roots, seeds	Ground bean, Indian potato, water chinquapin, arrowleaf, large yellow pond lily, pomme blanche (tipsin or pursh), Jerusalem artichoke, cucumber root, wild turnip.
Flowers, stems, leaves	Wild onion, lamb's quarters, sheep sorrel, yellow wood sorrel, milkweed.
Others	Corn smut, sugar syrup from soft maple and box elder, prairie mushrooms, Indian tea.

Sources: John Dunbar, "The Pawnee Indians," *Magazine of American History*, V, 1880, p. 323; Melvin R. Gilmore, *Uses of Plants by the Indians of the Missouri River Region*; Gene Weltfish, *Lost Universe*, p. 415; Waldo R. Wedel, *An Introduction to Pawnee Archeology*, Bureau of American Ethnology, Bulletin 112, pp. 59–60.

Table 2
Pawnee Cultigens
Maize/Corn

Wedel	Will/Hyde	Zweiner	Blaine, E	Murie, J
	blue flour	dark blue flour	blue	black (blue)
		Kiowa blue (Pawnee)		blue speckled
	blue speckled flour		speckled	
		black flour (Mandan)		
	white/red striped flour	Pawnee striped flour		Red speckled (red and black)
	red flour	red flour (Mandan)		red
	red flint			
		brown flour (Osage)		
	white flour	white flour (Tuscarora)	white	white
			very white	
	yellow flour		yellow	yellow
charred zea maize	yellow flint			
	sweet corn			sweet corn (2)
			a corn (color not given) described as having large short ears with large grains	
	popcorn			

Sources: Waldo R. Wedel, An Introduction to Pawnee Archeology, Bureau of American Ethnology, Bulletin 112, p. 121; Dan Zweiner, "Gardens of the Iowa, Garden Varieties," pp. 18–23, and "A Native American Seed Catalogue." George F. Will and George E. Hyde, Corn Among the Indians of the Upper Missouri; James R. Murie, in Corn Among the Indians of the Upper Missouri, p. 295; Garland J. and Martha R. Blaine, unpublished notes.

Table 3
Pawnee Cultigens
Beans

Gilmore	Will/Hyde	Zweiner	Blaine, E.
		Hidatsa red Kentucky Wonder, pole (Atik-taxhata)	red (Atipahat) yellow (Atiktaxkata)
spider beans		Great Northern, white beans (Atiktaka)	big beans (like lima beans)

Table 4
Pawnee Cultigens
Pumpkins, Squashes, Melons

Wedel	Gilmore	Zweiner	Blaine, E. and other Pawnee sources
In Hill site Bush summer squash (*Cucurbita pepo melopepe*)	No specific names		big yellow pumpkin, with grooves (*Pahukstarhi*)
		Arikara winter squash	small pumpkins (*Pahukskata*) green squash with curved neck; green squash, long like water melons, tapering at ends watermelons, very small

Sources (tables 3 and 4): M. R. Gilmore, *Uses of Plants by the Indians of the Missouri River Region*; Gene Weltfish, *Caddoan Texts*; Dan Zweiner, "Gardens of the Iowa" and "A Native American Seed Catalogue"; W. R. Wedel, *An Introduction to Pawnee Archaeology*; p. 121. Garland J. and Martha R. Blaine, unpublished notes.

The tables do not contain all the different Pawnee crop varieties. In the Hill archaeological site in Nebraska, Waldo R. Wedel found several seeds of the *Chenopodium nutalliae*. This plant, a leafy member of the family commonly called "lamb's quarters," is known to have been a cultivated food of the Aztecs. Wedel asked if the seeds had been brought from Mexico by the Pawnees, who were said to have traveled to that country. If so, had they seen it used and brought it back as a crop for their own use? He adds that it is possible that other crops grown by the Pawnees may not have been recognized as such by early observers.[12]

The Sacred Beings had said that women were to be the principal agricultural labor force, but men occasionally helped prepare the fields by removing heavy brush or felling trees. Such work was especially important in the latter half of the nineteenth century, when the opportunities to fulfill their roles as hunters and warriors decreased, and the government agent promoted the white man's form of agriculture.

Before the time of the horse-drawn metal plow, the prairie sod could not be broken with the Indians' traditional bone hoe made of animal scapula fastened to a short handle. Instead, use was made of fertile areas located at the bottoms of bluffs, at the mouths of ravines, along streams, and in other places where the soil was friable.[13] As soil depletion occurred near the villages, the one-half to three-acre family fields had to be located some miles away. This distance eventually increased risk to workers, who were sometimes killed by marauders, especially in the years from the 1850s to the 1870s. Fields where women were killed and scalped were sometimes abandoned because of fear of spirits that lingered there.[14]

After the hunt ended in late February or early March, the bands returned to their villages with thoughts of the awakening earth and the planting of Mother Corn and other seeds. But before any planting activities could begin, as Pitaresaru had told the agent, ceremonial events needed to take place in order to sanctify the activity and gain assurance of beneficence from the Spirit Beings and Mother Earth.

The first thunder heard in the new year was the sign of the reawakening of the earth and the beginning of the natural cycle of growth. Tirawahut talked to the people in the thunder, and they were glad to see the lightning flashes and hear the low rumbling of His voice. This was the time of quiet prayer within the lodges and of renewal of certain Sacred Bundles, whose powers helped sustain Pawnee life. For each step and phase of planting, growing, and harvesting, a certain Sacred Bundle and ceremony was a necessary part of the ritual that proceeded or completed a cycle. *

In the spring the fields were cleared of winter debris and crops planted, as Effie Blaine described. When the corn reached a certain height and had been hoed and weeded twice, the tribe left the fields to grow and ripen while they went on the summer hunt, usually in late June. The fields were protected by fences of bushes and branches of trees "skillfully woven together," or by earthen ditches or piles of dried corn roots and weed debris placed along the field edges over the years.[15] While the corn, bean, and other plants ripened, lookouts stationed in the fields on elevated platforms made of poles scared away birds and small raiding animals.[16] In late August, when certain wild plants matured on the prairies where the Pawnees hunted, the people knew it was time to return to the villages to harvest their crops.

After the Pawnees moved to Indian Territory, former superintendent Barclay White observed the corn drying process in 1877. The corn was kept in hot coals until the husks burned. At that point it was judged that the corn inside was partially cooked by the confined steam. After the ears were cooled, the husks were removed and a mussel shell used to scrape the corn from the cob by "running the edge of the shell between the rows." This shelled corn was then laid out on the ground on canvas sheets, or whatever material was available, and thoroughly dried.[17] Another method was to let the corn roast overnight in its husks in a bed of ashes and coals. One job for the small boys during this process

---

* In *Lost Universe* Gene Weltfish describes various activities and ceremonies in the Skidi agricultural cycle in Chapter 7, "The Spring Awakening," Chapter 9, "The Planting of the Crops," Chapter 12, "Closing Episode of Planting Period," Chapter 31, "Harvest Time in the Village," *Ceremonies of the Pawnee* by, James R. Murie, contains translations of descriptions of ceremonial procedures for agricultural events of all Pawnee bands.

A Pawnee wooden mortar made of a hollowed-out tree section. The pointed end was thrust into the ground to hold it firm. The pestle was a section of a sapling or branch with the bark removed. Photo by Dr. R. E. Venk. The Blaine Collection.

was to drive the horses away, for "it was almost impossible to keep them from eating the corn, but they were given the husks to eat." The pile of roasted corn for the extended Blaine family would fill a space approximately four feet deep and eight to ten feet long. "That represented a lot of work," according to Garland J. Blaine, who helped his grandparents prepare the corn in the traditional way in the 1920s.[18] "Late in the fall after harvest, the Pawnee used to go through the corn fields and say, '*heru atira, rak kutsu?*' (Mother Corn, do you have anything for us?), hoping to find an ear or two that were missed. We went through the entire field two or three times carefully examining the stalks and the ground. They would tell us, 'Children, look good now. If we miss any corn, the corn will cry because we have left it alone.' You would be surprised what we would find, an ear here and there, already dried, and we'd put it in the sack."[19]

All dried corn was placed in skin containers in underground caches either inside or outside the mud lodge. Later, old flour sacks were used. Caches were still dug in the 1870s, after the Pawnees were living on their reservation in Indian Territory.[20]

When it came time to use the dried corn for some dishes, it

was necessary to grind it into meal. One very old method was to place the kernels on a hollowed out rock, then use another rock held in the hand to smash and grind them into meal. The most frequently used instruments were the wooden mortar and pestle. The method of using these two implements was called "shooting something into a container," because the pestle was a long, rounded piece of wood like an arrow or spear shaft, which was lowered with force into the mortar. The expression was used because the quick, strong, downward thrust was similar to the motion used in thrusting a lance or spear into an animal or shooting an arrow with force into a quarry.[21]

Even after the Pawnee agency had a flour mill on Beaver Creek in Nebraska, the Pawnee women preferred to use the mortar and pestle.[22] Some of these implements were taken to Indian Territory, and later some were made there from local materials. Later day Oklahoma Pawnees remembered the older method of grinding with a stone mortar and mano, which was mentioned by observers in Nebraska.[23]

In summary, when the first Europeans entered the vast regions of mid-America in the seventeenth and eighteenth centuries, the Pawnees had long possessed a successful system of providing themselves with food and other necessities from their fields and forests. According to their origin accounts, their ways of gathering and growing plants and plant products had been revealed and taught to them by the Sacred Beings. They reached a time when knowledge and technique provided them with corn surpluses, which were used in trade with other tribes.

The system was interwoven with religious beliefs and sustained by annual ceremonies. Mother Earth and Mother Corn were revered and respected deeply by the people. The people believed that they, too, were a part of a larger natural system extending to the stars.

When reservation life began in the 1850s, and the U.S. government policy of changing cultural patterns began, the well-tuned native system of agriculture, based on religious beliefs and communal efforts, was seen as primitive. Efforts began to replace the old ways, and these became a means of cultural destruction under the guise of progress and civilization.

Part II

> The independent farmer was a model citizen and his virtues were
> the essential virtues of a free and enlightened people enjoying the
> blessings of a republican form of government.
>
> —Brian Dippie, *The Vanishing American*

Reflecting the values of their countrymen, the new American
nation's first leaders considered using their own farming system as
a means of changing Indian life ways. In his January 18, 1803,
message to Congress, Pres. Thomas Jefferson stated that Indians
should be encouraged to raise stock and become farmers and
"thereby prove to themselves that less land and labor will maintain them in this better than in their former mode of living."[24]
Of course, less land for Indian use would mean greater amounts
available for the new nation's non-Indian citizens.

Early beginnings and implementation of such ideas came in
the late eighteenth century with the devising of Indian treaties
that were written during the time of westward expansion when
the interests of resident Indian peoples and the intruding settlers
were in conflict. When Indians refused to yield peacefully, military force was used to persuade them. In the old Northwest Territory north of the Ohio River, Maj. Gen. Anthony Wayne's
forces defeated the Wyandots, Delawares, Shawnees, Miamis,
and other displaced and resisting tribes. In the treaty signed by
them at Greenville on August 3, 1795, there was a provision for
domestic animals and "implements of Husbandry" to be distributed among the signers' tribes.[25]

In the following years, most tribes encountered such provisions in the treaties they signed with the U.S. government. This
was particularly true when the policy of "civilization" of the
American Indian came into being. By 1819 Congress initiated
the Civilization Fund Act based on the concept of native peoples
taking their places as independent farmers in the new society.
Provisions were made that "persons of good moral character
should be employed to teach to Indians under federal treaty relations the mode of agriculture suited to their situation."[26]

Thomas L. McKenney was one of the most fervent and committed policy makers. His desire was to bring to Indian tribes the

advantages of his society's farming methods. In his words, "We want to make citizens out of them, and they must first be anchored to the soil, else they will be flaying about whilst there is any room for them in the wilderness or an animal to be trapped."[27]

As superintendent of Indian Trade from 1816 to 1822, McKenney promoted the use of government trading posts and factories as centers of influence on the tribesmen who visited them to trade their furs. He encouraged the post factors (commissioned merchants) to plant and care for model gardens with a variety of crops and to have seeds and agricultural implements to show Indians who visited. Agricultural pursuit would teach industry and commitment to individual efforts and rewards. It would also provide the stability and security that came from private ownership of land tilled by the individual farmer. Such agricultural efforts, he promoted, represented farming as it should be and would be for the Indian if the united powers of treaty, legislation, and Indian agent could bring about the change.

The Pawnees' turn to become part of the great scheme came on October 9, 1833, in a treaty with the United States, which contained in article XI the phrase, "The United States, desirous to show the Pawnees the advantages of agriculture, . . . [agrees] to break up for each village a piece of land suitable for corn and potatoes for one season." Article VII added, "The United States agrees to furnish each of said four tribes with a farmer for five years, and deliver to said farmers for the benefit of said nation, one thousand dollars in value in oxen and other stock."[28] Article 4 of the treaty of September 24, 1857, noted that "The United States agrees to furnish farming utensils and stock worth twelve hundred dollars per annum, for ten years, or during the pleasure of the President, and for the first year's purchase of stock, and for erecting shelters for the same, an amount not exceeding $3,000, and also to employ a farmer to teach the Indians the art of agriculture."[29]

Indian agents endeavored to carry out such treaty provisions and later regulations that required efforts to introduce agricultural methods intended to replace native ones. If the members of the tribe were not tillers of the soil, then the agents were to persuade them to change their ways. Often this occurred in areas where nature had shown, or would show, that farming was unfeasible, or at least only marginally productive. But the policy was universal in saying that civilization for all Indian peoples was to be found by walking behind a plow.

Thinking of the future, Indian Commissioner William Medill said in 1848:

> The idea is to colonize our Indian tribes . . . confining each within a small district or country, so that as the game decreases and becomes scarce, the adults will gradually be compelled to resort to agriculture and other kinds of labor to obtain a subsistence in which aid may be afforded and facilities furnished them out of the means obtained by the sale of their former possessions.[30]

The above statement hints at the fact that there was more to the policy of "civilizing" the Indian by teaching him to be a farmer than met the eye. The less land that the Indian needed to support himself in nomadic hunting and gathering activities, the more land that would be available for non-Indian use. The idea of allotting Indians their own farm homesteads was already in the minds of many policy makers long before the Allotment Act of 1886 was passed. In fact, Indian agents were trying to convince the Pawnees to take up individual farmsteads in the early 1870s. Six hundred ten-acre plots were actually surveyed for this purpose.[31]

The Pawnee agent met with the chiefs in council from time to time to make announcements and hear their responses to certain proposals, particularly about changes to be made in some aspect of reservation life. In September 1871, he warned tribal leaders that buffalo would soon be scarce and that they must raise stock for meat. He also suggested that they sell more of their land to supply funds for the purchase of farm machinery. Also part of their annual treaty annuity could be used to purchase hay rakes and pitchforks. After discussion the chiefs agreed to the agent's purchasing of the rakes and pitchforks.[32] This request was necessary because in an 1857 treaty, the government had agreed to supply farming equipment and seeds only for ten years, and the period had ended.

Later in the month, the agent reminded the chiefs that they had agreed in the spring to spend their entire cash annuity to break land and build houses on the aforementioned ten-acre plots. But now the chiefs refused the request due to the severity of Sioux attacks, which would make living apart from one another on individual acreages foolish and deadly. Somehow promotion of government programs blinded the agent, who adamantly insisted on the proposal although he was aware of the continuing Sioux attacks. He continued to promote the idea, and after persuasion, or perhaps coercion not recorded in the council journal, the chiefs agreed to the $3,000 expenditure.[33]

Occasionally the chiefs would object to certain innovations. Eager to introduce all sorts of garden seeds, in April 1872, the agent suggested garden peas. Sky Chief rejected the request to purchase these seeds, saying that beans were a better crop, but he agreed to purchasing seed potatoes for planting.[34] Both garden peas and cultivated potatoes were new crops to the Pawnees, but they had gathered the wild potato traditionally. Therefore, a cultivated form of potato was easier for them to accept. As for peas, they were an unknown food and not acceptable to the Pawnees, who were satisfied with their own foods. These had been given to their ancestors by the Sacred Beings, who had decreed which seeds should be planted, which plants should be gathered, and how these tasks should be done.

In May 1872, the chiefs told the agent that the tribe wanted to go on the hunt as soon as planting was completed. Rather unnecessarily, the agent told the chiefs to see that their people planted enough seeds for sufficient crops and to leave enough people in the village to care for the growing plants while the tribe was absent.[35] This was an effort to change the traditional patterns, which did not demand leaving behind individuals to care for the crops.

One of the chiefs was beginning to consider the new ideas. Eagle Chief of the Skidi Band indicated changes in traditional practices when he informed the agent at this time that "his people got through the work much faster, since before when only the women worked, the men do work now."[36] The council minutes do not reveal how many or how few warriors and others were involved. Because of the traditional resistance to changing the roles given to males and females in the origin myths, there may not have been many participants. But the agent reported any sign of success to his superiors.

In 1874 the records indicate a shift in field size due to plow use. According to the agent, besides the squaw patches worked by traditional methods, there were fields of between eight and twelve acres, which had been plowed for several years. The Skidis were making more use of the plow, and in this year they were better off than the other bands. Most of the working teams of horses were found in this band. They kept their horses in better shape than the other bands. "They do well if they manage to keep them alive with hay until green grass comes," commented the agent.[37]

This problem existed because the Pawnees were not able to take their animals to graze farther and farther from the villages as more forage was needed. This practice was constrained by the high risk of having horses stolen by their enemies. Since replenishment of the herds by one traditional means, that is, by stealing them back from tribes that had stolen from them, was discouraged and punishable, the Pawnees had to keep their horses close to the villages in order to have enough for the hunt. To offset the difficulty of poor winter forage, some chiefs began to gather hay in season, an innovation suggested by the agent.

The other three bands, the Chaui, Kitkahahki, and Pitahawirata, while more resistant to change, were obtaining some assistance with field plowing by the agency farmer in 1874. But for the most part, they continued in the traditional way, with women planting and tending the crops. In 1874 the agent said, "I approved of having them cultivate all they can among themselves, and in their own way if they choose."[38] The great need for food in these times of drought, grasshopper invasion, and poor hunts undoubtedly aided his acceptance of traditional and successful methods.[39]

The year 1874 saw the government increase efforts to turn the Pawnees into farmers living on individual allotments. On March 18, the chiefs agreed to give up $10,000 of their annuity for the purchase of seed, the breaking of five hundred acres of land, the purchase and repairs of agricultural implements, and the payment of Indian labor and teams.[40] This extraordinary amount represented the major part of their annuity, which, as events were to prove, could have been better spent for food and other necessities.

The Pawnee agent was pleased with the chiefs' agreement to spend their annuity in this manner. He saw it as a means to promote further the effort of turning Pawnee men into full time farmers. He then told the chiefs they were not permitted to go on the summer buffalo hunt, and they would have to depend *altogether* on what food they could raise on the reservation by their own efforts.[41] It had been decided that keeping the tribe on the reservation would prevent reoccurrence of the previous summer's hunt attack and massacre by the Sioux. From the Sioux annuity, the government paid for the loss of Pawnee life, belongings, and hunt products. There would be no Sioux annuity to help feed them this year, he informed the Pawnees.

The tribal leaders responses to this were not recorded, but it may be assumed that their not being allowed to go on the hunt was a serious blow, augmented by being told that they must go into the fields to work with the women. This was a serious affront to their culturally perceived roles as hunters and warriors.

These decisions also emphasized that their traditional life as hunters was changing rapidly. They were aware that the buffalo herds were diminishing, largely at the hands of white hunters who killed thousands of the great beasts for profitable sale of hides and tongues in the eastern market. For the most part, there had been curious interest in new ideas proposed by the agent to change the old ways. But the interest had been only half-hearted, not based on most leaders' true conviction. Acceptance of rakes, new seeds, and other items was mainly a way of gaining a concession here and there for something else that was seen as necessary in maintaining their status as chiefs and in promoting the welfare of the tribe. They wanted to maintain as traditional a way of life as was possible under the government's pressure for change and conformity. By 1874 it was obvious to even the most conservative Pawnees that their way of life was changing due to causes beyond their control. Other means, such as those suggested by the agents, must be considered in order to sustain the life of their people.

To add to the difficulty of the time, the summer of 1874 brought a serious drought to Nebraska, and crops of both Indians and

Forty thousand Buffalo hides, piled in yards of Rath & Wright, Dodge City, Kansas, 1877, ready for shipment.

Buffalo hides awaiting shipment East from the Rath and Wright yards, Dodge City, Kansas. During the 1870s, hide hunters slaughtered over three million buffalo. Col. Richard I. Dodge said that the Kansas plains offered the best buffalo hunting, although massive killing occurred in several states. This decimation led to near extinction of the animal and extreme deprivation of the Indian. Courtesy of Western History Collections, University of Oklahoma Library.

whites failed. What the drought did not destroy, massive clouds of grasshoppers did. A resolution proposed by the agent and agreed to by the chiefs allowed the remainder of the tribe's cash annuity to be spent for food for the hungry people.[42] Its amount was now $5,000, because it had been reduced by the resolution to use $10,000 for the above-mentioned items.

From the Pawnee point of view, not being able to follow traditional ways of coping with nature, and not going on the hunt when the season and ritual indicated, seemed to cause the balance between the Spirit Beings, the earth, its creatures, and the Pawnees to disappear.

The emphasis on turning the Pawnee and other Native American societies into male-oriented farming cultures increased after the Civil War. Signs of the times indicated that American farming may have reached its apogee as an individualistic enterprise by the 1870s. After that, the growth of cities and industry assumed greater economic importance.[43] Banking and industrial corporations increased in size and number and began to gain control of the economy. Farmers found that they had lost much of their extolled independence just at the point when they were making a turn from subsistence living to farming for profit.

But control of farming activities had left their communities. Railroad companies, grain elevator owners, and distant machinery manufacturers set prices for goods and services over which the farmer had little control. He became only the producer of raw products that moved along an increasingly complicated system of processes to the consumer. In the 1870s, when this trend began, new farmers' organizations sought to lobby the federal government for more rail rate controls and reasonable credit sources to assist their members in their struggle to compete against growing competition from European and South American agriculturists. The sad truth for the U.S. farmer in the 1870s, and later, was that "big corporations that were able to charge whatever the traffic would bear acquired their monopolistic powers by winning control, not of land and natural resources, but of capital and capital equipment."[44]

Yet government Indian policy continued to try to convert the Pawnees into replicas of the farmers of pre-Civil War days, rugged individuals, self-sufficient upon their land. In reality, white farmers now were taking collective actions to secure a fair share of the nation's wealth. The Indian as a farmer would have little chance to compete in what was becoming an increasingly mechanized and credit-oriented farming world.

✝✝✝
3

Horse Stealing

An Economic Necessity

Now Brother Horse comes flying,
Now I see my brother, the Horse comes flying.
                    —*Garland J. Blaine, family song*

After the Pawnees obtained horses in the late 1600s and early 1700s, those animals entered the realm of tribal legend and acquired magical and sacred characteristics.* Horses appeared in dreams and to vision seekers. Their earliest appearance is described in one origin myth. In it a boy has a dream of two beautiful horses. When he awakes he goes out and makes little horses of mud and pretends that they are alive, feeding and watering them.† Soon he dreams again of horses and hears Tirawahut singing a song. When he awakes he goes to the top of a hill and sings the song that he heard in his dream. He waits and in a vision he is told three wondrous things: Tirawahut has given him a dance; he shall become a chief; and the little mud horses are now

* In 1700, Jesuit Father Gabriel Marest noted that the Pawnees, Poncas, Kansas, and Missourias owned Spanish horses, and the Pawnees were said to have used them for buffalo hunting before this time. By 1719 it was claimed that the Pawnees had a limited number of horses they used for military endeavors. (See Ewers, *The Horse in the Blackfoot Culture*, pp. 4 and 335, and Secoy, *Changing Military Patterns on the Great Plains*, p. 28.)
† According to Garland J. Blaine, as late as the 1920s, he and other small boys made little horses of clay or mud.

living, just as he saw them in his dream. He is told where to find them and when he goes there, there are the two beautiful animals. He leads them to the village, "where people revere them as they are the first they have ever seen" according to the legend.[1]

Another legend reveals that the sixteenth-century horse, introduced into the New World by Europeans, soon took its place beside the sacred bison in Pawnee mythology. In one story a chief's son is plagued with misfortune. Numerous war parties of which he is a member are not successful, and finally other warriors refuse to allow him to participate in them. Rejected, he becomes despondent and leaves the village. During his absence he has a vision in which two clouds of dust appear in the west. The first cloud is made by two horses and the second by two buffaloes. The vision continues, and he finds himself in a sacred lodge under a lake. Here a group of men on the north side dance, imitating the movements of horses, while on the south side, men imitate the buffaloes. Eventually, they all turn into horses and buffaloes, and the leader of the buffaloes tells the boy that they feel sorry for him and will teach him the Buffalo Dance and the Wild Horse Dance. He will then become a doctor to his people.

After awhile, the horses give him a spear, a shield, and a black lariat. The buffaloes give him paint for his body and some of their wool. Finally, one of the horses returns with him to the village and serves him well in war and on the hunt. From then on, he is a successful warrior and hunter, and a respected member of his band.[2]

Some legends contain historical references. In one, of which there are several versions, a poor, sick, old horse is befriended by a poor boy and his grandmother. The horse is really a sacred horse, and in time he shows his appreciation of the care given him by becoming beautiful and spirited. He shows the boy how to hunt, vanquish the Sioux, and win the hand of the chief's daughter.[3]

Another story tells that long, long ago a party of hunters saw dust rising a long way off. Then they saw something moving, and there were small flashes of light in the sunlight. When they got closer, they saw an apparition, men-beasts dressed in metal clothing with hairy faces. They had never seen horses or Spaniards before, and they thought each horse and rider was all one creature.[4]

Not only legends but also songs told of the wonderful horse, Eagle Chief, a Pitahawirata, owned the following song and sang and danced to it in the Bear Dance.

> He said, the horse is shouting,
> I am telling it, the horse is shouting.
> Now I telling it,
> The horse is shouting at something he did.[5]

It has been observed that objects in a culture that have the greatest importance and use often generate in time a greater elaboration of language terms about them than in cultures where the same objects may not have, or may have lost, intensive use and importance. The classic example is in the Eskimo language, which contains many terms for snow, such as softly-falling snow, dry-wind-driven-snow, dry-packed-snow-suitable-for-cutting-into-blocks, and others.[6] The English language has words like bay, sorrel, and roan to describe horses. These words give a generalized mental picture of the horse's color but with no detailed characteristics. The Pawnee language carried the description of a horse further in a single term. These were not words added to describe, as English might, a roan horse with a black mane and forelegs but were complete descriptive words for a specific horse type. Some examples directly translated are:

Horse gray with iron-gray withers, forelegs; light-colored mane and nape.
Horse white; red ears, tail, and hooves.
Horse white; black ears, tail, and hooves.[7]

Such detailed names probably grew from large numbers of animals being herded communally and the need for an individual to identify correctly and claim his own horse or horses from the herd. This language development corroborates other evidence that the horse played an extremely important role in the Pawnees's daily and ritual life. Horses were held in high regard because of the basic belief that Tirawahut created and was a part of all creatures. Respect was due the horse, as it was the bison, for its supernatural origin and its part in sustaining life.

A Pawnee saying was, "Take care of your horse, and he may save your life by being in good condition. You addressed your horse respectfully by saying *Heru atiku*, or if a mare, *Heru tsu-at* [Greetings Male, or Female Horse]." Men spent time caring for a favorite mount. After a hard ride, a warrior would walk his horse for awhile to allow it to cool down, and he would use a corncob to curry it. Tallow was rubbed on a horse's groin if it were ridden for several days on long journeys.[8] Different plant medicines were used to heal or alleviate ailments such as saddle sores and distemper.[9] It was said that a horse had understanding. "If you see a horse and he rides toward people and puts his head down and tries to ride along the edge, someone is mean to him. If you take care of him and you curry him and you have compassion for him, when you get on him he is going to want people to know he is proud. Horses are smart when there are people about. He is going to nicker and hold his head up and people are going to see him. That horse is going to try to make you look good to others."[10]

Wichita Blaine, named He Overtook the Enemy, said only a bastard would whip a horse or treat it cruelly. Horses, he said, were creatures of Tirawahut, and they must be treated with respect. But, he added, noting the universal range of human character, "There are always those bastards who would mistreat anything."[11]

Among the Pawnees, as in most horse-owning tribal cultures, an individual's rank determined the number of horses owned. Although horses could be acquired as a gift and by natural increase in the herd, many horses were gained by raiding. Only chiefs and leading warriors could organize expeditions for this purpose. Therefore, the opportunities for their acquiring horses were far greater than were those of men of lesser rank. In addition, such leaders were given horses by younger men who were learning the craft when they accompanied such leaders on raiding expeditions and were successful themselves in capturing horses. Fifteen to twenty horses were about all one man's household could care for during early reservation days and for some time before that. A man having fifteen to twenty horses was a chief, a prominent warrior, or a doctor. A man with around five horses was probably coming into his own as a warrior, a hunter, or a man of means. Perhaps a man who was older might have only five horses or less because he had a smaller family to care for and less need. If a man had no horses, it did not mean that he was lazy but that he had bad luck on horse-stealing expeditions, or that he was not invited to participate, or that all his horses had been stolen by other tribes. However, a few men were cowards, fearful of facing the dangers in acquiring horses, so they had none. Some others were too old, ill, lazy, or poor to care for them.[12]

Women in the family had their horse-related responsibilities. Horses used as pack animals were in their care. They led the animals with the help of older children on the long treks to and from hunting country. If an animal should lose its pack or get free, it was the woman's responsibility to catch it, bring it back, and repack or tie it. Packing and unpacking of household goods and camping gear on the horse was hard work. At the camp, after the horses were unloaded, women took them to graze and be watered.[13] Some women were good riders; and Effie Blaine, who rode a horse to Indian Territory in 1873, continued to enjoy riding as long as she was able, preferring a "feisty" horse that would run fast.[14]

When a colt had grown old and strong enough to ride, it was trained and used to hunt, chase enemies, or escape from them, if necessary. When it became too old to use as a riding horse, it could be used as a pack animal. In the spring horses were used to carry burdens because they were stronger then than the mares with foals. In the fall the mares were used as pack animals, for it was said that then they could endure more than a horse. Young boys from ten to fourteen years took the horses to pastures located a day or two away from overgrazed village environs. This practice was dangerous and sometimes horses were stolen by marauding enemies and the young men killed.[15]

Such losses of horses became a serious problem in the 1860s and 1870s. It became necessary to guard and protect them continually. In Nebraska, during the 1860s, there was a big snow; one man who was a child then remembered that it snowed until the drifts reached almost higher than the mudlodges that were twenty to twenty-five feet tall. He said family horses had to be found in the deepening drifts, and as many animals as there was room for were brought inside the mudlodges. Some of the wooden wall supports had to be taken down so that the grass lining of the lodge walls could be eaten by the hungry horses. He added ruefully that it was fortunate that it had been a good crop year and that the people had enough dried meat, corn, and pumpkins. Otherwise, they would have had to consume some of the horses.[16]

In the twentieth century, a reminder of the great role the horse played in Pawnee history is retained in family names carried by Pawnee families. Some are (or have been) Horse Chief, Spotted Horse, Big Spotted Horse, Fancy Horse, Fancy Rider, Real Rider, Riding In, Riding Up, and White Horse. One of the earliest names recorded was that of Saritsaris (Shah-re-tah-riches) or Raging Horse, a Chaui signer of the 1833 and 1848 Pawnee treaties with the United States.

Horse Stealing and the U.S. Government

Horse stealing was not just a lark that the Pawnees indulged in for sport and adventure. It was a culturally accepted means of acquiring and maintaining status and wealth. Perhaps, more importantly, it was the method for replenishing a capital resource that was essential for use in the hunt, as a means for acquiring food, clothing, and shelter. Horse stealing was also necessary to maintain sufficient numbers of horses to offset thefts of Pawnee horses. Without the horse, attack and revenge against the horse-owning enemy was impossible and tribal survival became endangered. In the prereservation period, a balance could be more or less maintained between this capital loss and gain by stealing from distant places and peoples or from the enemy, who stole from you. The Pawnees were reputed to be excellent horse stealers. Garland J. Blaine, who listened to the old men from Nebraska, told what they said about their roles in this activity.

> Stealing horses was an ordered process with prescribed rules and roles. It was not a harum-scarum event but carefully planned. When he heard that an expedition was being planned, a young man without horses would ask an older man if he could accom-

pany him. Or an older man might ask a younger man if he could go with him and his party. Just a few men went together on foot in those days. When they got horses, and if the young man got six or seven, say, by his efforts, he would give them to the leader, other members, and his band chief when he got home. He divided them according to custom. Eventually he would be given one to keep for himself.

Then, when he was "practiced," he would go by himself, since he was yet too inexperienced to be responsible for anyone else's life. Sometimes he did not return. There was always danger from other tribes that might catch him alone on the long journey. But if he did return, he would again distribute most of the horses he got among his superiors in age and rank. And later he would keep some for himself. Finally, he would reach the time when he would go with others as a matter of course. As he got older he could lead parties, but this was assuming he had acquired or inherited the status to be a leader.

After the treaty period began this process began to accelerate and change. Horses began to be drained from the tribal stock more rapidly. This was due to many things, of which one was the increased raids on the Pawnee villages by foreign tribes. Also, as many tribes were moved by the government on to lands hunted by our tribe, it became more difficult to cross our country safely. There were Delawares, Potawatomis, Sac and Fox and others from across the river [Mississippi]. At this time young men did not always go through the preparatory period. They were desperate for a horse both as a necessity and as a symbol of being a man. Some went off to get horses without consent. In those cases some even stole from allies, such as the Wichitas. But when there was an organized group it never had more than four or five men in it. Small parties could more easily escape detection by enemy tribemen, and from an agent who did not allow our men to leave without permission.

After the Pawnees stole horses and started home, they would ride at least two days without stopping for more than a short time when it was time to feed and water the horses. They would find a stream in a valley with good grass. Then two men would stay on the rise as scouts. The horses they were riding would be taken with the others down the hill and driven into the stream and allowed to drink. The men with them would also drink and wash. Then the horses would be taken to nearby grass and allowed to

In October 1819, Maj. Benjamin O'Fallon held a council at Council Bluffs attended by the Pawnees. Samuel Seymour painted this scene. The original is in the Beinecke Library at Yale University. Courtesy of the Kansas State Historical Society, Topeka.

graze. The men on the hill would then run down and go into the water themselves to drink and wash. A short time later all would mount and continue toward home with the horses.

Fatigue, then exhaustion, occurred after so many hours riding without sleep. So a man would ride up to the leader and say, "Rekita, I am tired. Would you waken me?" Then he would ride in front and the rekita would pull out his cat-o-nine-tail-like whip and hit him across the back—not just once or twice, but more, until the man's senses were restored. The leader would ask, "How are you now, my son?" And he would reply, "Fine, Atias, [father, a term of respect]" and resume his place in the group.

Often men would arrive back at the village with their backs cut open with whipping. But this was a sign of honor. Some old men living when I was young had such scars. It was like a dueling scar. The more a man had, the braver he was and the more expeditions of *great* length and endurance he had been on. The Pawnee warriors would sit and drop their blankets so that the scars would show. When I first saw the painting of the Pawnee at the Council Bluffs council, and saw those blankets dropped to the waist, I thought, "Ah, those are Pawnees."

After stealing their horses, the old men had this to say about other tribes. The Mexicans or *Sustarus*, Hair Under Their Noses, were easy to steal from. They would chase us, but not over the river, the Rio Grande, because they didn't want to be chased themselves by the Indians on the other side, so they would turn back. The Kataka, western tribes like the Kiowa Apache, would give chase for four days. Then they would stop, but they always set the grass on fire at this point. When you saw the smoke, you could stop and rest for awhile. Those tribes hoped the prevailing wind would blow the fire so it would catch up with and trap you. Now the Kiowa and Comanche would only give chase for two days. Then you could rest and camp. We would not worry because those two tribes were cowards. They might try to get their horses back by stealing them, but they would never attack our men. As for the Cheyennes, we always went beyond their country. Then in later years the Cheyenne horses were never any good. They were always skinny and bony. My grandfather said if they ever had a good fat horse, they ate it. Riding a Cheyenne horse was like riding a knife blade!* The Sioux, Cut Throats, didn't take care of their horses. We only tried to steal back our own from them.

* In 1869, Big Spotted Horse apparently was satisfied with Cheyenne horses because he and his party brought back 150 of them to his village.

There is a story about a group of my family who were gone for a long, long time to find horses. My Grandmother Blaine descended from that family. The leader of this group was left-handed, as I was before my teachers made me change. This characteristic has always been a predominant feature in our family, and this particular group of men were almost all left-handed. Well, after these four warriors were away for a long time, they say that the family began to mourn in the evenings because they knew that after such a long absence that they were presumably dead. On one of the hunts in which game was scarce, my family and others went beyond the limits where they usually hunted. Some of the men went even farther. One evening here came one of the scouts who had been gone three or four days beyond our hunting range. He rode in saying, "They are still alive I think. There is a tree over there where I came from, and the must have been there because there are four figures carved into it. The leader is holding a pipe in his left hand which indicated they are the four men who have been away for a long time. And it is a fresh carving. It could not have been over a month old. So they must still be alive!"

So there was great rejoicing. Then some of the people got together with the family and decided to go look at the tree with the carving. The scout took them there and they saw those fresh-carved figures. And the details showed they wore what those men had worn. They wore beaver hats, what are now called otter hats. This man had a pipe in his left hand which indicated who he was. And each man had his robe on in a certain way that indicated the ceremonial organization to which he belonged. Not long after this the men all returned to our village. And they brought many horses with them.[17]

But the above described freedom to journey far from the villages and return with horses from many places was changed after the Society of Friends selected Indian agents, who became overseers of Pawnee affairs for the U.S. government in the 1870s.* The Pawnee horse shortage increased as agents demanded the return of stolen horses. They also tried to prevent the Pawnees

---

* President U. S. Grant initiated reforms in U.S. Indian policy to reduce inefficiency, graft, and mishandling of Indian affairs. Religious denominations, including the Society of Friends, received authority to oversee certain Indian tribes. Selection of Indian agents became a responsibility. The Pawnees' first Quaker agent was Joseph Troth, in 1869.

from recapturing or stealing an equivalent number of horses to replace those the Sioux or others stole from them. In the agent's view this practice only increased hostility between tribes. They said that if the Pawnees were stopped from going on "war parties," as the agents chose to call them, then perhaps the Sioux and others would not steal the Pawnees' horses. The Quakers did not recognize that their golden rule had nothing to do with traditional values, status, survival, economic needs, and demands of the region's plains and village Indians.

In stealing from other tribes, the Pawnees sought to offset their losses. Finally their agent recognized that the decreasing horse numbers were a serious problem. He reported the losses and repeatedly requested that something be done about successful Sioux incursions. The Pawnee tribal leaders were promised repeatedly that something would be done.

But nothing was effective during the 1860s and 1870s, although the government was quick to act if the Pawnee were the violators of the regulations regarding stealing and returning stolen horses. In January 1870, Pawnee Agent Jacob Troth wrote to the Comanche agent that some Pawnees had been on the warpath, and he was informed that they had taken a large number of Comanche horses. He replied, "I have made arrangements for the recovery of the horses and desire to turn them over to thee as soon as they can be reclaimed."[18] When Troth met with the Pawnee chiefs in late January about the matter, they said that they had friendly relations with the Comanches and wanted to maintain them; therefore, they would return the horses stolen by some of their warriors. At least that is what the agent said they said.

Earlier in the month, U.S. Army Gen. J. M. Schofield of the Department of the Missouri at Saint Louis informed Lt. Gen. Philip Sheridan, who was at his Chicago headquarters of the Military Division of the Missouri, that a party "believed to be Pawnee" attacked a camp of peaceful Arapahoes and Cheyennes led by Little Robe and Yellow Bear on Bluff Creek south of Fort Dodge, Kansas. Two hundred forty horses were stolen and driven off. He suggested that now or in the spring, Gen. Christopher Augur, commanding the Department of the Platte, could assist in recapturing them. Sheridan directed Augur to recover the horses stolen by the Pawnees, arrest those responsible for the thefts, and confine them with balls and chains attached to their legs at the nearest post.[19]

Supt. Samuel Janney, also involved in the matter, told the Indian commissioner that two "war parties" of thirty Pawnees were due to return to the reservation with over one hundred stolen horses. Their agent had inquired what was he to do with them? He had reminded him of the 1869 ruling that instructed, "Any horses in possession of Indians where ownership is questioned, that the agent and the commanding officer of the nearest post are to investigate and determine ownership. If the horses are taken from whites or friendly Indians they are to be returned."[20]

Agent Troth was instructed to proceed to Lone Tree, where the "war parties" were camped. There he selected two men from each of the three bands implicated. The prisoners were escorted to the Omaha military barracks as Sheridan had directed. The agent then elicited a solemn promise from the chiefs that their men should never be permitted to go to war (horse stealing) again. In return the chiefs asked him to intercede on the part of the six prisoners. He informed Superintendent Janney with satisfaction that, "I don't think they will give us any further trouble."[21] This group of Pawnees was imprisoned at the same time as the prisoners in the Yellow Sun case (see chapter 1).

The imprisonment of the Pawnee horse thieves caused official consternation when it was discovered that the accused were all U.S. Army Indian Scouts. General Augur stated that the prisoners were all "faithful soldiers of ours for the past two or three summers." He added that they had been of great service against the Cheyennes and probably thought they were doing a service by stealing the horses. Punishment should not be severe because they might be needed as scouts again.[22] Then the Secretary of War, Gen. J. M. Schofield, added that "in view of the facts stated by Augur as to the characteristics of the Indians engaged in the raid, their past service, and their probable ignorance of the relation existing between the Government and the Indians upon whom the raid was made, I would not advise any other punishment beyond making restitution as far as they are able."[23]

Nevertheless, the Pawnee Scouts continued to be prisoners while the Indian Office and the War Department continued to exchange correspondence on the matter. In late April, the Paw-

U.S. Army Pawnee Scouts in 1869. The Scouts were recruited and led by Maj. Frank North and Capt. Luther North. The last year that they were recruited and served was 1876. Their major engagements were with the Sioux and Cheyennes. Pawnee Scouts protected the men building the Union Pacific Railroad. Courtesy of Western History Collections, University of Oklahoma Library.

Big Spotted Horse, a renowned Pita-hawirata warrior, photographed in Indian Territory, ca. 1875. Courtesy of Archives and Manuscripts Division of the Oklahoma Historical Society.

nees were released from prison, and General Augur was authorized to see that the horses were taken to Fort Harker, a post in Kansas near the Smoky Hill River and the Santa Fe stage line.[24] Agent Troth was asked to select a suitable person to accompany the horse party to Kansas. He asked Luther North, a former U.S. Army officer in charge of the Pawnee Scouts, to do so.[25] According to North, whose account differs from the official version in some details, the horses were stolen in the fall of 1869 from the Cheyennes in Indian Territory. Big Spotted Horse, a Pawnee Scout from the Pitahawirata band and leader of the "war party," brought the horses back. In council the chiefs were reprimanded and reminded that they were never to go on war parties again. In the future, the Pawnees were to be friends with all the tribes. The agent then informed them that they had to take the horses back. The chiefs emphatically refused, saying they would be killed by the Cheyennes if they did so. Then, the chiefs were told that they were to care for and be responsible for the captured horses until they could be returned.

From time to time one or another of the chiefs would go to the agent and report the mysterious death of a horse for one reason or another. When it came time to return them, some months later, only thirty-five were said to be living. The party got together and drove the horses to Fort Harker. There they were delivered to the quartermaster by North, who was accompanied by the Pitahawirata chief, Fighting Bear, and eight young men.[26] An official letter states the horses were delivered by July 16, 1870.

After the imprisonment of the men, less was heard about Pawnee horse stealing, although it continued in the small secret forays mentioned in the Blaine account. While the traditional means of replenishment of the herd decreased, the stealing of Pawnee horses increased. In 1871 a large number were taken and the agent allowed the tribe to make efforts to recover them, except in two instances because Big Spotted Horse had "abused the privilege." Exactly what he had done was not explained, but it can be inferred that Pawnee attempts to pursue and recover stolen horses would not be allowed again.[27]

In July 1872, Baptiste Bayhylle, the Pawnee interpreter, and J. B. Omohundro, a scout, recovered some horses from an unnamed tribe by prearrangement between Indian agents. In the fall of this year, the horse scarcity became so serious that some of the tribe could not go on the winter hunt because they did not have enough animals to carry equipment, such as tipi poles and covers needed for shelter during the cold journey and the stay on the hunting grounds.[28] In October, it was reported that sixty-five horses had been stolen before this month and fifty-six stolen "last week." In November a large number were taken, and the agent wrote that he "hopes something can be done."[29]

The worst was yet to happen. The Pawnees who could go on the winter hunt left in November. In the meantime a large group of Sioux were observed leaving the Fort Laramie area in late October.[30] They found the Pawnees, surreptitiously approached the area where the horses were held, and drove off an overwhelmingly large number of 111, "almost all" of the horses owned by the Skidi and Pitahawirata bands.[31] The boys who were stationed to watch the animals were no match for the horsemen riding down upon them.

The hunt had to be abandoned and the angry and desperate hunters and their families walked the long way back carrying what they could on their backs. They had to abandon tipis, meat, and hides being prepared. Frank White, a Chaui, made his way to Fort McPherson, where he asked the commanding officer for help in recovering the horses. His request was refused; the excuse was that the post horses were sick and could not be used.[32]

The march back to their reservation was among the most bitter the Pawnees were to make. They had promised to stay at peace with all tribes and were no longer allowed to pursue the enemy to recapture their stolen horses. Now with many horses gone, and the meat from the hunt abandoned, they faced continuing hunger. Governmental control of the nomadic Sioux seemed to be minimal, and at this point, the Sioux seemed to have complete freedom to attack the village tribes and run off horses without the government taking any serious action against them. One reason for the lack of assistance from officials at Fort McPherson may not have actually been sick horses but a fear of taking sides with the Pawnees against the well-armed Sioux, whose lands were near the fort.

In January 1873, after the bands returned, the chiefs in council angrily demanded that two hundred soldiers be employed to help them get their horses back. The agent sympathized and attempted to pacify them by saying he would immediately inform the superintendent at Omaha of their plight and see what could be done. This was a familiar response, and the chiefs knew it. Still, they said they would wait awhile, but if speedy measures were not taken, they would take matters into their own hands and forget the peace policy forced upon them.[33] No action from the government was forthcoming, and on March 20, to further appease the angry and frustrated chiefs, Agent William Burgess sent the following petition to Supt. Barclay White.

> We the undersigned chiefs of the Pawnee tribe of Indians at a council held in the Council house this 20th day 3rd month, 1873, hereby agree to present the following, viz, That in consideration of our misfortune by the loss of many of our horses stolen from us

by our enemies and being entirely unsuccessful in catching buffalo or other game on our winterhunt, we are now in a very destitute condition and many of our number have little or nothing to eat. We have no robes or money to buy with and therefore on behalf of the tribe we request that the sum of Three thousand dollars ($3000) be taken from what has been represented to us as unexpended balance due to the Pawnees, and placed under the charge of our Agent to be used to purchase provisions and have the same issued among us as our necessities may demand. . . .[34]

Apparently this was not heeded, for in May, Superintendent White informed the agent that he needed a description of all the horses taken by the Sioux. This account would be sent to the Indian commissioner so that the total value could be computed and the amount deducted from the next Sioux annuity and then paid to the Pawnees.[35] Was this not bureaucracy at its pertinacious best? To question each Pawnee who had had horses stolen, and then to obtain and write down a complicated description of 111 or more horses, would certainly be time-consuming and even further delay settlement and justice. Why the surplus funds requested in the petition were not expended to feed the starving Pawnees is not said.

In the 1870s, the continual loss of Pawnee horses without their replenishment of supply by the traditional method of horse stealing hastened the tribe's economic decline. Feeble, few, or no attempts by the government to recover stolen horses, and reluctant or no compensation for losses sustained, caused not only a capital resource drain, but a loss of individual status and spirit. The economic base provided by horse ownership and use diminished until continual penury from this and other causes became the way of life for the Pawnee people after 1870.

✝✝✝

4

The Great Herd and the Pawnees

A Sacred Relationship

> *From where I come*
> *the Buffalo is standing in reverence*
> *with head low to the ground.*
> —*Pawnee song*

On June 1, 1871, Pawnee Head Chief Pitaresaru said to Supt. Samuel Janney in council that the Pawnees needed to go on their buffalo hunts for as long as possible because "we are afraid when we have no meat to offer the Great Spirit he will be angry and punish us."[1] This statement was made because the buffalo and the hunt represented a major religious commitment between the Pawnees and Tirawahut, the great God-Force of the universe and other Sacred Beings. The semiannual hunts were essential parts of the panorama of experiences through which Pawnee life moved felicitously when all rituals and acts pertaining to a particular aspect of that life were observed. The Pawnees hunted not only to obtain necessary products of the buffalo to sustain life but also to maintain the sacred order by killing and dedicating certain buffaloes to Tirawahut, who created and made all life possible. He would be angered if the rites that originated with the creation of the people were not properly observed. Pitaresaru himself had dedicated several buffaloes, four eagles and four wildcats to Tirawahut, and with these acts he had reached the highest favor with his God.[2] However, even if the superintendent had understood the significance of Pitaresaru's statement, he would have considered it only native superstition, irrelevant to the overall plans that the Society of Friends and the government had for attempting to "civilize" the Pawnees by eliminating their freedom of the hunt and substituting for it the space-confining life of the farmer.

Many Pawnee origin myths illustrate the early importance of the buffalo. The stories say that from the time of creation humans had kinship with the animal. A Skidi myth told that a certain female buffalo was the one that led all the other buffalo in their migrations, for she was humanlike and they followed her. Many times she would lead them to the villages so that they could be hunted by the people there. Illustrating the relationship between the Sky Gods and the Skidi, their legends add that the Evening Star gave the first buffalo to the people.[3]

The sacred relationship between man and buffalo was further sustained by men who sought visions. For some, a sacred buffalo might appear and give them songs and instructions about how to make Sacred Bundles, in which their powers would reside. Men who had been blessed with such experiences and owned Sacred Bundles formed or joined tribal Buffalo societies. They had the right and authority to perform rituals related to curing the ill, determining the time of the hunt, and officiating at ceremonies where sacred buffalo meat was dedicated to a Sacred Bundle. Pre-hunt ceremonies assured the Pawnees that the herds *agreed* to be located and hunted. Dried meat prepared during the hunt was also pledged to be used during the great ceremonies after the harvest of Mother Corn.[4]

During the vision experience, songs would be composed by divine inspiration. There are many sacred Pawnee songs that tell of a man-buffalo metamorphosis, such as the following:

> Coming suddenly, coming
>> Coming suddenly, coming
>> Coming, this man appears.
>> Coming, suddenly coming
>> This Buffalo is coming and appears as if it were a man.[5]

Another song goes

> It is as a buffalo I stand here.
> Chorus: As I stand, there I stood

Buffalo I, stand as, as I stand,
As I stand, there I stood,
Buffalo I, stand as I stand.
I refer to that place where I stood as a buffalo
That special place.
Chorus: (repeated).
To halt at a special revered place,
To halt at a special revered place,
Chorus: (repeated).[6]

Another set of two songs was composed by a Pawnee warrior who came upon five very old buffalo, far from the herd in winter. They were blind and were standing in a thicket near a stream and grass. He felt compassion for them and did not kill them. In a dream this song came to him:

The ground is not good [life is difficult].
Yet, they are still standing.
Five, they are that many.
No, their world is bad.

In the spring the man went out and found the five dead, lying frozen and desiccated. He then composed the second part of his song. In essence, it says:

Their ground is now good.
They have returned to Tirawahut.[7]

In Oklahoma in the 1920s, there were only three old men living who had Buffalo Doctor Sacred Bundles. During the ceremony, this song would be sung and these old men would arise. They were John Brown, Old Man High Eagle, and Wichita Blaine. They would be the only ones to dance first as these songs were sung. Then the others could join them. They each wore a buffalo tail and a matted tuft of buffalo hair on their heads. They carried baby buffalo hooves on sticks that formed rattles and whistles of wood about twenty-four inches long. There was also a bronze bell attached to each man's costume. Garland Blaine, then a boy, who was there remembered that their faces below the eyes were painted black. There were individual designs painted on their bodies, and they wore black leggings.[8]

The Sacred Beings gave the gifts of corn and buffalo to the Pawnees in ancient times. Both items were honored in ceremonies such as that of the Buffalo Horn Society, which included both elements. One song said,

> Coming there they stand, there they stand,
> As I stand near, suddenly, I saw them standing there.[9]

The reference here is to stalks of corn.

In the Skidi spring ceremony preceding the planting of the corn, both crop fertility and successful buffalo hunting were linked in the hoeing movements of the women dancers and the buffalolike movements of the warrior dancers around them. Small tufts of buffalo wool appeared as if by magic on the ground after the dance was completed, signaling that the time to plant the corn and other crops had arrived.[10]

The javelin and hoop or the buffalo stick game expressed another relationship between the Pawnees and buffalo. It was a man's game, played in the villages and in hunt camps. According to legend, the game represented the bond between man and buffalo. The hoop or ring, wrapped in buffalo vulva skin, with an attached blue or white bead, represented the female buffalo. In one legend a buffalo mother lost her daughter, then turned herself into a woman, and visited a village seeking help. She met a man who promised to help her and eventually located the game ring that was her daughter. He returned the ring-daughter to the mother, whereupon both changed into buffaloes. But before returning to the herd, the mother promised to help the Pawnees find buffaloes on their hunts, and the promise was kept.[11]

A Skidi version of the game's origin says that it originated as a means to call the buffalo to come to the hunters so that they would give permission to be killed.[12] The first game ever played was not between mortals but between the Sun and the Moon. The Sun lost and eventually the Moon, called Mother by the Pawnees, gave the game to them.

In a Chaui version, a man had a dream and saw two game

A hoop or ring used in the buffalo stick or javelin game of skill. This ring, wrapped in strips of buffalo skin, has a white bead attached. It represented the Evening Star that gave buffalo to man. Diameter approximately five inches. Photo by Dr. R. E. Venk. The Blaine Collection.

sticks as stars in the west. He was instructed how to cut the branches from which the sticks were made. One stick represented man and the other buffalo. In another band's account, the two sticks represented young buffalo bulls that had turned into game sticks. They had given instructions as to how the sticks were to be made, how the game was to be played, and what sacred songs were to be sung. The sticks were curiously fashioned with crosspieces representing hands and arms. Small, hooklike protrusions were ears, eyes, and one horn. The sticks were wrapped in tanned buffalo hide strips. The ring here also represented a female buffalo and was approximately four inches in diameter. If there was a white bead on top, it represented the Evening Star, who gave the buffalo to man; if there was a blue bead on top, it represented the heavens or Tirawahut, or the sacred female buffalo's daughter, previously mentioned.[13]

The game was played only by men on a special field in or near each village. The technique was to throw the ring along the ground, then hurl the two sticks in such a manner as to catch the rolling ring. Players received points according to which part of the stick caught the ring. Later in its history, this became a gambling game in which blankets and ponies could be exchanged between winners and losers.[14] Charles Augustus Murray, a European visitor who saw the game played on the hunt in August 1835, said the men played it for five or six hours at a time, gambling on the outcome.[15]

In other times two sides played against one another, and the side that won sacrificed a buffalo heart and tongue to the spirit of the buffalo and to a Sacred Being in the heavens. The losing side made the fire and cooked the heart and tongue. This ceremony was important for the maintenance of the bond between buffalo and man, for in essence it returned the spirit and body of the killed buffalo to the herd.

So it was out of this cultural tradition that in the 1871 council meeting, Pitaresaru insisted that it was necessary for the Pawnees to continue their hunt. For it perpetuated and acknowledged the ancient and sacred relationship with the Great Herd whose bodies fed, clothed, and provided shelter for the Pawnees.

Buffalo Hunting: Pawnee and Other Accounts

At one time the Chauis, the Pitahawiratas, and the Kitahakis or South Bands hunted separately from the Skidis or North Bands. Pawnee traditions say that at that time the Chauis lived farthest west; the Kitkahahkis dwelled in the center of the Pawnee lands; and the villages of the Pitahawiratas were to the east. Their hunting routes resembled the shapes of three elongated, adjacent flower petals. Each band started out separately and then, without crossing one another's paths, they each moved in a long loop, small at the top and large at the bottom. The movement is said to have been usually clockwise, following the sun's movement across the sky which was also symbolized in the clockwise movement of dancers around a center. These loops defined each group's hunting territory. The Chaui route went farthest west, into present-day southern Nebraska and western Kansas. The Kitkahahkis in the center journeyed through south-central Nebraska, Kansas, and sometimes into Oklahoma. The Pitahawiratas traveled through east-central Nebraska, then into east-central Kansas, and as far as the present-day Oklahoma border region. The North Bands, or Skidi villagers, followed a separate path due to their long separation from the others and their living to the north of the others. [16]

The Kitkahahkis and Pitahawiratas claim that in the past they had villages on the Republican and Smoky Hill rivers in Kansas; this gives credence to the above tradition that they hunted into Oklahoma and the surrounding regions. Kitkahahki villages in Kansas and southern Nebraska were described and visited by the Spanish explorers, and later by the American explorer, Zebulon Pike, in 1806. Archaeological evidence is present for two Kitkahahki village sites, but not for the Smoky Hill Pitahawirata sites mentioned in the account of the missionary, John Dunbar, who lived among them in the 1830s.

In 1835, Charles Augustus Murray, who hunted with the tribe, noted the routes of the different bands. As the bands journeyed south and west toward the hunting grounds from their villages on the Loup and Platte rivers, the Pitahawiratas and some Chauis went to the left, or east; the Grand Chauis were in the center; and the Kitkahahkis traveled to the right, or on the western side. He said the Skidis hunted by themselves, to the north of the main body of the Pawnees. [17]

In the Pawnee-described routes above, it is said there was an interband agreement that, if a bison herd was being hunted and it crossed into the hunting area of another band, it would be "left for that band," and not pursued into the other group's territory. [18] This tradition apparently existed before the earliest U.S. treaties with the four bands, or "tribes" as they were designated by the government. At that time their villages were at some distance from each other. Later their villages were nearer to one another

A Pawnee camp on the plains. The man in the foreground wearing a peace medal and eagle feather headdress is probably a chief. The photograph was taken by John Carbutt, working under the auspices of the Union Pacific Railroad Company in 1866. Courtesy of The Kansas State Historical Society, Topeka.

and concentrated along the Loup and Platte rivers in Nebraska. After 1833, their hunting territories were diminished by land cessions and by the U.S. government's movement of tribes onto reservations west of the Missouri River in Nebraska and Kansas.

The Pawnee said "we went up" when they went on the tribal hunt. This expression was used because, as the tribe journeyed south and westward, altitude gradually increased. Sometimes a small group would request permission to leave the main group and hunt alone. The chiefs would outline where the larger group would be going and tell the smaller group not to hunt in that direction. These smaller groups, led by important warriors, would go long distances. Some went up the Platte into today's southeast Wyoming or into the mountains of Colorado. Some traveled as far as Wyoming's present-day Yellowstone National Park, describing the hot water springs and the awesome geysers when they returned. The mountain goats in Wyoming were hunted and considered a delicacy.

Grizzly bears were feared and revered. Pawnees who were attacked by them shot arrows into their paws when they reared up. It was said this prevented them from running on all fours and charging the hunters. Once it was told that a grizzly bear was seen killing a buffalo.* It then buried it with only its horns showing. It went away and later returned with its cubs and dug up the carcass and fed on it.[19]

Going on the tribal hunt was a serious economic as well as a religious undertaking involving prehunt rituals, planning, discipline, and hard work for all. Not only would food be obtained, but robes of buffalo hides could be used in trade. Many forms of activity took place before leaving the villages. The sounds of knife sharpening could be heard throughout the village. This sound itself brought great excitement to the children, who anticipated the great adventure ahead. They would become greatly animated, running and shouting more than usual. "It was like knowing that you were going to be brought candy from the store in present times. You could hardly wait," one old man recalled. The men checked their gear—bows, arrows, ropes, knives, and horse equipment—and replaced or repaired any items that were not in good condition. The women would be busy making extra moccasins, preparing food packets of dried corn and other foods, and inspecting tipi poles, covers, and other items that might need repairing. Boys and girls were called upon to help wherever they were needed in fetching and packing supplies that were to go on the horses or on human backs. The latter burdens were held in place by a tumpline across the forehead.[20]

The summer hunt began after the spring Sacred Bundle renewal ceremonies and the planting of corn and other crops were

---

* In the Time of the Buffalo, by Tom McHugh, contains a Sioux Indian's sketch of a grizzly attacking a buffalo on page 199. The author states that buffalo "predation by the grizzly has been reported in only a handful of cases."

completed. When the corn reached a certain height and the fields were weeded, it was time to think of the long journey to the hunting grounds.

Later in the year, the Pawnees returned and harvested and prepared the corn and other crops for storage in underground cache pits. Then after the great harvest ceremonies were held and completed, preparation could be made for the winter hunting season. The time for leaving was not the same each year; it depended on the completion of the harvest and ceremonies. However, an effort was made to be on the way before the onset of the severe plains winter.

In each band village, heralds appointed by the chiefs were responsible for conveying council and other decisions to the villagers. Chanting loudly, they would walk through the village and call out that soon it would be time to leave on the hunt. For three or four days, they would go morning and evening calling out the news and urging the populace to make ready. When the day came, they again made their rounds, informing families of their places in the line of march, of the time of departure, and where the first stopping point would be. Departure day was decided in ceremony by the Buffalo doctors.[21]

The head chief's band took the middle position when all bands hunted together, a custom that began after the middle of the nineteenth century. The South Bands claim that the Skidis had no say in the route followed, but that they would come along if they decided to do so.* The South Bands had no voice in telling the Skidis what they could do, and they did not consider them in making their own decisions about hunting times and places before reservation years. This expression of separateness came about as a result of the long period when the Skidis had lived far north of the other bands, long enough to acquire a different dialect. They had also warred with the South Bands from time to time in the historic period, and had not come to aid a nearby South Band village when it was attacked by Sioux, it was claimed.

---

* Gene Weltfish, in *The Lost Universe*, claims the Skidis sometimes were the leading band on the hunt during reservation days; however, South Band sources, including Garland J. Blaine, say that this was never true. The Skidis could accompany but could not lead. The Skidis claim otherwise.

When it came time to start the hunt itself, after sighting the herd, the South Band chiefs would decide where each of their hunters would be. Then the Skidi chiefs, if they had elected to join the other bands, were invited to come and hear these decisions, so that they could find a place for their hunters. To plan this a map was drawn on the ground, and each band's positions marked.[22]

With a group numbering in the thousands, it was necessary that each band know its place to camp. Each morning as they broke camp and started moving, band chiefs or warrior society members policing the hunt stationed themselves on horseback and told band members where the next night's camp would be. Traveling over the same regions year after year, the people learned the locations of campsites near streams and timber. Wood was essential for fires to dry the butchered meat and water was necessary for both people and horses. If wood could not be found, buffalo chips were gathered for fuel.

On the march the children had especially good times. The younger boys took their small bows and arrows and shot at birds that fluttered up from the grass. They even took careful aim at butterflies darting before them. Then they would run and retrieve their arrows to take aim again at an elusive target. Other older boys would gather with sticks they had cut. Then they would walk in a line abreast, and drive out birds, rabbits, and other small creatures and kill them. At the day's end there would be enough game to take to the family camp fire for cooking.

It was considered important to remain healthy on the hunt, and women cooked soups with meat, dried corn, and other ingredients, sometimes added to prevent constipation, particularly among the aged. Very old people ate *oo*, a watery corn gruel, if teeth were gone and chewing difficult.[23]

When the day's march was over, a family might erect a small structure for a sweat bath. Stones, which were heated and then had water poured over them to produce steam, were not always available at a campsite, so they were taken with the family goods from the village. Salt was also carried. Both these heavy articles were sometimes carried on the horse-drawn *travois*, or sometimes in a sling worn over the shoulder and fastened to the belt. Family members took turns carrying these objects. One family would carry stones and another salt, and they would share them rather than duplicating unnecessary weight. Campsites needed to be in a spot where opportunity for enemy attack or ambush was minimized, and where dust would not blow into the camps.[24]

In areas that were considered safe, men rode carrying their bows unstrung. The bow string made of braided sinew would stretch and weaken if continually kept under the great tension that it had to have on the bow during the hunt. Long after the introduction of firearms, the Pawnees as well as other tribes continued to prefer the bow and arrow for hunting. Gunfire spooked the herds, and guns were far more expensive to obtain and maintain.

Wet clay and sand served useful purposes on the hunt. Clay was rubbed on the hunter's body as a camouflage and served to reduce the number of insect bites. At night after the hunt, the hunter would bathe in a stream, washing off the clay and soil of the day. Then sand was scrubbed onto the skin to further cleanse it. If the hunter had rubbed on a mixture of tallow and *parakaha,* a fragrant herb, to prevent sunburn, this, too, could be washed off with river sand. The sweat lodge also served as a place for cleansing. "The steam would open the pores and the dirt would just roll off."[25]

The buffalo was a multipurposed animal for the Pawnees and other tribes. In 1835, Murray described the ways he had seen the parts of the animals put to use in everyday life. These included meat for food (the meat was used fresh when on the prairies and dried for consumption in the village); hide lodge coverings; hide bales or parfleches used for storage and carrying purposes; bed coverings, clothing, saddles, lariates, and halters; sinew strings for bows, twine, and thread; softening and dressing skins with the brains; mallets made of the hoofs at ends of the shank bones; bone for scrapers, coarse chisels, and needles; bows of ribs, strengthened by strong fibers; dung fuel and water bags made of the bladders. He added that the buffalo hide had become the chief article of trade to whites for blankets, knives, beads, and other "produce of civilization."* [26]

---

* According to T. Lindsay Baker, hundreds of thousands of buffalo robes were traded by Indian tribes from before the middle of the nineteenth century until

Ceremonial uses of the buffalo included the use of its fat as a base for mixing pigments for body painting and as an ointment in certain ceremonies. It was mixed with sweet grass as a burnt offering and used as a medicinal agent.[27] Tufts of buffalo wool were worn in the hair of the Buffalo Dance performers. Tufts of wool also appeared mysteriously on the ground during one of the ceremonies preceding spring planting. Horn tips of varying sizes were utilized in cupping in curing practices. The entire horn, cut in half and scoured smooth, made a ladle or spoon.[28] The bison skull held a honored place on the low earth altar built on the west side of those lodges that housed a Sacred Bundle. Not all earth lodges could claim such an altar, although this has been inferred in some accounts.

Scouts were sent out to survey the entire hunt area, so that herd locations were known as the hunt progressed. In later times when competition for the valuable Pawnee hunting grounds intensified, the scouts were wary of enemies and took special precautions to prevent themselves from being detected, surprised, and killed.

One such precaution was that when stopping to quench thirst, Pawnees were taught to kneel on one knee with the right hand cupped to bring water to the mouth. Contrary to some popular illustrations, they never lay flat on their stomachs with their faces to the water. A rider would dismount, hold the lines in one hand and let the horse drink first. The horse would then stand guard while the rider drank. The old people would say that the horse was a far better watcher and more alert than a dog. If it were a gentle horse, the lines could be held in the left hand, and the right hand used to drink more rapidly. If, however, the horse was fractious, the lines would be held with the stronger arm and hand, and drinking done with the other hand, turning the head watchfully from side to side as one drank.[29]

Wichita Blaine remembered how the hunt scouts knew where the buffalo were on the plains. The herd would gather and stand grazing, pawing the earth with one foot, then the other, throw-

the animals' near extinction in the late 1870s. Buffalo hides were processed by Indian women for sleigh and lap robes, and in the East hides were made into overcoats and overshoes. The fur was woven into thread for stockings and cloth.

Polished buffalo horn tips used by Wichita Blaine in curing. A Pawnee doctor would place a tip over a wound or area of pain. The mouth would draw air or discharge by suction through the small end. Photo by Dr. R. E. Venk. The Blaine Collection.

ing dirt up over them. It was known that buffalo were in that distant spot because the dust would rise high in a straight, non-moving column over them. One method the scouts then used in signaling the sighting was to toss their buffalo robes into the air from a prominence. The robe was not just tossed loosely into the air but rolled compactly and thrown straight up over the head to gain greater height. It unrolled as it descended, presenting a broad surface for other scouts observing at a great distance.[30]

Once the scouts sighted a herd, and its location was reported, the Buffalo Society doctors or priests had an especially important role. An example of their influence is provided by an instance in 1835. Pitaresaru, the head chief, called a halt to the tribal procession and a ceremony was held. Murray described a circle composed of chiefs and Buffalo Society members. In the middle of the circle were two long poles "belonging to the medicine (Sacred Bundle) covered with feathers and shreds of cloth." He said that about an hour went by during which time speeches, prayers, and pipe smoking occurred as well as "medicine mummery," which he did not describe. This event, he explained, was to in-sure a good hunt. On another occasion, the priest decided that it was not auspicious to hunt, and the camp lay idle for several days. What natural or supernatural signs dictated this decision, Murray did not say. Later, when buffalo were sighted again by the scouts, the ceremony was repeated and it was announced that the "great Spirit" was favorable, and there would be a hunt.[31] While on the hunt in 1873, at the time of a Sioux attack and massacre of Pawnee hunters and their families, an observer re-ported that the "medicine man" stood on a prominence shaking his rattle and performing a ritual.[32]

Another function of the Buffalo Society occurred in the eve-ning after the day's hunt was over and the meat was brought back to camp. The society's members went through the camp calling out thanks to the "great Spirit" for the plentiful supply of buffalo He had supplied to the people. As they went, they distributed portions of the kill to the less fortunate in the camp who had no hunter in the family.[33]

Much has been written about buffalo hunt techniques, includ-ing the "surround" made by the Plains Indians. Wichita Blaine described to his grandson one Pawnee hunt pattern of the 1860s and 1870s and other aspects of the hunt.

> All the hunters would take their assigned positions forming a horseshoe with the open end toward the buffalo herd. All those men with horses would be in the most concave part or the top of the horseshoe shape. The men on foot would be lined at the ends closest to the herd. Those with the fastest horses were at the great-est distance from the herd. When the attack came the buffalo herd was usually sitting down. They could hear the rumble of horses hooves and they would turn their heads toward the sound. There would be a few bulls standing who would be looking at the oncoming hunters. The others would begin to arise, slowly stretch and eliminate their water and waste. Then they would begin grad-ually to move away and just before they began to break into a trot, the hunters would be among them. Those who were on foot would shoot the first one they could see and get close to, because after that, the animals really began to run and there was no way to

catch them. However, those who were on horse could be more selective and pick out what they wanted to shoot. Preferably a female was shot because the meat was more tender and easier to prepare for drying or to cook when fresh. A buffalo attacked only after it had been wounded, then it would stop and attack its pursuer.

Sometimes there was competition among some of the young hunters. The object was to see how many buffalo one could shoot with one arrow. When a buffalo runs he stretches a weak or thin area of skin behind his leg. There were some men who were able to shoot low through this spot and the arrow traveled with such force that it went completely through and into another animal. He said that once in a while a man would announce that he had killed three with one arrow. You tell it immediately, then your arrow is checked as well as the dead buffalo. There should be two wounded buffalo with no arrow, and one with your arrow in it. One thing about this was that the sinew on your arrow had to be carefully wrapped so that it would not unravel in the animal and the arrow come loose from the shaft and remain in the animal or be loosened and not be able to penetrate the next animal. Very few men could kill three with one arrow, but it could be done. Another place to shoot through was low in the front chest area where the body is more angular than flat. It was possible to shoot through this area, although it was a thin bony place and a man had to be an excellent shot. *

When sufficient buffalo were killed for food and other needs, the butchering began. This was neither a delicate or pleasant task. It was messy work done amidst the sound of death, dust, and in the winter, biting cold. At this time, skinning the buffalo was very difficult as the meat and skin would begin to freeze and the blood would cake and ice on the hands. In such a case the hunters would place their hands in the vagina which would warm them sufficiently to permit working and prevent their fingers from freezing. In the summer the flies and gnats would become unbearable and it was then the young boys would offer to wave willow branches over the carcass, and at the same time drive away the dogs that would follow the hunters from the camp if the kill site were not at too great a distance. The boys would do these same tasks in camp

---

* Tom McHugh said in his work, *In the Time of the Buffalo*, that the practiced archer could shoot with such force that his arrow would penetrate the buffalo to the shaft's feathers. Some claimed to be able to shoot through one and wound another animal (See pages 79–80.)

when it was time to slice the meat for drying. Another task that small boys did was to hold the lines of the hunters' pack and riding horses while they were butchering.

The warriors and older men butchered. The men who did not kill anything because of bad luck, or who were crippled, would go to some man and call him by his relationship name. They would say, "Dear, sir, I want you to feel sorry for me. Make my hands an extension to you," which means, "please have compassion for me and let me help you, whereby you can give me for my work anything you desire." Then the man would probably say, "Alright there is a buffalo right there that I have killed and you may start on it." This man was free to give him anything he wanted. He might be given the hide, but he always got all the bones with the meat that was left on them. He could also be given the backbone and the head. Sometimes, if the hunter had killed, say, four buffalo, he might be kind enough to give this man a half a buffalo. It depended on how many he killed, how large his family was, and what his ceremonial obligations were. The poor man was not always a member of his band, but he usually was. The men were all together in one group, so there were no band or village distinctions during the active part of the hunt and the later butchering. The poor men had a preference in asking. They knew who the kind men were, as well as those who were hard. Those mean men when asked to have compassion, might say, "If you wanted meat you should have been here, I cannot use you." There were always severe men. Now some young boys might come up to a successful hunter and say, "My grandmother is so and so, there are only she and I. I am too young to hunt. Could I hold your horse, take care of it while you butcher? Could you let me have some meat?" The man could say yes or no. If he said yes, the boy would hold the horse's reins. If the man put his knife down, the boy would get it and try to sharpen it a bit on any sharpening material available. He might also take the arrow and clean it off the best he could. He would unstring the bow if the man said he should. The more helpful he was the more meat the man might give him. He tried very hard not to be told what to do. It was part of the making of a man and naturally he was as observant as he could be. The easier it was for the man who was butchering, the more the man would think of him.[34]

Once the meat had been transported to camp on horse or human back, the processing continued. The object of cutting the meat now was to make very thin sheets that could be dried in a minimum amount of time to reduce the weight and prevent spoilage. After cutting, the thin strips would be pounded on the skin side of a hide, then hung on a pole framework to dry. They would be turned frequently and pounded again to flatten them and to thin the fibers. After this the meat would be returned to the frame. After a few days, it would be dry. Hot summer sun and warm wind acted as drying agents. In the winter the meat was still cut thin, but then it was held over a fire to sear it. It was turned again and seared, then pounded flat, then hung up to dry on the scaffold or frame.[35] Searing over the fire could also be done in summer, if there was a need to hasten the process.[36]

Charles Augustus Murray made several observations in 1835 that can be compared with the conditions of the 1860s and 1870s. In the later years there were fewer Pawnees on the hunt. The population had fallen below three thousand, due mainly to epidemic diseases, enemy attacks, and, perhaps, lower reproductive rates. In 1835, Murray estimated that there were six hundred lodges, with about five thousand people in all, and one thousand hunters present.[37] An official 1833 estimate of the total Pawnee population was eleven thousand.

In 1835, there was greater freedom in choice of hunting grounds and perhaps much less danger from enemies because of the greater number of Pawnee warriors present. Murray mentions that the Cheyennes attacked once. This tribe lived in nomadic groups on the plains east of the Rocky Mountains in present-day Colorado. Their hunting grounds seem to have overlapped or impinged on the Pawnee grounds. The Sioux are mentioned but not as being especially worrisome.

He also noted the Pawnee hunting technique. To attack the herd, the hunters were mounted in three parallel lines, with the head chief and his band warriors in the middle line. At a given signal, all lines surged forward, toward the middle and on both sides. Even the poorest man had two or three horses, he claimed. The richest chiefs had between eight and twelve, and the head chief, Pitaresaru, had at least thirty. The Pawnee horses were of American, Spanish, and wild ancestry, he said.[38]

As told in the previous chapter, in later years the number of horseless men grew as horse thefts by other tribes increased and the government agents refused to allow the Pawnees to pursue and retrieve their losses. The strategy of the bison surround and attack changed to accommodate this loss of horses. It was changed, as described above, so as to maximize the kill to allow each hunter a more or less equal chance to kill at least one. In 1872, there were 509 men, not all of them able bodied hunters. There were 876 women and 1,082 children, or a total of 2,447 people.[39]

When there was enough meat prepared for the coming season, the bands returned to their villages. In the years after 1860, the success of the hunt became unpredictable. Herds decreased in numbers and the competition for animals from eastern tribes settled by the U.S. government west of the Missouri increased. The Pawnee treaty of 1833, which ceded land south of the Platte, said in Article II, "The land ceded and relinquished hereby shall remain a common hunting ground during the pleasure of the president for the Pawnees, and other friendly Indians who shall be permitted by the president to hunt on same."[40] Sac, Fox, Ioway, Kickapoo, Potawatomi, Delaware, Shawnee, and other tribes removed from their original homes and now living on reservations in Nebraska and Kansas were given the right to hunt on the traditional Pawnee and other tribal hunting areas. For the Pawnees the possibility of warfare became a part of the hunt journey, and scouts not only had to watch for the signs of a distant herd, but for the presence of the lurking enemy who came to steal horses or to count coup by attacks on the hunters. The balanced relationship between the Pawnees, the Great Herd, and the Sacred Beings became difficult to sustain.

The Government's Role in Changing
Traditional Pawnee Hunting Patterns

Conditions imposed by the federal government also added to the strain of carrying out requisite patterns to maintain the sacred ways. Once the Pawnees had signed away most of their lands and were moved onto their Nebraska reservation, federal control began to alter traditional ways. Now, instead of the secular and religious leaders planning and carrying out the decisions made regarding all phases of the hunt, the Indian agent, superintendent, military officials, and often the commissioner of Indian Affairs decided the matter.

In the early 1870s, the Quaker agents wanted their charges to begin farming as a full time occupation. They were not pleased when they learned that the Pawnees were away from the villages and fields an estimated two to three months in the summer and three to five months during the winter.[41] But once they became acquainted with reservation life, it became apparent to them that without the buffalo hunt there was not enough food or other needed items that the buffalo produced. Grudging permission to hunt was given but always with the admonition that times would change and there would be no more hunting.

In June 1871, Supt. Samuel Janney reluctantly gave consent to hunt but told the chiefs that the buffalo were disappearing and in time there would be no more. * When it was explained by Pitare-saru how important hunting was in relation to their religious beliefs, Janney replied, "We don't give the Great Spirit meat, and he favors us. . . . What he requires is a good heart."[42] Again in April 1872, the chiefs persisted in requesting permission to go on their hunt. The winter hunt had been poor, and the tribe was hungry. The agent asked if they would rather purchase beef with their annuity money than go hunting. The chiefs answered no.

In September of the following year, the chiefs impatiently went through the process of asking permission to hunt, and the agent told them he had to get permission.[43] During a June 1874 inspection visit by a Friends committee, the chiefs repeated their request. The visitors promised that they would use their influence to gain consent from the Indian Department in Washington and from the superintendent in Omaha.[44]

This Pawnee appeal came after an April 16 meeting when the assembled tribal leaders were informed that they would not be allowed to have a summer hunt. From now on, they would have

---

* It had been observed that the bison herds were decreasing as the hide hunters began their relentless forays. Dan Flores suggests that perhaps brucelosis, tuberculosis, and anthrax, which causes aborting, may also have caused a decrease in bison herds. These ungulate diseases may have been introduced by infected cattle herds in New Mexico and other areas.

to turn their hands to farming and rely on what they could raise to feed themselves. It was added that the previous year's poor hunt, when many Pawnees had been killed by the Sioux, was partially responsible for the government's decision. It is suspected that this was seen as a good opportunity to stop the tribal hunt and implement the policy of full time farming once and for all.

But in July 1874, the Pawnees had not yet accepted the reformers' values and push for work pattern changes. The chiefs of the three South Bands appeared determined to start on the hunt with or without permission. Agent William Burgess wrote Supt. Barclay White, "I did not deem it advisable under the circumstance to issue a mandatory order that would lead to bad feeling and a disobedience that could not be immediately controlled as the chiefs and leading warriors were leaders in the movement."[45] The chiefs told Burgess that the sympathy shown them during a recent Friends committee visit convinced them that it would not be wrong to go, and as long as there were any buffalo to hunt they *must* go. The more difficult life became, the more imperative it seemed to try to continue those essential activities woven into the cultural fabric that would bring life back into balance.

The U.S. Military and the Hunt

The line of the frontier settlements has steadily advanced during the year, especially in Kansas, Nebraska, Minnesota and Dakota, gradually absorbing the country, which only a year or two since was in the possession of the Indian.
   —Lt. General Philip H. Sheridan, in a Report to the Secretary of War, 1872

Not only were agents, superintendents, the Friends committees, and Indian officials in Washington involved in decisions concerning tribal hunts, but also the U.S. military. In the early 1870s, the Pawnees lived under the jurisdiction of the Department of the Platte, Division of the Missouri army organization. Part of U.S. military policy from about 1845 to the 1880s was directed toward controlling Indian tribal movements.[46] Particularly this was true in the 1860s and 1870s west of the Mississippi and Missouri rivers, where the large nomadic tribes such as the Sioux,

Cheyenne, Arapaho, Kiowa, Apache, and Comanche were resident. These tribes were not yet all confined to reservations and seemed little inclined to respect the government's long term plans to accomplish this. The continued and increasing intrusions into their hunting and homelands by white settlers and other Indians brought about confrontation and hostility.

But for those tribes, such as the Pawnees, who had relinquished the greater portion of their lands and were on reservations, army policy dictated that under certain circumstances tribal members must stay within the reservation borders. This policy became action when hostile tribes hunted on each other's lands or settled old scores when they came in contact with one another. The Sioux or Lakota bands were particularly aggressive toward their more settled neighbors, such as the Poncas, Omahas, Otoes, and Pawnees. Their bands roamed at considerable distance from their centers in the Dakota Territory, and they were often in Pawnee hunting grounds or near their villages. This activity increased as the years went by, the buffalo supply decreased, and tribes scoured the plains for food. The Pawnees called these the "scarey years." During the 1870s, intermittent drought covered these same areas, and the crops failed. Grass on the prairies dried up, and the buffalo sought new areas for grazing.*

Men would travel in all directions for four or five days and never see a buffalo. They stayed longer to hunt and left the villages largely unprotected. Then the Sioux came and attacked, but there was no other choice, because food had to be found.[47]

On June 3, 1870, Supt. Samuel Janney informed Indian Com. Ely Parker that Gen. Christopher Augur did not want the Pawnees to go on their summer hunt. The army was pursuing hostile Indians in the general area where the Pawnees would be traveling. It was feared that the Pawnees might become involved in the conflict or be mistaken for them.[48] The same directive was issued in the previous summer of 1869, and by now the Pawnees were in real need. Pawnee Scouts now reported buffalo were quite

---

* Flores points out that areas along the southern plains' periphery to the east, where bison had migrated during historical and prehistorical drought peiods, were not unavailable due to human population increase in the U.S. government settled Eastern tribes such as the Cherokee there.

near, and again General Augur was asked. This time he consented if the Pawnees would carry a large flag with PAWNEES inscribed on it so they would not be misidentified. A certain route was laid out for them, so their location would be known.[49]

In November 1871, the time for the winter hunt was overdue, and the chiefs were informed that the army refused to allow them to go. The reason given was they disobeyed orders on the previous hunt. They were to give a letter to Captain Edwin Pollack at a predetermined location, but they were accused of being in the area several weeks before "he knew you were there." The chiefs defended themselves by saying that they had sent the letter by courier but had not delivered it en masse, as apparently was expected. So both General George D. Ruggles and Captain Pollack informed their superiors and the Pawnee agent of the infraction. In council the agent now told the chiefs, "You have always suffered when you went contrary to my direction. General Ruggles says that the Pawnees can't go on the hunt because they behaved so badly last summer."[50]

Apparently other accusations were made regarding Pawnee behavior, for Pitaresaru arose and said, "We told you in council that the South Indians [Wichitas] invited us to go down there. . . . I camped near to where the soldiers were. The buffalo were there. I sent my son with the letter [to Pollack]".

Then reacting to Ruggles's accusation of stealing, he continued, "We came through a settlement but the crops were not fit to eat. We don't want to be with the Poncas again. They steal. I saw at the Ponca camp corn laying around. I told the Ponca chief it was not right. We did NOT steal." Another chief, defending his people, arose and accused the Poncas and added that the Pawnees purchased some corn and did not steal any.[51] The Poncas were mentioned because from time to time the smaller tribes in the area would ask to accompany the Pawnees on the hunt as a matter of protection from enemy attack.

Later in the middle of this same month, a welcome change in policy came when General Augur informed the agent that the Pawnees could go on the hunt. What brought the change is not certain, but it is possible that the Pawnees were proven not to have committed the corn stealing depredation.

U.S. Army Maj. Gen. Christopher C. Augur commanded the Department of the Platte in the early 1870s. He often determined whether the Pawnees went on the buffalo hunt. Courtesy of Western History Collections, University of Oklahoma Library.

In 1872 Maj. Gen. Edward O. C. Ord commanded the Department of the Platte. In July he was informed by Agent Jacob Troth that the Pawnees, following directions, were starting on the hunt with each of the four bands carrying a large flag, three by four feet, with a large letter P in the center. They were instructed to follow a route up the Loup Fork on the south side until they were opposite Grand Island, where they would cross the Platte. They would then travel up the Platte on the south side a short distance, then strike across to Capt. J. D. Devin's Ninth Infantry camp at the juncture of the Red Willow and Republican rivers.[52]

Not only was the route spelled out, but to prevent deviation from it, the tribe was accompanied by J. B. Omohundro, a scout for the government at Fort McPherson, and Baptiste Bayhylle, the mixed blood Pawnee agency interpreter. Not only General Ord, but Lt. Gen. Philip Sheridan had given consent.[53]

In October 1872, Troth wrote again to General Ord. His old aversion to hunting had been put aside for the time, and he wanted the Pawnees to go because they could "aid in their support and there is nothing for them to do on the reservation in winter."[54] Permission was forthcoming and on November 9,

1872, the tribe was on its way. Apparently the vigilance, if there was any on the part of the army to prevent intertribal hostility, did not succeed. The Sioux attacked the hunting party and drove off 111 horses, bringing the hunt to an end because there was no way to carry equipment, hides, and dried meat back to the villages except in minimal amounts on peoples' backs.[55] In great anger the Pawnees went to Fort McPherson and asked that soldiers be sent to recover their horses. The request was refused. Yet about this time, when the Sioux, Whistler and Hand Smeller, had been killed, fifty soldiers searched for and found the Pawnees to ask accusingly if they had done it.[56] The chiefs emphatically denied the allegations, and they later proved to be correct in their denial.

This incident showed a disparity in the treatment of the two tribes by the military. The army could supply men and horses to search for the Pawnees about a presumed assault on the Sioux, but they would not pursue the same policy of search for Pawnee horses known to have been stolen by the Sioux. One reason was that the army was not afraid of the reservation Pawnees but was highly concerned about its ability to control the erratic and hostile Sioux.

When the Pawnees finally returned to their agency, frustrated by their attempt to get swift redress for the terrible loss of their horses, they demanded that the agent request that two hundred soldiers be sent to assist them in recovering their animals. In a revealing letter to Supt. Barclay White, Agent William Burgess said, "I think it advisable to tell them at once what may be expected so they may get reconciled to their condition or make such demonstration as they intend. We shall, of course, encourage them to continue in their peaceful pursuits."[57] No military assistance was forthcoming.

After the above incident the bands separated into smaller groups as they found their way back to the reservation. The agent sent a message to Col. J. J. Reynolds, Third Cavalry, commanding at Fort McPherson, saying that some of the Pawnees had not yet returned. "They have all been ordered home, but some are tardy in complying since they have been unsuccessful and are much discouraged. . . . I hope they will not trouble you in the future, but if any more should visit your camp, please order them home."[58] To be ordered "home"—what a change for the proud Pawnees, who were called the noblemen of the prairies by one early observer.

In July 1873, General Ord was informed that the Pawnees were about to depart on the hunt and was told their destination, so that the army would know their location. It was to be another tragic journey. On August 5, in southwestern Nebraska at a place now called Massacre Canyon, an overwhelming number of Brulé and Oglala Sioux fell upon the hunters and their families.

Although the Pawnees made a stand and fought through the day, over a hundred were wounded, killed, or raped and mutilated. Again the survivors had to flee, leaving all their belongings and the buffalo meat that had been drying. A visitor to the canyon two days later said that bodies and possessions could be seen as far down as the timber grew, about a mile and a half from the battle's origin point.[59]

A cavalry unit under Capt. Charles Meinhold was camped a dozen miles away at the mouth of Blackwood Creek. They claimed to know nothing of the battle until a few survivors struggled into camp. When the chiefs asked for help in pursuing the Sioux, the captain sent them away, saying he would visit the site of the battle later. He thus made no attempt to follow the Sioux immediately but later attempted to trace their trail north, although he could find no signs of the rapidly moving tribesmen.[60] This was the second unsuccessful direct attempt by the Pawnees to get the military to aid them in redressing Sioux depredation and decimation. It led them to say in later years that the government wanted the Sioux to destroy them, thus ignoring the justice and protection due them according to Pawnee understanding of the U.S. treaty obligations to them.[61]

During these years, military men serving on the plains expressed their ideas, often in frustration, about Indian policy and the Indians who inhabited their territorial range of authority. In October 1872, Maj. Gen. Winfield S. Hancock, commanding the Department of the Dakota, expressed his opinion that the time had come to interfere with the Indians' nomadic habits even though, ". . . it should be necessary to violently place them on reservations and rigidly keep them there."[62] His troops had been under attack by Indians while accompanying railway surveyors who were working and moving westward at this time. He complained of the government policy that supplied food, guns, and ammunition to Indians who in turn used them against his troops.

Maj. Gen. John Pope, commanding the Department of the Missouri, which included Kansas and other areas westward in which the Pawnees hunted, voiced the view that Indians on reservations should be confined to them, and not even under the pretext of hunting be allowed to roam where they had no business to be.[63] He and others seemed to be unaware of or ignored the fact that Indian land cession treaties often included the specified right to hunt in certain ceded lands. He referred in his 1872 report to the Osages, who left their reservation to journey upon the plains. But in an 1837 treaty with the Osages, Kiowas, Creeks, and others, the U.S. government agreed that these tribes would be allowed to hunt on the great prairies beyond the natural timberline called the Cross Timbers, which extended north and south from Kansas to Texas. Subsequent Osage treaties did not retract this right.[64]

The Pawnee treaty of 1857 does not mention the right to hunt on certain lands, although the 1833 treaty, as mentioned before, allowed the right to hunt in the aforementioned areas. The Fort Laramie Treaty of 1868, with the Sioux, Arapahoes, and others, reserved their right to hunt on lands north of the North Platte, and on the Republican Fork of the Smoky Hill, "so long as the buffalo may range thereon in such numbers as to justify the chase."[65] Pawnee traditional hunting grounds were contained in part of these regions, so that possible contact between tribes could occur and did with consequent hostilities. It is wondered whether, when these areas for different tribes' hunting usage were designated, the Indians and U.S. government were identifying and designating the same areas. There were conflicting claims, and river names and areas were in the native tongues and distances were calculated in different ways. It is not surprising that territorial overlapping and intrusion, willful or otherwise, occurred.

General Ord, commanding the Department of the Platte that lay between the two previously mentioned departments, had little to say about Indian depredations or hostilities in his report of 1872, but he did mention the Indians to the north. He said they had committed offenses in his region, then escaped north of the Platte to take refuge in the "extensive Indian [Sioux] reserves there." Then, "the Indian Department has not deemed it politic to allow a pursuit, which if attempted at all would have required a large force and perhaps led to war." An 1869 Indian Office circular and a military order issued at the same time stated that all Indians who confined themselves to their reservations were considered "friendly subjects of the Indian department," and "all others were consigned to the army to be treated as friendly or hostile as circumstances might justify."[66]

This would explain a major reason that the Sioux were never seriously pursued, if at all, after their constant aggressions against the Pawnees and other tribes in the Department of the Platte. In addition, the nonaggression policies of Quaker officials in the Northern Superintendency were against military action, which it was believed would only acerbate Sioux retaliation against other Indians. Neither the Indian Office nor the military were that eager to antagonize further the Lakota bands, a far more numerous and dangerous group than the sedentary reservation Indians to the south in Kansas and Nebraska. At this time it was more politic to prevent the hunt and confine the Pawnees and others to their reservations so as to lessen the chances of military involvement in intertribal hostilities.

The Composition of the Pawnee Hunting Group Changes

For centuries, the whole village or band abandoned their earth-lodge villages to go on the hunt. All individuals went, except for the very infirm who could not possibly make the effort to go. With cession of their lands to the United States, and the beginning of reservation life, there were changes in the hunting group. The agent assigned white men to accompany the tribe to and from the hunt in the early 1870s. With these men overseeing their route and behaviour, Pawnee hope for the feeling and expression of freedom away from the authority of the agency and its personnel diminished.

Another change occurred when the agent kept some Pawnee children in agency school for the 1872 summer hunt. Superintendent White approved of this, saying that the "demoralization" resulting from going on this venture would be avoided as well as the effect of absence from school.[67] The great hum of anticipation that caused the children to run and play harder in former years was missing for these children as they watched, from behind the schoolyard fence, the preparation and the movement of their families away from the villages.

In this same year in November, the agent reported that a third of the tribe would not go on the winter hunt in order to protect their timber from nonreservation white men who were cutting and hauling it away by the wagonload. But some of them could not go because they had no horses.[68] This third was a sizable portion of the tribe, and it forecasted a substantial economic loss resulting from fewer individuals involved in the killing and processing of the kill. That there were fewer men on this hunt may have contributed to the Sioux being able to steal the 111 horses, as mentioned previously.

In a letter Superintendent White wrote to Indian Commissioner Parker, he foretold the doomed journey, "Their object was hunting alone and they are not prepared for fighting the Sioux."[69] At this time, there were 2,447 Pawnees, of which approximately 800 stayed in the villages.

The most radical and controlled change came in the 1874 summer hunt. Although the commissioner had restricted hunting, the agent gave permission for only fifty men from each band to go. He gave permission because by now the Pawnees had little food, and there would be less and less until the crops matured. Passes were now required to leave the reservation. The hunt was to be a short one, and only small game was to be sought.[70] As it turned out, twelve women went anyway, their presence being necessary to process the kill. But what a contrast this group of 212 made to the great retinue of 5,000 that Murray reported stretching across the prairies for miles in 1835.

Besides government control of who went on the hunt and

where they went, there was also control of the time of departure and the length of time that could be spent away from the reservation. Dangers increased as the government discouraged and prevented the distribution of guns to the Pawnees. In spite of repeated requests for arms and ammunition to protect themselves from the enemy, the Quakers never wholeheartedly believed the Pawnees should be armed.

Sky Chief prophetically declared in exasperation in a November 1871 council: "We take our horses out to hunt without arms and I expect the next thing you know you may hear that I am laying dead because I had no arms to defend myself."[71] He was referring to the Sioux and Cheyennes, whom the Pawnee claimed were always better armed than they were and seemingly had greater access to or at least were not so carefully prevented from obtaining arms.[72] General Hancock's statement above about the Sioux obtaining arms from the government seems to bear this out. In the summer of 1873, while on the hunt, Sky Chief met his death at the hands of the Sioux as he had feared.

The Pawnees had become accustomed for many years to intertribal visiting, often to take the Sacred Pipe and ceremony of adoption to members of other tribes. One of the tribes for which they felt special kinship was the Wichitas, also a member of the Caddoan language group. For many years after the hunt was completed, rather than returning directly home, it became customary for groups from different bands to travel southward to visit their adopted kinsmen among the Wichitas and stay for extended visits.[73]

But when reservation life began, restriction on such visits also began. It was necessary to gain permission to go and to have passes signed by the agent, as well as prior approval of the Wichita agent and later the Indian commissioner. However, Pawnees considered this to be unnecessary and they resented the restrictions. In one council Superintendent White spoke in anger to the chiefs, demanding to know why three hundred Pawnees had gone to visit the Wichitas without permission.[74]

So even intertribal visits, an adjunct activity of the hunt cycle, were prohibited in the 1870s. Part of the government's growing reluctance to permit friendly intertribal visits was the disruptive effect agents believed they had on its Indian "civilization" program. An Indian away from the reservation visiting and enjoying the friendly intercourse and maintenance of intertribal bonds was not learning how to be a full time farmer. He was also practicing autonomy and self-direction and not under direct agency control. Such prolonged visits might also lead to alliances against the government.

Beyond that there was concern over Indian-white relations. The number of communities that were springing up across Kansas and Nebraska increased as the land was opened to settlement. Most settlers were afraid of Indians or hated them, and depredations did occur from time to time as Indian groups with hungry stomachs passed isolated farmsteads. Whenever the Pawnees left to go on their hunts, the agent always sternly demanded that they should keep peace and not steal any crops or possessions of white men and told them that if they did, "punishment would be administered." [75]

Thus Pawnee life changed radically with the curtailment of the hunt and its control by outside forces. For the American Indian, hunting had far greater meaning than was understood by others then and now. It was an activity that entailed an insistent need for the fulfillment of sacred obligations that maintained a reciprocal bond between the Creator, the Spirit Beings, and the people. It was a part of the sacred order that had existed since the Pawnee origin time. Visions, songs, sacred societies, and games were inspired by the Buffalo. Buffalo Society Doctors cured the ill with rituals obtained from the great animals in visions and dreams. Fear of Tirawahut's anger and abandonment, if ritual was not sustained, intensified as government policy severely restricted the concomitant practices and freedom of the traditional hunt. It is difficult now to relive the frustration and feelings of helplessness and despair of a people who for centuries had maintained their relationship with the Great Herd so that it never seemed to decrease but was always willingly available to feed and clothe them.

Long before their fate and that of the Great Herd had been determined, when the first light-skinned explorers arrived on the shores far to the east and in the warm waters to the south. Subsequent nineteenth-century historical and ecological events culminated in the termination of the hunt, the near extinction of the buffalo, and the growing belief that the Sacred Beings and the Great Herd had turned from the Pawnees in spite of their endeavors to maintain the relationship.

✝✝✝
5
The Pawnee and Sioux Relationship

The Sioux of Dakota, however, seem to be most the belligerent. Since
these Indians have ceased their war with the whites, they gratify their
thirst for blood by raiding upon weak neighboring tribes, and no argu-
ment can induce them to abandon the practice.
　　　　　—Ely Parker, commissioner of Indian Affairs, 1870

The Pawnee and Sioux relationship was rarely one of trust or
amity. From the 1830s to the 1870s, their relations consisted of
horse stealing raids and warfare upon one another, with revenge
and retaliation constant factors. Accounts by traders, missionaries, military men, and government officials testify to the long-
standing enmity between the tribes.

From the 1830s to the 1850s, Edwin Thompson Denig spent
his life among the Sioux and other northern Plains tribesmen.
He was first a trader, then a *bourgeois* in charge of a fur company's
transactions at Fort Union and later at a trading post located in
North Dakota at the mouth of the Yellowstone River. He became
an excellent chronicler of Dakota life, including their relationships with other tribes in the region.[1] He observed that the Brulé
generally were able to get the best of the Pawnees and "seldom a
summer passed but many a scalp of these enemies were brought
to camp." Their enemies were not unresponsive, and in 1835 the
Pawnees and Arikaras stole between forty and fifty Brulé horses.
They did not escape without being pursued, losing twenty-two
men and all the horses, it was claimed. Burlé patterns of warfare
included bringing back heads, feet, hands, and other body parts

to the village.* Here they were carried impaled on sticks, and the scalped heads were dragged through the village amidst cries of triumph. Finally they were pounded with rocks and shot at by the young boys.[2] Referring to the Lower Yanktons, Denig said they were the least hostile of the Siouan bands, but occasionally they went on war parties to the Pawnee villages "in quest of scalps or horses."[3]

In the 1840s, the Presbyterian missionary, John Dunbar, saw at first hand the enmity shown by the Sioux against the Pawnees. He said that the main Sioux objective at this time was to steal horses. "The Pawnees defended themselves as well as they could, but they were at a disadvantage against the well mounted and well armed Sioux."[4] In 1843, one band fortified its village by digging a ditch and erecting a turf wall around it. They had requested two hundred guns from the agent to be paid for with their annuity in order to defend themselves.[5] In one encounter the Sioux rode into a village and began to burn the lodges. They did not all attack at once. Some stayed mounted at a distance, and at intervals rode furiously into the village to kill and count coup. In this attack on June 27, 1843, they drove off all the Pawnee horses and burned twenty of the forty lodges. The battle lasted from daylight until noon. The Pawnees, fought fiercely but were no match for the well-armed Sioux. A Sioux Indian agent, according to Dunbar, informed the Pawnee agent that he had influenced three small bands to stop their incursions against the Pawnees, but the others were "resolved at war, and if possible to exterminate the Pawnees."[6]

Not only did the Sioux attack the Pawnee villages along the Loup and Platte rivers, but they also assaulted the hunters and their families while they were on journeys to and from their hunting grounds. Lt. Percival G. Lowe observed on August 12, 1858, "Twenty-five hundred Pawnees, men, women and children passed east, running from the Sioux with whom they had had a battle." There were losses on both sides, but the Sioux got most of the Pawnee horses.[7]

* Samuel Allis, Pawnee missionary and school teacher, observed this practice after a Sioux attack and battle with the Pawnees in 1844. He assisted the Pawnees in burying their dead and observed such mutilations had occurred. (See Allis, "A Presbyterian Mission in Pawnee Country," p. 730.)

The Pawnees were settled villagers for a great portion of the year. This put them at a distinct disadvantage when crop fields had to be tended, and the women working there became easy targets for the enemy. The Sioux were mostly nomadic bands that mainly occupied several regions in the present states of North and South Dakota and Minnesota, and also parts of Iowa and Nebraska. Because they were mainly nomadic, and with a few exceptions had no settled villages, their people were not the easy targets that settled people were, no matter how capable and aggressive their warriors were.

In their relations with the Pawnees, the two most predatory bands seem to have been the Brulés and Oglalas of the Teton Sioux division. The Yanktons and Santees were inconsistent in their relationships, sometimes professing friendship and exchanging tribal visits with the Pawnees, and at other times indulging in horse stealing, raiding, and killing. Part of this inconsistency may be explained by the leadership and organization of Sioux bands. According to Preston Holder, there was no unified Sioux Nation, but bands consisting of "loose aggregates of more or less closely related family groups." They were usually held together through the male line "and their continuance depended to a great degree on the exploits and adventures of the men. . . . A strong leader of one season might through a series of reverses become a mere follower in a completely different band within the passage of a year." The status and power of a leader could shift with his fortune or misfortune in war and his ability to gain and distribute wealth, such as horses. There was "a plethora of leaders vying with each other for the allegiance of followers," and there were "many small groups with little stability of allegiance and considerable mobility of residence."[8] Thus if band leadership changed in this manner, it is possible that the relationship with the Pawnees might change from hostility at one point to nonaggression at another, depending on the leader's war experience and who his enemies were.

The ultimate effect of Sioux warfare on the Pawnees was its partial contribution to the decline of the Pawnee population. From 1830 to 1875, a period of forty-five years, Pawnee numbers decreased from an estimated 10,000 to 12,000 to 2,276.[9] The Sioux numbers compared to the population of their enemies was overwhelming. A careful estimate of all Sioux bands in 1888–90 gave a total population of 43,000. Of that number, 4,373 were Brulés and 7,730 were Oglalas.[10] Earlier figures are unknown or are rough estimates, and it can be assumed that the numbers were always larger than the later Pawnee figures. Even though there may have been close to a one-to-one death rate in Pawnee and Sioux hostile encounters, it is apparent that the ability to replace Sioux warriors in greater numbers than the Pawnees could was a factor in the continuing Pawnee population decline. This is not to say other factors, such as epidemic diseases and malnutrition, did not play a major role, but the Sioux stealing of horses and killing of women who were population and economic producers took a substantial toll at this time. Such events affected not only the ability of the tribe to provide adequate sustenance from the hunt and from fields abandoned because of fear but also to reproduce itself at a normal rate of increase. As an example, in the Blaine family, Wichita and Effie were very young children in Nebraska when their mothers were killed by the Sioux. Wichita had no siblings, and Effie had one brother who survived only to his teen-age years. Stories about orphans living with grandparents or other relatives are common for this time. Figures in official reports do not give numbers of women murdered by the Sioux in these years.

The Pawnee Remember the Sioux

Pawnee Death Song
Here I come. Here I come. Here I come.
Here I will go. Here I will go. Here I will go.
Tirawahat, as a ghost,
Where could I go?
Here I will go. Here I will go.
—Blaine family song

In remembering the bitter last years in Nebraska, the Pawnees recalled that they were on "rigidly unfriendly" terms with the Sioux, called *Tsu-ra-rat*, or Throat Cutters.[11] It is remembered that the Tsu-ra-rat became relentless in their attacks, and the Pawnee tribe summoned all of its decades of experience as efficient warriors to defend the people and survive. The times were called *we-tuks*, or scarey, for it seemed that the Tsu-ra-rat were always around ready to pounce, raptor-like, on small groups of women in the fields and young men herding the horses.[12]

To warn of impending attack, the Pawnee tactic was to maintain a system of scouts who went out from the villages each morning to take strategic positions on vantage points. Here they observed any persons or parties approaching from any direction. Early travelers described seeing solitary sentinels stationed on nearby prominences silently watching their approach to the Pawnee villages.[13]

> All men who were warriors did scouting. No one came around and said you were on a list, it's your turn. If a man was not going to be away from the village, then every other morning, he would take it upon himself to get up about 3:30 to 4:00 just as it was getting gray in the East. He would go out from the village and take his position on a high place. When the sun came up it was a good time to be alert. You could see a long distance. It was silent so you could hear well. Alertness at this time was necessary. You had to be alert to see the enemy who often chose this time to stealthily approach the village. If you were hunting and scouting, this was a good time not only to see the enemy but a buffalo herd.[14]

Associated with scouting duty were songs that were composed to express certain relevant feelings and events. They revealed a great deal about the men who were called on to preserve the lives of the people on a day to day basis. One good example is the one written at the beginning of this section. The reference to "ghost" is a term for a person who has been scalped, but is not dead. These individuals were feared and not allowed to enter the village or live near there. They were living dead, or ghosts, and had to fend for themselves. A warrior preferred to be killed by the enemy, rather than be scalped and left living. Sometimes women in the fields were scalped, mutilated, and survived.[15]

Some scouting songs were said to have been composed before the time of horses. The older songs were sung to a trotting cadence that a man maintained as he ran and sang coming into village after leaving his scouting post. While on their posts, men

The Scalped Ones, *by Albin R. Jake, Pawnee artist. Women working in the fields were often scalped and mutilated by marauders. The painting shows circular, red-lined areas on the top of each head and distorted features. A surviving scalped person was feared and not allowed to live in the village. Some were said to band together to survive. One Scalped One is said to have followed the Pawnees to Indian Territory and lived by himself in a ravine pointed out to the author. Photo by Dr. R. E. Venk. The Blaine Collection.*

sometimes sang their own or family songs in a low voice to keep alert and pass time. One of the older songs says,

> Here he comes [the Sun]
> As I see Father [the Sun]
> As I see him. [16]

Roaming Chief (Roan Chief) sang this song:

> This is my world
> Using a rock for a pillow
> Who is watching me? [17]

Roaming Chief, sometimes called Roam or Roan Chief, was born in 1852 in Nebraska. Later, in Indian Territory, he became head chief of the Pawnees. Courtesy of the Kansas State Historical Society, Topeka.

The question, "Who is watching me?" is said to have meant that he was alone in a world of his own with no members of his family nearby.

As was said, the Sioux used to attack early in the morning, and when they did they sounded like the cries of many crows in the distance. Old men who had been warriors in Nebraska would say that when they were walking or riding, "And I suddenly heard a sound like a crow, I knew immediately I was being attacked. Even to this day, if you are out on the prairie, the only bird that can sound like a man's call and be as loud as a man from a distance is the crow. It was a teaching for all in those days, 'When you hear a crow, stop and look sharply. It may not be a crow. We all knew this.'" [18]

Attacks on the Villages

The Sioux rode into villages to steal horses, to count coup, or to kill. A Pawnee woman remembered that

> Once my family was in their earthlodge when shouts were heard outside. My father, a very young man then, ran out and noticed much activity, men running about getting their horses. It was customary when under attack to jump on your horse and yell, "I am . . . . I am here to defend against the enemy!" This time when Leading with the Bear ran toward his horse, he experienced for the first time in his life that feeling in which you cannot move, you are frozen in your tracks. Charging down on him, ready to kill him, was an enemy on a horse. He was unable to move, until his sister screamed from the door of the earthlodge, "You are Leading with the Bear and you are going to defend me against the enemy!" Instantly he gained his senses, raised his bow and shot the man. My father never knew why the man had not counted coup or killed him first. [19]

Death was always close. Saritsarusa, or Raging Horse, was a chief. His son was Sirerirutkawi, or Taken as a Leader. One day the chief's wife was in the fields working with her two daughters. The Tsu-ra-rat came down and killed and scalped them along with other women and children in the field. After this, Saritsarusa had only his son left to talk to, and he would encourage him and tell him that whenever the Tsu-ra-rat came, "You must be a man and go out no matter where the Sun is, fight and you may save some wives or mothers or sister of other men. Your mother is killed, and so are your sisters killed and scalped, and this is what you must do, and what I must do."

Taken as a Leader used to sit with a mirror in front of him. Every day he would sit there for two or three hours to put on his paint, comb his hair, and fix his braids. But whenever the Tsu-ra-rat came, he would go out and fight fiercely. He was becoming a great warrior, and he had counted many coup and killed many enemies.* He was still a young man, very young. But one day he was killed. It was one of those days when there were too many Tsu-ra-rat for the number of Pawnees, and he was killed. His father found him where he had fallen after the battle. He got down from his horse, lifted his son up across it, and rode back to the village. Here he cried out loudly as he rode, "I have done the right things in encouraging my only son to be a leader and fight for his people." He rode across the village from side to side, mourning his son and praising him before the people. The Pawnees have a song that commemorates his death.[20]

Wichita Blaine said that when the Sioux attacked his village, the chief would let the warriors pursue them, but only so far, because the chief, a Pitahawirata, said, "I have given my word in the treaty." Before that time, "We used to pursue the Sioux and kill everyone, but one, so he could go back and tell the others."[21] Small secret groups of men would leave the villages unknown to the agent and fight a type of preventive or guerrilla warfare so as not to break the treaty. These groups did not go to the Tsu-ra-rat camps but tried to intercept their war parties as they approached

---

* Kenneth Bordeaux, of Brulé and Oglala descent, discussed the coup system with Garland J. Blaine. He said, "If you ride in and touch a man with a stick or arrow that was a great honor. If you can ride in and touch a man and get away from him alive, that was bravery. You had really done something. You were looked on as a coward if the guy was too good for you and you had to kill him. You weren't good enough to get away from him after touching him." Blaine agreed that this was the Pawnee way also, adding, "My people would tell about some man who would come back and say, "I killed so and so." And someone would say, "Maybe he was turned the other way, and you sneaked behind him and killed him." This was said in ridicule and indicated that you were not as brave as you wanted others to believe.

and entered Pawnee country. This was not aggression, it was reasoned, but a way of preventing it by deterring the enemy from
reaching the villages. These were mostly seasoned warriors, but
even very young men wanted to join these parties, usually after
they had had a family member killed. In their grief and anger,
two or three youngsters would go to an older man and say, "Uncle,
I lost my sister, or my mother, to the Tsurarat. We know more
war parties will come here. We want you to lead us to the enemy.
We can stay out of sight, then drive off their horses, then attack
them afoot." Often the older man would reply, "Just as angry as
you are now is as scared as you would be when we attacked. You
are too young for me to take you." [22]

But sometimes age was not sufficient for wisdom in leadership,
as the following account reveals.

My Grandfather Blaine was a teenager and his two cousins were
probably in their early twenties, and they asked their uncle to
take them out and show them the art of warfare—to show them
what to do for protection purposes. He consented and while they
were getting ready, I guess it was obvious what they were going to
do, an older uncle of the leader asked them if this was their inten-
tion and they said, yes. He said he was getting to be an old man,
his wife had been killed in the fields, too, and he wanted to go
with them. "I do not want to become an old man. While I can I
want to contribute my service to the protection of our people."
He presented such a strong argument that they were persuaded to
take him. He was about fifty years old and the uncle who was to
lead was about thirty.

When they were well prepared with dry corn and extra moccasins they left the village early in the morning. They were about
two days from home on the grasslands west of the agency, when
they saw a band of Tsurarat. They counted and there were about
twenty-five men in all. Before the five of them could hide, the
Tsurarat saw them and came in force toward them. This thirty
year old was leader and supposedly what he said was obeyed.
There was never any question about that. The man who was
leader was to obeyed without hesitation on any war party. He said,
"We will run over this little hill. We won't run to the creek. After
we get over the hill, they will figure we will run around this little
knoll back to the creek. Instead we will run over the next hill and
get out of sight in hopes they will not see us when they get here. I

am hoping they will think that we ran toward the hill, then to the creek to hide in the trees there, and that is where they will go. That will give us more time to go in this other direction and then to the creek that runs on around the hill. That way we will have time to get there and be concealed and be ready to fight."

But the old uncle said, "Oh, no. I am the oldest here and you are my relatives and you all have to listen." While he was arguing about what action to take, the Sioux were getting closer and closer. The young leader said, "Old Man, you are killing us. You can go where you want to, but you young men follow me." They ran over the hill and the old man followed them. Then as planned they ran over the second hill and lay down in the tall grass. In a minute or two there came the enemy riding to the top of the knoll they had just left. They looked around, wheeled their horses and galloped down toward the creek sounding like crows.

About this time my grandfather noticed a little black cloud take form and begin spreading out. He said he could see the Tsurarat arrive at the creek. Then they stopped. They spread out and rode up and down the banks, being careful not to get too close. They thought we were hiding in there someplace. After we lay there a short time watching, the leader said, "We will get up and make a run toward the creek. When we get there, which was a distance from the Tsurarat, we will find a good camouflage and will be ready for our protection." About this time the enemy figured they were not in that area of the creek, so they stopped, talked, and rode back up to the place where they had come over the hill to find the trail. My grandfather Blaine said, "At that time the little cloud had grown darker and down came the hardest downpour, just a blinding sheet of rain. It washed out their trail and the Sioux turned and rode down to the creek farther north of where they had been searching. This left the way clear for us to follow my uncle's plan, and we ran around the hill down to the part of the creek that the Tsurarat had already searched. We crawled under some foliage and were ready in case they returned. We stayed all afternoon, then came out and went back up to where we had come from. We looked and looked but could see no sign of the Throat Cutters."

The young leader said, "We got out of this very lucky, and we should not press our luck. The best thing to do is to return. You young men did get some learning. It should now be very apparent that where there is a leader there should only be one leader and everyone respect his decisions. This is the way it is. This is our practice, our way, but my old uncle here, maybe he is getting old.

When you are old you have second thoughts. This is dangerous. There is no time." So they returned to the village.[23]

In 1875 only a few old, ill, and young Pawnees were left in the villages. The others had gone to Indian Territory to the new reservation. The ill had been left to recover and some children were still attending the agency school. Even then the Sioux used to ride into the villages and stab at the empty lodges with their lances, counting coup. One time, after being alerted, the Pawnees gathered at the school for protection. All that is, except one old man, who stayed by himself in the village and fought the Sioux for awhile, then was finally killed by the circling horsemen as he stood his ground for the last time singing his death song. *[24]

The Pawnee Way of Warfare

According to Garland J. Blaine, who was named Tirawahat wesitawa, or From the Heavens Two Eagles Come Flying, two Pawnee expressions give examples of tactics used by the tribe in warfare. *Skiri ki ku ru ri*, or Those Who Were Like Wolves, described Pawnee warriors who had the ability to fade into the landscape and conceal themselves where there seemed to be no place to hide. The expression *Ti rar ri ri wi si sat*, or They Went Side by Side (to fight), was used to described a battle formation used by the Pawnees. It was a straight line of men shoulder to shoulder facing the enemy. When advancing, the movement was sideways, exposing less of the body surface. In the straight line battle formation, the men arranged themselves in groups according to the specific warrior lance society to which they belonged. †[25]

This Pawnee formation is confirmed by George P. Belden, who lived among the Santee Sioux for a time in the 1860s. He joined them and a group of Yanktons on a horse-stealing raid against the Pawnees. He observed that during the ensuing battle after the Pawnees discovered them, the Pawnees "deployed a long line, and advancing, began the battle by hurling clouds of arrows

---

* Some Pawnees stayed in Nebraska to try to avenge the deaths of loved ones. One Pitahawirata, Tirawa resaru, chose to stay because his wife was killed by the Sioux.

† The Pawnee warrior could belong to one or more of several different lance societies. They were called this because the emblem of each was a special lance uniquely decorated with different symbols of that particular group. Eagle, crow, owl, and other feathers, as well as otter fur, buffalo tail, red and blue strouding

against us. . . ." Then, "while one party had been holding us in front, another body had moved downstream, under cover, and crossed over, completely outflanking my warriors." He continued that the attack was a total failure for the Sioux and they retreated in defeat.[26] According to Garland Blaine,

> Each Pawnee battle group consisted of ten to twenty men spaced about ten feet apart. Each group was distinctively dressed with the insignia of its society, such as a lance with different feathers fastened to the shaft. Body paint was of different colors, and members of the same society did not necessarily wear the same color or design. Some wore white streaks all over the body. Others had the left side of the face painted blue and the right side red. Different designs resulted from vision quest experiences or dreams. These special designs were unique to an individual and were worn by him to any event.[27]

> In major encounters before "treaty times" a band or village chief assumed leadership. Mounted on his horse he chose a good vantage point apart from his warriors where he could observe and direct the action. His scouts brought him notice of the location of the enemy or where they were coming from. This was relayed to the groups of warriors in their society groupings. He was particularly watchful of any flanking movement attempted by the enemy, and warning of this would be sent to the warriors. Within each of the groups, such as the Iruska, one great warrior might lead its movements, but each man according to circumstances, could act independently in a fluid rapid encounter where men horses, cries and dust might obscure the leaders' commands or other sign communication with the warriors. One man, or perhaps, more, might say, "This is a good day to die." If so, this man was carefully painted and dressed in his best. In case of death, then, no one would have to dress the body. If a man stripped off everything,

strips, and other items were attached to the lance carried on a war party. These societies had the sanction of certain Sacred Bundles, and ceremonies, songs, and dances were associated with them. Membership was by invitation and an outstanding warrior could be asked to join more than one. Some societies were strictly for policing, escorting, and scouting on the hunt, while others were concerned only with defence and attack of the enemy. Others had both these functions. The names of some of the Pawnee lance societies found in one or more of the four bands were: Brave Raven Lance, Red Lance, Two Lance, Black Heads, Those Coming Behind, Fighting Lance, and Knife Lance. (See Murie, *Pawnee Indian Societies*, p. 558 ff.)

that could also mean he intended to win or die. When he did this he took off his breech cloth which was about three to four feet long and six to eight inches wide. He tied it around his head with the ends hanging to the side or back. Otherwise, if worn in battle it would bind and chaff, especially when riding a horse, where in quick maneuvers it could hinder the rider. Another reason for removing clothing in battle was that if a warrior was shot there would be no cloth to enter the wound. Wounds with cloth in them went bad even with the best medical attention our Pawnee doctors gave them."[28]

Col. Richard Dodge, who was familiar with the Pawnees, described his experience with a Pawnee warrior in Nebraska as follows*

In 1867 I was with a party of officers elk-hunting on the Loup River. We had an escort of twelve or fifteen soldiers, and six Pawnee Indians. We established our camp in a fine position, and each officer, taking one or more Indians, went hunting as it suited him. One day I was out with one Pawnee, and, not finding game, had ridden some twelve or fifteen miles from camp, when we were discovered by a band of between forty and fifty hostile Sioux, who immediately set upon us.

About four miles back I had noticed a splendid defensive position, one of the very best I have ever seen. Putting our horses at half speed we plunged into the barrancas of the "bad lands," and in half an hour emerged on the spot sought for. Here we dismounted and made our preparations for fight. The Pawnee positively refused to fight on foot, and when I was ready I found him ready also; not a rag of clothing on his body, and nothing but a bridle on his horse. From some receptacle he had fished out a lot of narrow red, blue, and white ribbons, which he had tied in his hair, and in the mane and tail of his horse, and which, as he

---

* Regardless of some criticism of Dodge's historical accuracy and embellishment of events, this description of Pawnee behavior contains accurate details. His description of preparation for battle, including the stripping off of clothing, and the warrior's decorating himself and his horse with red and blue ribbons, seems authentic. Perhaps the ribbons were strips of blue and red strouding, which was used in decorating the sacred lances of certain lance societies and would identify him as a member. Warriors often fought without clothing so that if shot, clothing would not be forced into the wound, which then could not be adequately cleansed and could cause incurable infection.

moved, streamed out for yards in the rear. Sitting perfectly naked, with unwonted ease and grace, on his barebacked horse, with fire in his eye, determination in his face, a Spencer carbine in one hand, the reins and a Colt's revolved in the other, he looked no mean ally in a fight for life. I had hardly time to admire his "get-up" when the whole plain in front seemed alive with yelling savages, charging directly down upon us. When they got within about two hundred and fifty yards I drew up my rifle; but before I could get an aim the whole band threw themselves on the sides of their horses and, swooping in circles like a flock of blackbirds, rushed back to the limit of the plain, about six hundred yards. Here they halted and held a consultation, and some of them, going off on the flanks examined all the ground and approaches. Finding no line of attack except in front, they again essayed the charge, again to be sent to the rear by the mere raising of the rifle. This was again and again repeated with like result. Finally they withdrew beyond sight, and I wished to start, but the Pawnee said, "No, they will come again." They were absent for nearly an hour; I believe they were resting their horses. It was very hot, the whole affair was becoming very monotonous and I was nodding, if not asleep, when the Pawnee said, "Here they come." I started up to find them within shot, and brought up my rifle; whereupon all ducked, wheeled, and went away as before, entirely out of sight. During all the charges the Pawnee had evinced the greatest eagerness for fight, and I had no little difficulty in keeping him by me whenever the enemy ran away after a charge. Answering yell for yell, he heaped upon all the opprobrious epithets he could think of in English, Spanish, Sioux and Pawnee. When they wheeled and went off the last time, he turned to me with the most intense disgust and contempt, and said emphatically, "Damn coward, Sioux, now go." So, after a four-hours' siege, we saddled our horses and returned to camp without molestation, but were followed the whole way; and from that time we had no sport or comfort in our hunt, the wretches preceding us by day, driving away the game, and trying to burn us out every night; constantly making their unwelcome presence felt, and yet never giving us a chance for even a long shot at them.[29]

Garland Blaine added his own account

Warriors, who returned from a successful encounter in which enemy were killed, entered the village or camp and shouted, "There they are alone in a prone position bloated!" Although only a few hours or a day or so had past since death and the enemy bodies were not yet in that condition, it was known that they would be. It was a derogatory statement. That is the way Pawnee victims were left, except if they did anything to them such as removing hair. Then they always left the enemy face down and ground their faces in the earth before leaving them. . . .

When an unknown group of warriors was sighted or encountered on Pawnee lands, rather than attack them, the Pawnee chose to discourage any aggressive behaviour by the newcomers. To do this and to surprise them, they would ride through them and horsewhip them and ride on. The Pawnee would attack and kill if attacked, but to avoid this, the above practice of showing strength to protect themselves and prevent killing was practiced. It was considered even braver to ride in through the group, hit someone with your whip, ride out, then circle and hit someone else on the way back through the group. That was brave because you gave them all the chance to kill you both coming and going. Killing was not considered as brave an act as was the above whipping. It was said you could kill someone by shooting him in the back from a distance. This was far removed from what we considered braveness and facing danger.

Loss of kinsmen at the enemies' hands was the chief reason for seeking revenge and preventing or discouraging future attacks. However, after treaty times this was discouraged, although revenge killing continued without the chief supposedly being aware of it. Pawnees would also reprimand other tribal visitors who came to their villages and who were suspected or known to have wounded or killed Pawnee. It is said that on rare occasions, visitors were sometimes killed by irate kinsmen if it was known that they were guilty, or that the tribe they represented was guilty of a serious act. But any man who was unprovoked and killed a visitor was subject to public censure by the village and his band chief.

When confronted by the enemy while hunting or riding out on the grasslands, the size of the opposing group was considered before attacking. When the whole Pawnee tribe was moving with families and warriors, they traveled in their band groupings. We would spread ourselves across the prairies in all directions so that other tribes would hesitate to attack us knowing that large numbers of warriors would come to the assistance of any segment of the tribe that came under attack. When the Pawnee population numbered in the thousands they were formidable opponents. The opposite was true if a small group of Pawnees, say three of four, encountered a larger moving group of horsemen. They would avoid being seen and go around the larger groups, fading into the landscape.

If different tribal groups of similar size with their families should encounter one another, a few representatives of each tribe would approach one another some distance between the main bodies. If the language was not mutually understood, then sign language was used. It was customary to invite friendly or nonhostile tribal representatives to visit the camp for a meal at the fire of some chief or important warrior. After the visitors sat and ate, they indicated they would now leave and return to their own people. "Thank you for feeding us," they would say, "We, the rest of us, are over that hill. We and you are hunting, and we will go in another direction to hunt." This was courtesy and also let the host know that there were others of the visitors' tribe nearby in case treachery was contemplated.

It was believed there was a relation between brave men and the buffalo. The bravest Pawnee warriors were members of a Buffalo Dance Society, and only those who were exceptionally brave could become members. They closely associated or identified themselves with the Sacred Buffalo given by Tirawahat to the people in the beginning. Occasionally such a warrior would be out alone, perhaps scouting, hunting or seeking a vision. He might be caught and surrounded by a group of Throat Cutters. When a man alone was attacked he would find a place and there he would make his stand. Now a single buffalo could make a wallow as big as a pond one hundred feet across. And in the hours that followed as a Pawnee fought alone, he darted to avoid blows, or being shot or speared. In time the ground would become disturbed until it looked like a buffalo wallow. Sometimes he could hold off his attackers until dark when he would try to make his escape. His lips would be all cut from biting them, and his tongue would be thick from having no water. His arm where the bow rested would be bloody, and his fingers raw from use of arrows and bow string. Sometimes he would be killed. Later when other warriors passed by they could see what looked like a buffalo wallow and in it human bones. And they knew that someone brave had died there.

But others returned. Two Chiefs was one of the men who faced death and killed to keep his life. No one ever argued with him for he had killed several enemies in hand to hand combat. It was a practice of the Pawnees never to cross or upset such men because they had done enough for the people. He had had to kill and he had the deaths and those times on his mind and he had to live with that.

Wetitah haharah, he tastes himself, was the expression used by the Pawnees that meant one could almost taste death in one's self. This was said when a group was surrounded by fifteen or more enemy to one man. It meant to stand your ground until your lips bleed from biting them from concentration, from fear and the desire to survive if it was at all possible, although one could almost taste death. And yet a warrior knew he would someday die at the hands of the enemy, and in the scarey time, *we-tuks,* that was expected. Thinking of that time of death such a song as belonged to John Luwak, Chaui, was composed.

> Woman, I will not be tasty to her
>   when she is crying,
> Woman, I will not be tasty to her
>   when she is crying.

This was explained as meaning that after my death she will be crying and there will be no relationships between us and she will not know me again.[30]

While the Pawnees grew to fear and hate the treachery of the Sioux in the middle and later decades of the last century, they were also derisive about them as Colonel Dodge's account describes. Another story told by the Pawnees says, "The reason there were so many bands of Throat Cutters was that each time a Sioux got hold of a Pawnee to count coup or killed one, it was thought to be such a big deal that he was made a chief and then he took his family and made another band."[31]

Nor were the Pawnees reluctant to tell on themselves in recounting an event where an erroneous judgment made a decisive difference in the outcome of a Sioux encounter. The following story illustrates this.

Some Pawnees were out riding and wanted to cross a stream. Suddenly a Throat Cutter appeared and told them in signs they'd better not cross there or they would be killed. The Pawnee signaled that this was their land and they would cross anywhere they pleased. The Pawnee leader figured somehow that the Sioux were on their way somewhere and needed to be there at a certain time, and would skirmish a little, then flee from the Pawnees who would pursue and catch them in the usual fashion. Another warrior appeared who spoke bad Pawnee. The Pawnee figured it was a Pawnee who had been captured and who had been away from the tribe a long time. But since he had not escaped, they had contempt for him. He spoke in broken Pawnee telling them that the "road" everywhere else was good, but here it was bad, so they should go another way. The Pawnee then proceeded to call him the worse names they could, one which was in English, "dirty wretch!". If you scrape him he is so dirty, it would show white, like the whites. They then hurled various other epithets at him across the stream. So they crossed anyway, and in no time encountered a larger group of Sioux, and "got the hell beat out of them." So they retreated back across the stream and found another place to cross. This story is told in good humor in all three Pawnee South Bands.[32]

Pawnee Attempts to Make Peace with the Sioux

The Pawnees continue to say they promised in their last treaty with the United States in Nebraska in 1857 to live at peace with other tribes and give up acts of hostility toward them and the whites. They claim that, in exchance for this and other concessions, the United States promised to protect them from their enemies and prevent attacks upon them. Article 5 of the treaty of September 24, 1857, as finally written, gives the following agreements:

> The Pawnee acknowledge their dependence on the Government of the United States and promise to be friendly with all the citizens thereof, and to pledge themselves to commit no depredations on the property of such citizens, nor on that of any other person belonging to any tribe or nation at peace with the United States. And should any one or more of them violate this pledge, and the fact be satisfactorily proven before the agent, the property shall be returned, or in default thereof, or if injured or destroyed, compensation may be made by the Government out of their annuities, nor will they make war on any other tribe, except in self-defence, but will submit all matters of difference between them

and other Indians to the Government of the United States, or its agent, for decision, and abide thereby.[33]

It is possible that in the interpreter's translation of the treaty from English to Pawnee he or the Pawnee signatories misinterpreted or misunderstood the phrase, "And should any one or more of them violate this pledge. . . ." They may have thought it referred to the sentence before it, which mentions other tribes. The phrase, "except in self defence" seems to have been conveniently overlooked by Quaker agents after 1869. They insisted for the most part that no form of aggression occur under any pretext.

There was misunderstanding or misinterpretation of this treaty by both sides, it would appear. The Pawnees always insisted that the government did not live up to its commitment to them to keep the Sioux from breaking the peace and attacking them after they had promised not to attack the Sioux or any enemy. This is how they understood the treaty.[34]

The Pawnee leaders took their treaty agreements seriously, as numerous entries indicate in the 1870s council minutes with the agent in Nebraska.[35] Differences and hostilities between them and other Indians were brought before the agent for settlement as their treaty stated should be done. The numerous attacks and horse thefts by the Sioux were discussed heatedly. With few exceptions little action was taken to compensate the Pawnees for the continuous losses, although correspondence between agents, superintendents, and the commissioner of Indian Affairs continually discussed the rapacity of the Sioux against their neighbors. It did not take long for the Pawnees to suspect and then believe that the government's words were not to be trusted.

The Sioux treaties of 1865 and 1868 with the United States show some interesting differences in government demands and reactions to tribal infractions when compared to the 1857 Pawnee treaty. On October 28, 1865, at Fort Sully, Dakota Territory, many but not all of the Sioux bands signed individual treaties. Among those not present were the Brulés, one of the most frequent attackers of the Pawnees. In the 1865 treaty, the Oglalas and others agreed to "discontinue" for the future all attacks upon persons or property of other tribes unless first attacked by them."[36] It would appear that for the most part little attention was paid to this agreement. The Oglalas continued to attack the Pawnees, seemingly without provocation, unless there were more secret Pawnee forays to count coup, seek revenge, or steal horses than were reported.

Of significance is the fact that unlike the Pawnee treaty, nowhere in the 1865 Sioux treaty did they agree to return stolen property. The Fort Laramie treaty of April 29, 1868, was signed by the Brulés, Oglalas, and other bands. In Article 1, it was stated that if any Sioux committed a "wrong or depredation upon any person or property of anyone, white, black or Indians at peace with the United States, then the wrong doer shall be turned over to the United States for trial under its laws, and in case they willfully refuse to do so, the person injured shall be reimbursed for his loss from the annuities or other moneys due or to become due them under this or other treaties made with the United States." [37]

There is a fond Pawnee memory of one Nebraska agent, who was small in stature, and who would get on his horse and ride after the Sioux with the Pawnees when the villages were attacked, though his name has been forgotten. They approved of him because he would jump on his horse, catch up with them, and take his whip and thrash any Sioux he was lucky enough to catch up with. Now this was the proper way for an agent to handle the Sioux, they said. [38] After the Quaker agents came in 1869, the Pawnees rarely were allowed to pursue the Sioux when they attacked the villages. This counter measure was stopped by Agent Jacob Troth, as mentioned in the horse stealing episode when Big Spotted Horse went beyond what the agent thought was proper behavior.

By 1870, it was unnecessary to tell the Pawnees that their condition was deteriorating. Hampered by the Quaker assumption that nonaggression would beget nonaggression between tribes, the Pawnees were held back from traditional warfare methods by a shortage of arms, horses, and agents' demands, and by threats to withhold annuity funds if they took defensive action towards other tribes. * Sioux agents who were not of the Quaker faith

* How truthful was Agent Jacob Troth in 1869, when he reported that the "chiefs desire part of the half of the annuity usually expended on dry goods,

often approached the problem of Indian aggression with a different point of view.

Unable either to retaliate adequately, except for making minor secret sorties, or to seek peace traditionally, in March the Pawnee chiefs requested permission to have a council with the Sioux chiefs in Washington in order to make a peace treaty. After a recent raid, they had asked the agent for permission to pursue and retrieve their stolen horses. The agent would not allow it.[39] It was obvious to the Pawnees that the government was not able or would not prevent the Sioux from attacking them or stealing horses, and this request for a traditional face-to-face peace council might solve a deadly dilemma resulting from these conditions.

In June, Superintendent Samuel Janney suggested to Commissioner of Indian Affairs Ely Parker that on their way home from a visit in the capital city, the Sioux chiefs could be invited to meet with the Pawnee chiefs at Omaha or Columbus, Nebraska.[40] Spotted Tail's presence was important because Brulé warriors were said to be the perpetrators of many raids on the Pawnees. His animosity against the Pawnees was said to come from his belief that U.S. Pawnee Scouts killed his brother while the former were guarding the crews on the Union Pacific railroad construction a few years previously.[41] By now, Sioux hostility had increased Quaker concern that the civilization program for the Pawnees was at a standstill. It was impossible to make the Pawnees carry out the government agricultural program calling for settling on dispersed homesteads when the risk of life was so great. This impediment contributed to their promoting the Pawnee request for a council to seek peace.

In June, Janney received a letter from Capt. Dewitt C. Poole, Indian agent at the Whetstone Agency, Dakota Territory. He said that Spotted Tail's band camps were from twenty-five to one hundred miles from the agency. Not volunteering to take the Pawnee invitation to counsel to Spotted Tail, he added that at the chief's next visit to the agency office, he would bring up the matter of the Pawnee request to make a peace treaty with the

---

blankets, guns, etc., be used for the purchase of cattle and farm horses, and that no more of it be expended for purchase of guns, pistols, and hunting knives." (Commissioner of Indian Affairs Annual Report 1869, p. 350)

Brulé band. However, he added, he had discussed the matter with several other Brulé chiefs who had come to the agency, and they said they would not agree to any arrangements that Spotted Tail should make. He advised that the Sioux did not submit to the authority of one chief, and thus the success of "the peaceful measure proposed is somewhat doubtful."[42]

In the meantime, Janney had spoken directly to Red Cloud of the Oglala band. In responding, Red Cloud informed him that at one time the Pawnees and Sioux were like one people, but the Pawnees turned against them, joined the white soldiers, as scouts, and killed them.[*] He could not make a peace without consulting his people, he said. Other Sioux chiefs present repeated Red Cloud's statements to Janney. Nevertheless, Janney hoped optimistically that he had made a good impression on the chiefs and that they would eventually consent to meeting with the Pawnees.[43]

So the Pawnee hope that the Sioux would meet with them in council was not to be fulfilled immediately. It would seem that the Sioux, individually and collectively, were not eager to establish a relationship with the Pawnees that would prevent coup counting, horse stealing, and other depredations. What would they have to gain? They had superior numbers; and the Pawnees, hampered by the circumstances in which they found themselves under Quaker control, were no longer the unfettered foe they had been or could be. As if to emphasize their disinterest in the peace overture, soon after the Red Cloud-Janney meeting, a group of Sioux attacked a Pawnee village. The Sioux were surrounded by the Pawnees and one was killed. The Pawnees lost one man with three wounded.[44] Although there may have been other unrecorded instances during the summer of 1870, it was not until October that the Sioux attacks were again officially noted. Some Pawnee women gathering wood were killed and scalped early one morning. There happened to be U.S. troops in the area and they pursued the Sioux. In this instance, the agent allowed some Pawnee warriors to ride with the troops. One Sioux was killed.[45]

---

[*] Sioux attacks on Pawnee villages and other hostilities antedated the enlistment of Pawnee Scouts by several decades.

Red Cloud, Oglala Sioux chief. *Courtesy of Western History Collections, University of Oklahoma Library.*

Spotted Tail, Brulé Sioux chief. *Courtesy of Western History Collections, University of Oklahoma Library.*

Soon after this, Janney visited the agency and found a hostile group of Pawnee chiefs. Forcefully they stated that they were always willing to pursue the Sioux as far as was necessary, but except for the recent event, they were restrained by the agent. They spoke in "strong terms" and believed that some of the attackers were Brulés and Oglalas from Whetstone Agency. The frustration of their situation was made clear when they said *they* were required to give up Cheyenne horses that they had stolen and that their young men had been imprisoned for that offense. Therefore, the Indians of the North, the Throat Cutters, should be required to give up horses they had stolen from the Pawnees, and those who had murdered Pawnees should also be punished. None of this seemed to have happened. And why was that? One chief declared what the Pawnees should do was to form an alliance with other tribes and wipe out the bands of molesting

Sioux. Janney urged them not to do this but reported to the commissioner that "they are strongly inclined to do so."[*][46]

Janney had not yet heard from Captain Poole regarding his request to discuss peace overtures with Spotted Tail, and the depredations from that quarter had continued. Gen. Christopher Augur agreed that the "Pawnee have just cause to complain."[47] Somehow, in late November, Spotted Tail was convinced to meet with the Pawnees. General Augur suggested that he could accompany the Sioux chiefs to Sioux City or Omaha and meet the Pawnee chiefs there as soon as the latter returned from their winter hunt.[48]

With this turn of events, the Indian Office in Washington and the War Department began to plan for this important council. However, Janney informed Acting Commissioner W. W. Clum that a meeting of the two tribes should be held in April. Although the Pawnees would return from their hunt in March, it was a bad month to travel. Rather that Omaha or Sioux City, he suggested that the Santee Agency located south of the Missouri in northern Nebraska would be a good place to gather because the Pawnees could go there directly in wagons from their reservation. The Santee agent would be consulted to see how the Santees felt about having the event at their agency.[49] The only hitch to all this was that Pawnee chiefs said the Santees did not treat them well on a previous visit, and they were not eager to return to that place.

The cost of such a council was estimated by General Augur to be about $1,000. Janney, aware of the importance of gift exchanges in expediting friendship and agreements, believed that they would have to be purchased for the Indians if they had no funds to purchase them themselves. He said, "The object in view is so very important that we should not spare any reasonable expense to effect it."[50] The government took complete charge of the proposed event by determining site location, transportation, and supplying gifts. Traditional ways of conflict solving among

[*] George Hyde in *The Pawnee Indians* (page 308) expressed his opinion on the differential treatment of the Pawnees and Sioux by saying, "The same humanitarians who were so solicitous for the welfare of the fierce and ungrateful Sioux, left the Pawnees to shift for themselves."

reservation tribes were now prevented, and the government or-
chestrated and controlled such efforts.

In January 1871, by suggestion of the government, the Santee
chiefs and headmen invited the Pawnees and Brulés to their
agency. Theirs was more than a magnanimous gesture. The Santees hoped that in such a meeting there also might be an agreement made between the Brulés and themselves that would convince the former not to steal Santee horses! The Pawnees were
interested in that important problem also, but they wanted as
much to receive satisfaction in monetary compensation for the
loss of their women killed by the Brulés. Monetary compensation
was a practice that the government had instituted some time before to prevent revenge and retaliation, and since the Pawnees
were largely prevented from taking active measures to right the
wrongs done them, they expected compensation to be made in
monetary form. This would not substitute for the terrible losses,
but it was their only option for satisfaction at this time. Janney
said, "If the latter (Brulés) cannot pay from their own resources,
I think it would be a good policy for the government to assist
them in reparation [payment]."[51]

To affirm the Pawnee agreement of meeting their adversaries
in council, their agent framed the reasons, supposedly given by
the chiefs, for sincerely wishing peace. One was that they could
not settle on farms as long as the Sioux attacked isolated individuals, and they looked forward to beginning this new life in the
coming spring.[52] For the village living Pawnees, extended family
responsibilities took the form of community work groups such as
the corn planting and harvesting events described by Effie Blaine.
For them, separate homestead living would seem to have had the
lowest priority.

In the posthunt Pawnee council held in the Pawnee Manual
Labor School on March 27, 1871, the agent took up the proposed
meeting with the Sioux. He said the Santee agent had spoken to
Spotted Tail and that he had said that he wanted to make a
treaty with the Pawnees and would use his influence to prevent
his men from warring on the tribe. If a treaty was completed with
Spotted Tail, then their agent would see that if the Brulés broke
the treaty and raided the Pawnees, "then they will have to pay
you." He continued that Spotted Tail and his people had been

assigned a reservation farther from the Pawnees than before, and it was hoped that this greater distance would be a deterrent to Brulé raiding parties.[53]

After these opening statements, the agent asked the chiefs if they would like to comment. Sky Chief spoke first, saying the Pawnees wanted to make peace and would agree to the agents' plans. He thought Spotted Tail might speak the truth, and if peace was made then they wanted their horses returned to them. He now revealed that one year some of them had gone as U.S. Indian Scouts with white soldiers to hunt Spotted Tail but were unable to capture him. He said that he did not want to make peace this summer but later, in Washington. There he would see if Spotted Tail told the truth and was sincere. The idea seemed to be that a peace made in Washington would have greater force and validity if it were made under the eyes of the officials there.

Terrecowah explained to the agent that the reason that Sky Chief wanted to defer the peace council was because he had lost three women in his family. This can be inferred to mean that he still sought revenge for their deaths, and peace would prevent his personal mission from being accomplished. Terrecowah added that "we have all lost some women" and said that he did not trust Spotted Tail because he did not fight like a man, but killed Pawnee women. He ended his remarks somberly by saying that he did not think that even the Great Father could make the Sioux keep peace.

A chief of the Kitkahahki band said he, too, lost his wife to the Sioux. He did not want to seem contrary but preferred to go to Washington to meet with the Sioux rather than go to the Santee Agency. Agent Jacob Troth then showed his displeasure by telling the chiefs he had worked two years on the peace council plans, and he had been directed by Washington to do so, and "What I do is the same as if your Grandfather [the President] had done [it]." Now the chiefs came, he continued, throwing obstacles in the way. He accused them of acting like children. In order to stop the killing of their men, women, and children, and the stealing of their horses, they must make a treaty with the Sioux *now*, he stated emphatically.[54]

Pitaresaru said that if they went to the council, the Pawnees would do no talking and that the Sioux must talk. Sky Chief agreed with him, but others did not, including the interpreter, Baptiste Bayhylle, who said that if they went and did not talk, he would not go.

The second Skidi chief arose to say that he had a "brother" among the Sioux whom he had heard was the cause of all these troubles, and he wanted to talk to him. This statement would indicate that, as Red Cloud had said, at some time the relationship between the some of the Pawnees and Sioux had been amicable. The role of the adopted brother among the plains tribes was an old custom. Tribes or segments of tribes visiting one another often held ceremonies in which brothers were chosen and gifts exchanged. Strong bonds were created that often endured for many years.* If the Skidi chief had a brother among the Brulés, he believed that he could talk and appeal to him and perhaps modify his attitude toward his Pawnee brother's people.

Doctor Chief commented that if such a council should occur, he intended to ask the Sioux to pay for the Pawnees they had killed, and in turn the Pawnees should pay for the Sioux they had killed. It is supposed his reasoning was that if the slate could be wiped clean, then no further reason would exist for seeking revenge by either tribe. Having reflected on the comments heard, old Terrecowah spoke, "If we go, I am going to speak. If I was a young man and had hard feelings, I would fight, but because I am an old man, I will try and make peace." Sky Chief ended the discussion by saying that they would go and talk together, and they would come again and perhaps be of a better mind tomorrow.[55] On the next day, March 28, they gathered again. Pitaresaru began the talks by stating that he thought he was right yesterday in not wanting to go to the Santee Agency, but the agent had disagreed. So now, he thought, they would go to that place, but they would need clothes to go in and guns to hunt with along the

---

* In the present century, Garland J. Blaine, Pawnee, and Calvin Arkekita, Otoe, became "brothers" when they were young men. Later, they each named a child after the other. They kept in touch over the years, and when Calvin became confined to a wheelchair early in middle age, Garland visited him in Marland, Oklahoma, until his death. They always addressed each other as "brother."

way. Their fear of Sioux treachery demanded such protection. Their request implies that compared to the Sioux, the Pawnees were poorly armed. Sky Chief, who had wanted to postpone the treaty making attempt until it could be held in Washington, arose and explained that when he saw his empty lodge, his wife having been killed by the Sioux, he became so angered that personal feelings of revenge overrode his desire to make peace. He feared, too, that there would be no one to defend the women if they left the villages to make peace. Although he preferred to travel to Washington, he would rather go to Omaha. As chief of his band, he hoped the Sioux would be made to do the right thing, and he thanked the agent for his efforts on the tribe's behalf.

Other chiefs agreed to follow the agent's plan and hoped that the outcome of such a council would be favorable. The agent then gave more details of who would attend the meeting at the Santee Agency, including the Brulés and Santees and their agents, the superintendent from Omaha, and other white men. He relayed the information that Spotted Tail said that none of his men had been to the Pawnee country for six months, and he would prevent them from coming. He also said that he had "persuaded some Northern Sioux from going. . . ."[56]

The subject of being properly dressed was mentioned again. The Pawnee leaders wanted to look as they should look for such an occasion, both splendid and impressive, not poor and neglectful. The loss of wives and daughters who made or repaired their garments made their need apparent. Guns were again mentioned. One warrior said, "Father, if we go without arms the Throat Cutters will kill us." The agent reacted with, "I thought the Pawnees were very brave. I am not afraid to go." Of course, this told the Pawnees that they would not receive any guns and that the agent knew that he was in no danger from the Sioux anyway. Records of a meeting the next week, on April 3, make no mention of the proposed council.

Two months went by, and Spotted Tail had not yet sent word that he agreed to council at the Santee Agency. But on April 20, the news came. The agent informed the chiefs that a letter from Gen. Ely Parker, the commissioner, said the Sioux were not willing at this time to make peace with the Pawnees. He hastened to add, as he observed their reaction, that the Sioux would "be fixed so that they cannot molest you as they have done."[57] The old Pitahawirata chief, Terrecowah, who previously professed to be too old to fight, now immediately responded, "Say the word and we'll go and fight the Throat Cutters." Sky Chief stated that he did not know what to say about this turn of events, but if the Sioux did not want to make peace, he would like to send the young men to recover their stolen horses. This thought was reiterated by the others. Surprisingly, or perhaps as a consolation, the agent said that if the men obeyed him, they could go and see where the horses were located. They must not take any Sioux horses or kill any Sioux. If they found any of their horses at Whetstone Agency, they were to tell the agent there, and they would be paid for them. This was a surprising statement, considering this agent's previous adamant attitude about the Pawnees taking any action of this sort. He was as frustrated as the Pawnees at this point, having fervently hoped that peace could be obtained for the tribe—and the process of teaching agricultural and other skills continued.[58]

In June, Superintendent Janney came to the Pawnee Agency to discuss future congressional Indian appropriations and the Pawnee requests for their annuity goods. During the council, he repeated that Spotted Tail had said that his people would not disturb the Pawnees, and he would try to influence other Sioux chiefs to restrict their warriors from attacking or raiding. Janney added hopefully that he thought the Pawnees need not be afraid of the Sioux from now on. Bristling, Eagle Chief replied that he was not afraid of the Sioux, and young Pawnee men felt glad to know their enemies face-to-face. They could defend their people, run the Sioux off, and go get their horses back.[59] Apparently Troth's spur of the moment offer to let the Pawnees go to the Whetstone Agency had been rejected by the superintendent because he now refused to allow the Pawnees to leave.

His misguided optimism about Sioux tractability came to an end in this same month, when two young Pawnee men, agency farm workers, were killed four miles from the agency while hauling wood in two wagons. General Augur was of the opinion that the attackers were "Minnecouas" [Miniconjous] who had been lurking around Fort McPherson.* He said he would send soldiers to pursue and try to catch them and recover the two government-owned mules that had been taken from the government wagons.[60] Having government property stolen apparently got immediate results in contrast to Indian losses by theft. The culprits turned out to belong to Spotted Tail's camp. This was discovered when they went to Whetstone Agency in August, and the agent heard that they had been talking about killing and scalping two Pawnees and capturing two mules. At this same time, the agent was informed that Spotted Tail had said that, although he was willing, he could not make peace with the Pawnees without the consent of the chiefs of the other bands. For this reason he had deemed it unwise to have traveled to the Santee Agency to make peace.[61] This same reason had been used by Red Cloud to avoid a council with the Pawnees, and now it seemed that Spotted Tail, too, did not have authority over all chiefs in the Brulés. This is what Captain Poole, Brulé agent, had concluded when he told Agent Troth that some of the chiefs informed him they would not abide by Spotted Tail's decisions.

In Janney's opinion, the two Sioux who had murdered the young Pawnees should be arrested and tried, and the two mules returned because the Pawnees had not retaliated for the last two Sioux attacks in which Pawnees had been killed. For this reason it was proper for the government to take some action.[62] The Pawnees grimly waited for government action with little hope of a peace treaty council in the fall of 1871. If the government had abided by its treaty obligations, no treaty between the two nations should have been necessary. However, it apparently wanted to shift responsibility for peace keeping elsewhere. Or else it was concluded that the government could not control Sioux aggression. This attitude was reflected in Ely Parker's statement, ". . . and no argument can induce them to abandon the practice [warfare]."

Barclay White of the Baltimore Friends Meeting replaced Samuel Janney as superintendent of the Northern Superintendency. On his first visit to the Pawnee Agency in October 1871,

---

* The Miniconjous were a Teton Sioux band, living between the Cheyenne and Grand rivers and in the Black Hills in Dakota Territory.

he met with the Pawnee chiefs and leading warriors. With the aim of making a positive impression, he told them the government would protect them against their enemies. He was greeted with a wave of derisive laughter. The chiefs immediately asked why the government did not prevent the Sioux from attacking them, and what had been done to arrest the Sioux who had murdered on June 8th two young educated Pawnee men? In reporting this meeting, White said, "My situation was embarassing and I could only assure them that something would be done."[63]

For the most part, 1872 was to be the most peaceful year the Pawnees had had in their warlike relationship with the Sioux for many years. No attacks were reported in the first six months, although in June an Omaha newspaper reported that sixty-seven members of Spotted Tail's and Red Cloud's bands, all splendidly armed, were on the warpath. This news was part of a dispatch received by General G. D. Ruggles from Maj. N. B. Sweitzer, commanding the Second Cavalry. He reported a scouting expedition up the Middle Loup had encountered a group of warriors. They told him they were on a raid against the Pawnees. He talked to them, and they agreed to give up their plans. When he last saw them, he observed that they had struck off toward their own reservation. However, he added with some skepticism, "They might go down the Cedar River and give the Pawnees a whirl. I will telegraph to the agent so they can look out. . . . I think since they were so unexpectedly overhauled by my party that they will give up the raid against them."[64]

Capt. Luther North, who often led the U.S. Pawnee Scouts when they were called up for enlistment, spent this summer of 1872 acting as a scout for Major Sweitzer. He gives an account of an encounter with the Sioux in the same month on the South Loup some sixty miles up the river from the town of Saint Paul. It differs from Sweitzer's account. As an advance scout, he first sighted the Sioux camp, which contained families as well as warriors. He returned to tell Sweitzer, who waited for the ammunition wagons to catch up with his troops. Then he issued 100 rounds to each man. He asked what tribe the Indians were, and North told him they seemed to be Brulé Sioux from the Spotted Tail Agency. According to North, Sweitzer asked him to summon the Sioux, a few of whom had gathered on a hill overlooking the cavalry. When they came near, North made signs asking what they wanted. Sugar, coffee, and flour were indicated. Then, "Major Sweitzer made a speech to them that they could not in the least understand, telling them they must go home and be good Indians and gave them sugar, coffee and hardtack. They went away rejoicing and that was the last that was seen of them."[65] This would not seem to be that group that Sweitzer mentioned in his dispatch. However, North was the scout on this month's expedition, and he mentions no other Sioux encounters. A few days later, after taking some dispatches to Grand Island, the troops met some Pawnees who were following the trail of some Sioux who had stolen a great many horses from them at their agency. North, who spoke Pawnee, talked to them for awhile, and on returning to report to Sweitzer, he told him of the encounter. Sweitzer's comment was, "If you run across any more of them in this country, tell them to go back to their reservation and stay there; that any Indians found from their reservation will be considered hostile, and will be treated as such." "I thought of telling him, that if he treated all the hostiles as he did the party of Sioux we had met a short time before by giving them sugar, coffee and hardtack, they would all be hostile, but I kept still."[66]

There was less active hostility by the different Sioux bands toward the Pawnees in 1872. One reason for this was that they were concerned with the invasion of their lands by the Northern Pacific railroad and were harassing the crews and attacking the troops who accompanied them. The army was greatly concerned about this, as the report of Gen. Winfield S. Hancock, commanding the Department of Dakota, indicated. He said the Indians resisted the building of the Northern Pacific railroad west of the Missouri River. The line ran through the "great hunting ground of the Sioux tribes," and because of their large numbers, they could effectively prevent the operation of the railroad. Several attacks on his troops had occurred during the year. In his opinion, it was essential to compel the Indians to recognize the authority of the government and the territory.[67]

During this summer, Agent Troth finally could report some success in his efforts to gain peace. Though details are sparse, he reported that Pawnee soldiers met with Red Cloud and his company in Omaha and talked and traded blankets and other items.

They "returned home quite pleased" with their meeting.[68] Good relations continued. In July, several young, educated Pawnee men were given passes to visit the Santee Agency. They were Ralph J. Weeks, Martin Pritcher, Abraham Lincoln, Andrew Murray, Mathew Simpson, and Joseph Treat.* Their purpose was to promote peace and friendship, and he hoped that they would be treated kindly, Troth wrote to the Santee agent.[69] For this visit to happen indicates a fortitudinous change in Sioux attitudes, at least among this segment of the tribe, who had been accused of stealing Pawnee horses in the past.

The Pawnee chiefs were apparently not involved in the Omaha visit, since Troth called the representatives "soldiers" and not chiefs. But while on the summer hunt, Terrecowah, the Pitaha-wirata chief, came near the Sioux, camped, and had a peaceful encounter, even though he was told by the Sioux that they could not make peace at this time because some of their chiefs were in Washington.[70] Brave old Terrecowah! He was the one that said he was too old to fight, so he would make peace, then changed his mind and said he would go fight the Sioux when he heard that the Sioux did not want to meet at the Santee Agency. Now he was acting traditionally, with peaceful intent, in hopes that the Sioux could be persuaded to stop their damaging aggression against his tribe.

Troth watched summer outside his agency window disappear into the September autumn of 1872, and he wrote that no Sioux raid had been made on the Pawnees for over a year, since June 1871, ". . . and the prospects of a permanent peace between them is very promising. . . ."[71] He may not have known about the Pawnee group that North encountered that summer following a Sioux trail to retrieve their stolen horses. Or to make the picture look good, he might have neglected to mention it.

Pitaresaru, maintaining pressure for a formalized peace with the Throat Cutters, asked the agent in October to write to J. B.

---

* These are examples of English names given in school or by the agency to eliminate the hard-to-spell Indian names and to give family surnames. They were selected from the names of agency personnel, traders, or well-known public or historical figures. The name "Julius Caesar" was given in several tribes. This name continued in the Pawnee tribe until the death of the well-known silversmith of that name in the 1980s.

Omohundro, who knew and had contacts with the Sioux and who had accompanied the Pawnees on their last winter's hunt. He wanted him to seek out Whistler, a chief of the Brulés and ask him if he would consent to make peace with the Pawnees.[72]

But this short period of progress toward peaceful coexistence was abruptly ended in December. Although a group of Yankton Sioux visited the Skidis and were hospitably treated and shown the Pawnee Manual Labor School early in the month, the Pawnees suspected they were guilty of stealing thirty horses in the month before their visit.[73] To make matters worse, during the week of the Yankton visit, fifty horses were stolen, and it was thought that Red Cloud's band had committed the crime.[74]

Signs of hostile intent increased. A large party of Sioux under Big Belly was observed traveling toward the Pawnees hunting on the Republican River. The agent reported that in four years the Pawnees had not sent a war party to the Sioux.[75] But small Pawnee parties may have left the reservation secretly and returned successfully, as Wichita Blaine related. Big Belly may have acted in hopes of retaliation.

While 1872 seemed to have been a year during which the Pawnees and a few Sioux leaders began attempts to diminish the patterns of warfare and theft, it was only a flicker of change that died in the winter of 1872–73 and was completely extinguished in the late summer of the latter year. As mentioned previously, many horses, so necessary for Pawnee survival, were stolen on the winter hunt. Pawnee reaction turned from desire for conciliation and peace to revenge. Their new Quaker agent, William Burgess, and the superintendent heard their threats to go after their horses but turned them aside with promises that steps would be taken to ameliorate their suffering and loss.[76] Unfortunately, as mentioned above, in February, Whistler, Fat Badger, and Hand Smeller's deaths were thought to have been caused by the Pawnees, who were accused and harassed by the military. They denied the charge and later evidence indicated others were responsible.[77]

In March, they were allowed to follow the trail and search for stolen horses. They traced them to a Yankton camp and were allowed by the agent there to take as many horses as they had had

U.S. Army Lt. Gen. Philip H. Sheridan commanded the Division of the Missouri. Under his command were the departments of Dakota, Missouri, Platte, and Texas. Courtesy of The Kansas State Historical Society, Topeka.

stolen from them. But not long after, the horses were again stolen by Sioux, unidentified this time.[78]

Now the Pawnees sought to establish peace again as their situation became more and more intolerable. In July 1873, while on their way to their Republican Valley hunting grounds, seven Pawnee chiefs and Baptiste Bayhylle, turned and made their way to Fort McPherson. They carried a letter from Burgess, who had decided to let the Pawnees ask the officers of the Third Regiment of Cavalry for help in contacting the Sioux in hopes that a peace council might be arranged. The post commander sought instructions from higher authority. A telegram to Washington to William D. Whipple, assistant adjutant general, from Lt. Gen. Philip Sheridan at headquarters, Military Division of the Missouri, stated that the Pawnees told the fort's officers that the Sioux were too strong for them; they could not cultivate their ground for fear of attack upon their women, and they wanted peace. Gen. Edward O. C. Ord recommended prompt action by the Indian Office through its personnel. At this time, the War Department was reluctant to become involved in intertribal arrangements, particularly with the Sioux, who were actively aggressive against United States troops at this time. So they turned the responsibility back to the civilian Indian Office.[79] It is possible that Burgess knew all this but consented to the chief's request to go to Fort McPherson to turn aside their constant demands that something be done. Nothing was accomplished except more correspondence between government bodies.

The main body of the tribe continued on their way to the hunting grounds. With them was John Williamson, a young man of twenty-three years, who worked as an agency farmer, and who had been assigned the duties of travel agent for the hunt. He was accompanied by another young man, Lester B. Platt, a relative of another agency employee. Williamson's job was to see that the tribe followed a prescribed route and to prevent any depredations. Settlers were eager to make claims often for depredations not committed or to blame the wrong parties, and Williamson was a safeguard against such claims.

The summer before had been a peaceful summer when Terrecowah camped peacefully near a Siouan group. Now Agent Burgess and others believed that this summer would follow a similar pattern. As the Pawnees traveled, small groups of Sioux were seen from time to time watching them from a distance, but the Pawnee chiefs were not alarmed and said that if it were necessary, the could drive them off.[80] The officers at Fort McPherson also assured the Pawnee chiefs, requesting help in arranging a council, that they were in no danger while hunting, and if the Sioux did trouble them to come and report it.

The predictions and hopes for a peaceful hunt was wrong. On August 5, 1873, after the Pawnees had located a buffalo herd and had shot and skinned some of the kill, a cry of alarm was heard, and the Sioux fell upon the hunters. Pawnee tribal accounts vary from the official version and tell the story in this way,

> They were attacked in the morning and were overrun by three waves of Sioux. Immediately they left the line of march and ran down into the canyon to try to reach the creek and the trees and brush growing along it which would give advantage against the

attacker. The old Pawnee claimed that the Sioux were never known to pursue any Pawnee warrior into undergrowth near a creek or stream for fear of ambush and death. When the group ran down into the ravine or canyon they probably did not all move into it at the same place, but were in scattered groups extending along their line of march along the edge of the canyon. They went over into it as soon as the alarm was sounded, moving quickly, abandoning much equipment, catching ponies if they could, and riding as fast as possible down the ravine toward the main canyon where there were trees and undergrowth near the area where they had camped the previous night. They knew this canyon area well from generations of experience in hunting there, and there is no doubt in the author's mind [Garland J. Blaine] that they knew where the undergrowth and trees were located between them and the Republican River. *

The author's grandmother, Effie Blaine, said that during this run everyone became disorganized. A short time later the warriors and chiefs grouped and made a stand. The women and children—and older people who were able to do so—found shelter in trees near a creek. Robert Taylor, who said he was a young man at the battle, recalled that people started to seek shelter and protection and ran into the nearest ravine. The warriors then told them to run until they could find the nearest timber where they might find shelter. He noted that it was long ago established never to pursue Pawnee when they were in brush or trees for they were invincible in that kind of cover. Taylor said that suddenly a riderless horse came running in his direction. He ran toward it, but saw that he would not meet it at the right spot to get the reins. Hence, he ran to a small rise and made a desperate leap that put his foot directly into the stirrup. He threw his other leg over the horse's back and sat upright all in one swift movement. He said having a horse saved his life. Later in his life he talked to Sioux who had been at the battle and who told the following story to him: There was a young Pawnee warrior who had found a cave-like depression in the steep canyon wall. From this vantage point he killed many

---

* Much has been written over the years about this battle between the Pawnees and Sioux. Examination of the article, "Pa-re-su, A-ri-ra-ke: The Hunters that Were Massacred" by Garland James and Martha R. Blaine in its entirety will give various military and agency views of the events, which do not always coincide with Pawnee recollections. The senior author of this article, Garland J. Blaine, gave tribal accounts he had heard as a boy and young man by survivors of the tragedy. These, too, have a bias.

Sioux. One of the Sioux chiefs had lost a son recently and his men said to him, "Come here and look at this Pawnee. He looks like your son." The chief said that it was true and made signs that if the boy came out, he would not be harmed. He looked so much like his son that he offered to save him and adopt him as his own. He said, "I am still crying. I have lost my son. You are brave. If you come out you can be my son."

The Pawnee signed back, "No, you Sioux have killed all my people now and in times past. There is no reason for me to live. I will stay here." The Sioux tried to dislodge him because he had ignored the chief's request, but the chief finally said, "Let him go, we will leave him here." But whenever they tried to leave, he would run out and shoot at them with the arrows he had picked up that they had shot at him. Finally, after the chief went away, the Pawnee wounded in his bow arm and no longer able to shoot, was captured. Sioux warriors were dismembering him when the chief came back and tried to stop them, but it was too late. Robert Taylor said he was told that the chief ordered that the legs be returned to the leggings, the rest of his body clothing, and the corpse buried on the top of the hill nearby.

The Pawnee warrior's name was *Sireritawi*, or He Is Known By Them, a Pitahawirata band member. Once some Pawnee went to Trenton and were unable to find the grave from the Sioux description of the place. The location has been forgotten now.

Another person who survived the battle and told about it in later years was Old Lady Washington, *Tsupiriktaka*, White Star. She was said to have been born in 1844 and would have been about twenty-nine years old at the time of the battle. She told my grandmother and me that she was shot in the back and so was her baby: "I couldn't turn it loose, even though I knew it was dead." She claimed the fight started at noon and went on into the afternoon; some of the old men, women and children got away, and made the younger men go, too. But all the warriors and chiefs had made declarations that they were "through living" when they saw how many Sioux there were. Many men had lost wives, sisters, and daughters previously to the Sioux and were now determined to fight to the death. White Star heard them shout, "*Tirawahut*, this is where I shall remain. I do not wish to see the sun come up." They made a covenant that this was their last day. White Star continued, "The Sioux would make a charge and ride by. When the dust cleared our men would still be standing there. Then there would be another charge and the men would roll and jump and fall, zig-zagging, shooting at the same time. When the dust cleared our warriors would still be standing there. Some made it through the day but many were killed, but not a man was taken captive.

John Haymond of the Kitkahahki Band, who was about ten to eleven years old at the time of the battle, said he was so young at the time of the battle that he didn't realize what it was all about, and was just sitting on the packed meat they were going to take home, and was looking around at what was going on and eating some of the fat and dry meat they had prepared, with his coat lying on a pack of meat back of him, and his horse tied nearby. Suddenly to his right he was aroused by a sound and saw a bunch of Sioux headed his way. He grabbed his coat with the meat in his mouth and mounted his horse to escape.

One of several Pawnee Scouts who survived was *Kuruksrawari*, Traveling Bear, who, according to Luther North, had distinguished himself in past battles. He was left for dead at the canyon, and when a Sioux stooped over to scalp him, Traveling Bear threw his arm around his neck, took a knife away from him and killed him. Though seriously wounded, he later made his way to Plum Creek Station, 150 miles away, and eventually returned to Genoa, where he died a few months later.

One of the curious differences between the account of John Williamson and the Pawnees at the battle is the fate of Sky Chief, *Tirawahut Resaru*, the leader of the expedition. Williamson said that, "Sky Chief, the leader in command of the Pawnees, was shot while skinning a buffalo and also scalped." However, there are various accounts by Pawnees that he lived for some time and that he effectively rallied and led the Pawnee warriors against the Sioux. Sky Chief, called "uncle" by the author's grandmother, came to their earth lodge and visited her mother, his relative, at Genoa (that is the Indian village) where Effie Blaine, grandmother of the author, was born. She mentioned his bravery to the author many times, and his behavior during the battle was cited as an example of the sacrifice Pawnee chiefs made for their people. This is what she said:

When a handful of Pawnee warriors made their stand against the overwhelming number of Sioux, Tirawahut Resaru made a gesture to the Sioux to take notice. He made hand signs to them that his two daughters and his wife had been killed by Sioux while

Pawnee survivors and descendants visited Massacre Canyon near Trenton, Nebraska, in August 1925. Courtesy of Hastings Museum, Hastings, Nebraska.

they worked in their fields. He went on to say that he no longer cared to live—that where the sun stood this day he would fight to the death. He then took his three year old son who was with him on his horse and slew him with his knife, after saying that he would rather do that than to have him fall into the hands of the enemy.* He then rode behind his warriors shouting encouragement to them and saying *Ti-ra-sa-ka-ri-ki ke-tu-re-tsis a-ki-ta-ru rus-ku-ra-pa-ku ti-ta-ku. I-ri-wa-ru-tu-tsi-ra-ru. I—ri-he-wi-tu-ra-he ku-ra-hus ha-ra-ra-ku-a-ra. Ra-wa pi-te-sut-ki-pi-ta-ra-ku-u,* May I see here today, you protect the tribe. This is the end. It is supposed to be better old man not to become. Now, men, a man be![81]

In spite of their greatest individual efforts, the Pawnees were overwhelmed eventually by the superior numbers of Brulés and Oglalas, and Sky Chief and over one hundred others died in aptly named Massacre Canyon. The survivors made their way back to the reservation. Some wounded did not complete the journey, such as the woman who died at Indianola and was buried by sympathetic white people.†

This disaster moved the Indian Office to decisive action, and the Sioux bands involved were made to pay reparations for the loss of life, meat, hides, equipment, and horses stolen during the battle. The sum was taken from their annuity.

The early winter months of 1874 saw no let up in Sioux raids to steal horse from the Pawnees. Between one hundred to two hundred were stolen in two reported raids, one in January and one in February.[82] In the February raid, the Pawnees followed, killed seven Sioux, and recaptured their horses.

---

* In the 1920s, some Sioux occasionally visited the Pawnees. They and old Pawnee men would talk about the old times in Nebraska. They would ask about Sky Chief, wanting to know why he had killed the little boy. It was explained that "we called the Sioux, Cut Throats, and it was known that when any one made a good stand against them and they killed him, they cut off his head, and Sky Chief did not want that to happen to his son."—G. J. Blaine.

† As a Bicentennial project in 1976, this Nebraska town, which had cared for the grave for over a hundred years, moved the remains to the town park where a small fence and marker were erected. The Pawnee head chief, invited to speak at a commemoration in the park, thanked the people for this act of humanity and kindness.

In 1866, a Society of Friends' statement regarding Indian relations read: ". . . for government and its officers to try the effect of just and pacific measure; to substitute for the sword the benign and winning persuasion which flows from the spirit of the Gospel, and teaches us to do to others as we would that they should do to us."[83] Now, after the 1873 massacre, the realities of Indian life and values became clear, and Burgess, particularly, was able to see that the noble goals of Quaker beliefs were not yet to bear fruit on the western frontier. He allowed the Pawnees to pursue the Sioux, as described above, and began to seek peace on the Indian level. In February, he allowed Baptiste Bayhylle, an interpreter, to go to Oglala country and seek out some of the chiefs. No response for peace was made, instead, he reported in the council that "indications of war were given."[84]

In May, the Yanktons, through Agent J. H. Gassman, invited a group of forty to fifty Pawnees to visit them at their agency. It was located north of the Missouri River, between Fort Randall and the town of Tyndall, some one hundred miles north of the Pawnee villages and agency near Genoa. The purpose of the visit was to renew friendship. They were not to stay over two weeks, the Pawnee agent stated, because a longer stay would keep them away from their farming efforts. In his opinion the "better classes" in both tribes were in favor of making peace and so this visit should be allowed and encouraged.[85] The Yanktons had consistently been less aggressive against the Pawnees than some other bands. In 1862, they had remained neutral in a general Sioux uprising in Minnesota and had warned whites of coming attacks.[86]

Although unsuccessful in February in his overtures to the Oglalas, Bayhylle was given permission to try again in July. He was to visit Plum Creek Station, where it was hoped that, through one of the Sioux traders he knew, an interview might be arranged with Oglala chiefs. Seeking approval for this venture from Superintendent Barclay White, Agent Burgess wrote, "It is not the right method probably to arrange peace matters between that tribe and the Pawnees, but a friendly interview might be a preliminary step in the right direction if anything further can be done." Speaking of recent events, he disclosed that the Yanktons, Poncas, and Otoes had made friendly visits to the Pawnees, but the tribe was much chagrined because they had no horses to spare to give as gifts as was proper and traditional.[87] It is possible that at least the Ponca and Otoe tribes understood this because they too were victims of Sioux horse thievery.

Superintendent White approved of the visit, and Bayhylle was issued a pass dated July 22, 1874. It was in the form of a letter "To Military officers or others whom it may Concern." With him rode Spotted Horse, a soldier of influence in the Skidi Band, which was also the band of the mixed blood, Bayhylle.* The two men were not to expose themselves to danger in their mission, which would seem to have been considerable considering that they went by themselves into comparatively hostile country.[88]

During this month of July, rumors and reported sightings of Sioux near the agency and village area kept those Pawnee who had not gone on the summer hunt and the neighboring whites apprehensive.[89] Earlier in March, whites were attacked north of the reservation, and the Pawnees were quickly blamed. The agent denied their complicity. In the present instance, he said the Pawnees kept constant watch, "but have no mode of protection equal to necessity."[90] Is that to say that they did not have sufficient guns or ammunition to repel the well-armed Sioux? There was still resistance to arming the Pawnees adequately so they could defend themselves. On this point, the Quakers did not waver. In February, the chiefs had asked that sixty guns be obtained for each band so that they could defend themselves against the Sioux. The agent informed them it would not be possible because the government did not furnish guns to any Indians or allow the agents to do it. If they wanted them, they would have to buy them themselves. In saying this, he knew there were not many personal funds available for such an expenditure.[91]

As long as the Pawnees were in Nebraska, they were never able to bring any of the Sioux bands that were their enemies to a peace council resulting in the termination of warfare. Devious attacks, horse stealing, and killing continued. In 1875, when

---

* Spotted Horse, or Spotted Horse Chief, was a name also found in the Kitkahahki Band. Big Spotted Horse was a renowned warrior in the Pitahawirata Band. It is not always clear which band's warrior is referred to in some reports or accounts.

most of the Pawnees had departed for a new reservation in Indian Territory, those left in the villages, consisting of the old, ill, and school children, were attacked on August 22 and again on August 23. The first attack came while a company of U.S. infantry was stationed at the agency for the Pawnees' protection. Nevertheless, the hostile party escaped without discovery. The next day's attack was made by fourteen men, "dressed as Indians and thought to be Sioux."[92] According to the Pawnees, this was when the old man came out alone singing his death song and without hope tried to defend the others.

✝✝✝

6
The Way to Be "Civilized"

Alter and Conform

To do what they called civilizing us . . . was to destroy us. You know they thought that changing us, getting rid of our old ways and language and names would make us like whitemen. But why should we want to be like them, cheaters and greedy? Why should we change and abandon the ways that made us men and not the beggars we became?
—Overtakes the Enemy, Pawnee

One goal of acculturating the Indian was to produce a reflected but limited cultural image of the white man, ignoring the suitability, worth, integrity, balance, and values of an Indian culture as it was. In colonial and early United States history, this was seen as necessary. There was mistrust of others who differed radically in appearance and lifeways. To make the nearby stranger more like one's self was to make one's own position in relation to him more comfortable and safe. As the white man termed it, to "civilize" the Indian was in some measure to be able to predict his behavior and control him by insisting that he follow the norms of society. The civilization process became imperative with the rising resentment and hostility manifested by the Indian, who saw his lands lost to invaders playing a game with treaties. Getting the Native American into society's class structure was seen as practical, Christian, and an economic necessity. Once there, he should know his place and conform to the expectations associated with that role.

Even among the most traditional societies, no culture stays the same or resists change absolutely. Centuries ago, the Indians saw that the white man's ways were quite different, but some of the

143

objects he possessed were distinctly useful to have. These objects were often those that would make the performance of certain economic activities more predictably efficient and successful. Manufactured metal objects, such as knives, guns, and kettles, were an example. These could be obtained from the white man in exchange for furs and hides. Jacques Cartier in his first New World voyage in 1534 noted that the Micmac Indians of Canada were so eager to obtain French ironware that they traded all the furs they had, including their own clothing, and promised to return the next day with more furs to trade. Before 1600, guns and ammunition were introduced into trade. This motivated widely dispersed tribes to travel long distances to exchange their products with the French.[1]

The matter of "civilizing" the Indian of the distant frontiers and interior of America in those times was not a compelling concern. Native contact with white men was limited to intermittent encounters with those employed in the fur trade and by others interested in making tractable the "savage" heart by saving souls among a few tribes in the interior Great Lakes and river regions where posts and missions were established. When the English made their entry into the New World, the acquiring of Atlantic coastal land for settlement by a growing population of family-oriented farmers and townsfolk resulted in a different type of relationship with the Indians. Cultural conversion of their indigenous, "backdoor" neighbors became part of the colonial scheme in order to promote their own safety as well as economic and other purposes.

Treaty commissioners at first proffered only the hand of friendship, but later began to offer, in exchange for Indian land, items such as plows, cattle, seeds, schoolhouses, agents, and other things for containing and civilizing the Indian. By the end of the treaty period after the middle of the nineteenth century, an Indian agency with its employees reflected many facets of social, religious, and economic life, as the so-called civilized world perceived it. There were teachers, farmers, doctors, blacksmiths, school matrons, traders, millers, preachers, administrators, clerks, and others, all brought together in the small world of the agency and reservation to play a part in the "civilization" of their tribal charges as dictated by treaty and government policy.

In the nineteenth century, some humanitarians believed that to "civilize" the Native American was to save him from extinction. By now, Indian populations were radically decreasing due to European diseases, warfare, hunger, and other factors. To prevent this, it was rationalized, the people must be placed under government protection, influence, and control. As more and more land was taken from the Indians by treaty, they were forced to live on smaller tracts of land, called *reservations,* where they were deprived of freedom to follow traditional endeavors. Here too, malaise, malnutrition, whiskey, and disease continued their ravages.

Humanitarian groups, such as the Society of Friends, or Quakers, viewed with sympathy the suffering and losses of the Indians, whom they had called brothers since the time of their leader William Penn. Although his primary motivation was not to save the Indian from extinction, Pres. Ulysses S. Grant, in the late 1860s, asked the Friends and other religious bodies to take charge of certain Indian agencies and reservations to implement his policies. It was hoped to gain better Indian affairs' administration by honest and efficient management. For the Friends, this was to be done in their way, through honorable dealings, efficiency, and respect.

Their philosophy and goals for the Indians, including the Pawnees, under their supervision in the Northern Superintendency, were given in an 1869 report. It was written after Benjamin Hallowell of the Baltimore Yearly Meeting, Franklin Haines of the New York Yearly Meeting, and John H. Dudley and Joseph Powell of the Philadelphia Yearly Meeting all made a long journey of inspection to the agencies and tribes under Quaker jurisdiction west of the Missouri River. Overall their report showed great respect and admiration for the Indian. They said it should be remembered that the ancestors of the Europeans now in America were once members of tribal societies themselves. Their forefathers had been able to advance up the ladder of civilization, and the Indian who possessed many fine traits of character would also become "civilized," if given the proper treatment and instruction. It was emphasized that many of the Indians' problems were not due to inability but to the injustice and negative attitudes that had been directed against them by white men.[2]

After seeing various Indian reservation living conditions, the report stated that several changes in Indian life were necessary to implement "civilization" programs. From their totally different point of view, the close-knit, extended family living in a single Pawnee earthlodge was seen as crowded, with lack of light, cleanliness, and sanitation facilities. These conditions, the Friends' observers believed, produced illness. Each family should have its own individual plot of land or allotment and homestead, so that the Indian man would "feel the dignity of manhood from possessing personal right" and—as if this were totally alien to the Pawnee—have "something to care for and something to love" by husbanding his land and raising food for the support of his family.[3] Then, in their businesslike manner, they suggested that to pay for the agricultural changes needed, that is for teaching farming skills, as well as the purchase of farm implements and animals, it might be necessary for the Indian to sell more of his tribal land.

Education of the Indian children was considered most important, and it was thought that establishing tribal industrial training schools to teach skills found among their white brethren would civilize the young for life in a new society. Because of the nature of their own beliefs, the Quakers did not discuss the need to change Indian religious practices to the degree of some other faiths, which saw belief in Christ as the means of conversion to "civilization."

Many of the suggestions and "civilization" schemes suggested by the Quaker report of 1869 had been a part of Indian-federal relations for some time and were included in many treaties. Several Pawnee 1857 treaty articles illustrate this. Article 3 said, "In order to improve the conditions of the Pawnee and teach him the arts of civilized life" the United States agreed to establish two manual labor schools, and if necessary four would be built, one for each band. In them, common school education and also mechanical and agricultural arts would be taught. In Article 4, the United States agreed to furnish shops and tools for a blacksmith, gunsmith, and tinsmith. Iron and steel would also be supplied. The Pawnee tribe agreed to furnish two young men to work as strikers (a blacksmith's helper who wielded the sledge) and apprentices in these shops. Also farm implements and stock worth $1,200 a year for ten years were to be supplied as well as a barn. A farmer was to be hired for an indeterminate time. In addition, a steam mill was to be built, suitable for grinding grain and sawing lumber. A miller and an engineer would be furnished for ten years. The mill was included with the thought that agency buildings and eventually Indian houses would be constructed from lumber produced there. In expectation of a speedy civilization effort, the last part of this article stated that whenever the President should become satisfied that the Pawnees "have sufficiently advanced in the acquirement of a practical knowledge of the arts and pursuits to which this article relates, then, and in that case, he may turn over the property to the tribe and dispense with the service of any or all the employees herein named."[4]

In Article 6, six laborers were to be furnished to teach the Pawnees how to take care of farm stock and to use the farm implements mentioned above. For every laborer hired by the government, the Pawnees were to supply three men to work with and learn from them.[5]

In all of the 1857 treaty articles, it was assumed that civilization would be accomplished by the above stipulations and that the Pawnees who would serve as apprentices would learn new crafts and in turn become acculturating agents for all their people. It was hoped that others in the tribe would see the advantages in the new ways of life their kinsmen were learning and by which they were profiting and bettering themselves. When the Quakers came twelve years later, there was little evidence that the Pawnees had accepted to any great extent the civilization goals of a government that assumed that Indian culture was inferior and that it was necessary to change it for the good of everyone.

Condition of the Pawnee in the Early Years of the Quaker
"Civilization" Effort

But, poor things, hungry and destitute as they are, we did sincerely wish they could be employed in a way which would produce a supply to their needs.

—From a Quaker report, 1869

The Pawnee condition had been deteriorating for many years for several reasons. One was after their contact with white men, European-introduced diseases such as smallpox drastically reduced tribal populations during the eighteenth and nineteenth centuries. In 1845, the estimated Pawnee population was 12,500. By 1872, the census indicated that there were only 509 men, 876 women, and 1,062 children for a total of 2,447 people.[6] This tremendous loss of population in less than thirty years would seem to affect the psyche of any group and its interactions and responses.[*]

Besides disease and hunger, often starvation faced the people. Food sources derived mainly from crop growing and hunting were severely curtailed. Drought and hoards of grasshoppers caused frequent crop loss in the 1870s. One Pawnee recalled that in Nebraska the insects were so thick that they blocked out the sun, and it got dark during daytime. They ate everything, "our fields and even the leaves on the trees. We had nothing to eat then."[7] Fear of going to fields where the enemy lurked and killed women workers became another contributor to decreased food production.

Intermittent government refusal to allow tribal hunts added greatly to deepening tribal impoverishment. There were several reasons for this stance, as previously detailed. One pertinent here, was the explanation that, if hunting was discouraged or prevented, then the tribe must turn to "civilized" farming to support itself. The agent in 1867 had said, "Until the buffalo disappears little hope can be entertained of the Pawnee making much progress in the arts of civilization."[8] All agents agreed that hunting jaunts were a detriment to Indian pursuit of full time farming and the education of the children by agency teachers. They did not know or did not acknowledge the adequacy and accomplishment of traditional Pawnee agriculture that produced surpluses used in trade with other tribes in previous times.

During one period of destitution in 1873, the superintendent and Indian commissioner discussed the possibility of giving weekly

[*] Richard White in *Roots of Dependency* (pages 199–211) gives a fine historical background of the social and ecological factors that brought about the conditions of poverty and other problems that faced the Pawnees on the Nebraska reservation.

rations to the tribe to get them to stop wanting to hunt.[9] Although they had previously refused beef rations, now in January, when they had been refused permission to hunt again, Pitaresaru in council pleaded. He said, "We would like you to give us some beef to eat." Good Chief added, "We want you to give us something to eat. We have nothing. We want beef and flour."

To this Agent Jacob Troth replied, "I can give each band a beef. We can hardly get enough flour for ourselves." Pitaresaru retorted, "There is plenty of flour in Columbus [a nearby town]." Troth exclaimed, "No, there is not. I'll get two sacks of flour for each band."[10] This was a paltry amount that was insufficient for the number of people to be fed and their adequate nutrition.*

Then the chiefs asked that money recovered from whites for theft of reservation timber be used now for purchasing food. They were told that such monies had to be deposited in the U.S. Treasury but that the agent would present their case to the superintendent. The chiefs argued that such money was due them directly by treaty rights.[11] Nevertheless, these funds were not forthcoming. Examination of Pawnee treaties does not indicate that such a provision existed. But again, what was said and agreed to by the Pawnees and the government, and what appeared in the final written treaty, appear to have been two different things.

It should be remembered at this point that funds due the Pawnees for thousands of acres of land ceded by them to the United States had not been paid to them. Only the small amount of annuity funds promised in treaty were available.

During these times of extreme duress in the early 1870s, the agent requested, and the chiefs felt pressured to consent to, large portions of their annuity being spent on repairing the agency mill or dam. Some of the annuity also was used in purchasing agricultural implements such as mowing machines for the agency farm, from which the tribe derived minimal benefit. These requests by the agent were made because the ten-year period in which the government had agreed to supply and pay for such items had expired. Now annuity funds were desperately needed to buy food

---

* Garland Blaine said that flour mixed with water and cooked as gravy or made into "fry bread" was all the food that his people had many times in Nebraska and Oklahoma as late as the 1920s, when he was a child.

and other essentials. The agents, concerned mainly with the government's goals of civilization, was able to convince the chiefs that they would be better off if they would agree to his proposals rather than press for fulfilling their immediate needs. At least, records were written to indicate that they agreed.

In March 1873, the agent visited the villages and reported the people were in quite destitute circumstances. Even the better-off members had little food, usually a few beans and a little dried corn. "They all beg for help," he said.[12]

After this visit, the agent called the chiefs together on March 20 and proposed to aid them if they desired and really needed it. They replied that of course they needed food and that their condition was the same that it had been for many months. He replied that he thought food could be obtained, but they would have to sign a petition to Supt. Barclay White, which said, "We are now in a very destitute condition and many of our members have little or nothing to eat. We have no robes or money to buy with. We request that the sum of $3,000 be taken from what has been represented to us as an unexpended balance due to the Pawnees."[13] In sending the petition, the agent suggested to the superintendent that not much money needed to be spent on meat, that corn meal and potatoes would go farther.

During these "starving times" as the Pawnees recalled them, the people used ingenuity to try to survive. Garland Blaine's grandfather told him this story:

> When we lived in Nebraska in the mudlodges, the people used to place a little grain outside the entrance of the lodge. It was not put directly in front of the doorway, but a little around to the side in view of the black birds that followed the buffalo herds and stayed around the villages. We made a rawhide thong with knots tied in it at about eight inch intervals. It was about eight feet long. A man would take it and sit quietly in the entrance of the lodge. He waited until a few birds came and began to eat the grain. When they were busy he would quickly whip the thong out and around the corner of the entryway. He kept it low to the ground. With skill the birds would be hit and stunned or killed. They were picked up and taken immediately into the lodge and roasted whole over the fire. For my family, we would have a pile about ten inches high and about eighteen to twenty inches in di-

ameter for a meal. The feathers burned off. The children, of which I was one, were given the heads which we ate except for the bill. They were filling. *Te-ki-rus-pa-ku* is what we called this. It means "chewing the bones in the mouth."[14]

The condition of the Pawnees beginning at and under Quaker administration of their affairs was one of physical and emotional stress. An increasing rate of decline in their population can be attributed mainly to hunger, disease, and enemy attacks on the village, in the field and on the hunt. The civilization programs promoted during their last years in Nebraska, 1870–75, were often accepted on empty stomachs in hopes that accommodation might benefit and ease an often desperate condition.

The Pawnee Chiefs' Role in the Acculturation Process

It has been mentioned that the Pawnee chiefs had the principal role in accepting or resisting the new concepts and items of "civilization" brought to their people. Some description of their traditional place in the society needs to be made here.

In the majority of tribal decisions, the chiefs traditionally had paramount power. There were two chiefs chosen from the chiefs' bloodline in each band. They represented their bands in all negotiations with other bands, tribes, or foreign nations. Consensual council decisions were made after each man in turn had the opportunity to voice his opinion. In the villages, they arbitrated and settled disputes brought to them and decided on punishment for infractions or crimes. Their decisions were conveyed and carried out by responsible and respected warriors, some of whom served as village law enforcers.

The chiefs concurred when the hunt priest decided the day for starting the tribal hunt. They chose the Lance or Warrior Society that had the responsibility of scouting and guarding the people on the hunt. The leading Lance Society's members were chiefs and male relatives. The chief had to give permission for war party formation and departure, and they selected the village heralds. They had seats in all sacred societies and their influence and control permeated all aspects of Pawnee life.

John B. Dunbar, whose missionary father and family lived

Pawnee children near an earthlodge in Nebraska. Photo by W. K. Jackson. Courtesy of National Anthropological Archives, Smithsonian Institution.

among the Pawnees in the late 1830s and 1840s, knew them when they were living in a more traditional way, and not yet under pervasive agency control and the strain of confined reservation life. Before this cultural catastrophe, the Chaui, Pitahawirata, Kitkahahki, and Skiri (Skidi) bands acted autonomously for the most part, living at some distance from one another in villages under their own chiefs. Band cooperation occurred when assembled band chiefs met to take part in councils with foreign nations' representatives, such as treaty commissioners from the United States. On some occasions two or more bands would hunt together, aid each other in defense of their villages, or be part of certain interband ceremonial events, such as the Hako, or the

Pipe Dance as it came to be called. At this time, one band would send representatives to visit another band's or tribe's village and participate in several days of complex ritual, feasting, and gift giving during the adoption of a band member by the visitors.[15] Otherwise, the bands lived and acted separately in pretreaty times and were identified as separate tribes by some early observers.

During historic times, the Pawnees had a head chief, who it appeared made decisions on his own in some matters regarding tribal actions. For example, in 1840, Dunbar reported that the Pawnees would not move to another location due to the absence of the head chief. "The other chiefs told us he was like our President, they could do nothing without him."[16] More often than not, there were occasions when a council of band chiefs aided him in the decision making process by individual deliberation, discussion, and group consensus. This council could be called by the head chief on his own initiative or at the suggestion of a chief or chiefs. If the matter to be brought under consideration was of such importance that secrecy was required, then it was held in such a place that only those men entitled to participate were allowed to be present. Dunbar continued, that Pawnee chiefs "used their influence steadfastly for promoting the welfare of their bands, often making great personal sacrifice to that end, and proving themselves in reality the fathers of their people."[17] Ideally they were expected to give presents to their people and to not expect any in return. They were also expected to provide food for those who were destitute. These traditional commitments, among others, became increasingly difficult to fulfill as time lived on the reservation lengthened and their power and options were continually curtailed by governmental regulations.

The Pawnee chiefs were the first and last line of resistance to the continued pressure and threat exerted by the government to control and change the life of their people. They may not have understood the pervasiveness of the effort at the beginning, because no society as a whole grasps the total meaning or future impact of technological or other changes coming from the "outside." That is, an acceptance of one type of change does not mean that only that aspect of life will be made different but that many contiguous and interrelated behaviors may change with each new cultural innovation accepted.

As leaders of their people, it is assumed that the Pawnee chiefs and other traditional leaders were either covertly or overtly opposed and resistant to the United States' authority, when it proposed ideas that countered their beliefs and rights as opinion and decision makers. The agent was charged with control of his Indian population, and the chiefs were expected to be subordinate in their relations with him. Father-child, teacher-student, warden-prisoner, variations of these roles began to be played out as years under the reservation system passed.

One U.S. Indian policy goal was to eliminate the opposition of the chiefs and other opinion makers to change. Old values and beliefs must be eradicated if the ways of "civilization" were to be instilled. Tribal leaders stood as guardians of those cultural beliefs that held the tribal society together.

After the installation of agents among Indian tribes, the government's policy leaned toward the "coercive disruption of tribal governments." Chiefs and other leaders were often ignored, downgraded, or deprived of power. Reservations would often resemble penal institutions in which Indians would be reward for "civilized" behaviour and punished in some manner for nonconformity.[18] In 1872, Com. of Indian Affairs F. A. Walker declared that no one would rejoice more than he would when the Indians "no longer dictate in any form or degree to the government . . . and . . . if they stand up against the progress of civilization and industry they must be relentlessly crushed."[19]

As part of the domination of Indian political life, the time came when some agents would choose tribal leaders, or at least approve or disapprove of those selected by the tribe. These men would sit before him in council agreeing to his proposals, making those directed decisions that often required their signatures or marks. Some agents pursued tribal political control assiduously, selecting only those men who would agree with them. Among the Ioway living on a reservation in southeast Nebraska and northeast Kansas at this period, one of the great Ioway chiefs, Notchininga, died. A council was called on October 23, 1862. Tohee, who was among others who had been appointed a chief by the agent, said to him, "Tell our Great Father our head chief is dead, and now the chiefs are young men, and we want to see if our people cannot become like white men." Agent J. A. Burbank in reporting the situation said he would designate a successor after he received instructions from the superintendent.[20] In 1848, White Cloud, the Ioway head chief, was removed from any government-recognized position of authority when he led a war party against the Pawnees. The warriors had successfully ambushed a traveling party killing one Pawnee. For this he was removed as chief. Prior to this he had consistently defied and argued against U.S. intervention in Ioway affairs. The war party seemed like a good pretext for removing him from power once and for all.[21]

Although it does not appear that any of the Pawnee chiefs were ever removed from their positions, Pitaresaru and other chiefs were threatened by Superintendent White in 1873. At this time over four hundred Pawnees had gone to Indian Territory without permission to visit the Wichitas, a tradition they had followed for many years.[22] White accused the chiefs of not having control over their people and said sarcastically that they were nothing but women. He added, if they could not manage their people according to government regulation, then "we will find men who can control their bands," and "I want Pitaresaru and every chief to know when the Government speaks it will be obeyed."[23] This definite effort to curtail the chiefs' decision making powers and their control of tribal actions could not have been stated much more forcefully than that.

There are a few known instances in which the Pawnee agent had a hand in the selection or naming of chiefs. Traditionally, this was done within the band power structure. However, in 1871, Good Chief of the Pitahawirata Band asked the agent to name a chief to replace one who had died.[24] Why the band was unable to do this itself is not clear, but the situation indicates the inroads made by the agent in gaining political control. By 1874, chiefs and leading warriors or soldiers were accustomed to receiving certificates from the agent validating their positions. Agent William Burgess requested new papers be sent for several men who had lost or misplaced theirs.[25] Exactly what meaning and significance such a document had for the Pawnee chiefs is not known.

Although on the surface, Quaker agents rarely seemed to have involved themselves in selection of chiefs, there was one important group of men who were selected, or at least approved of, by the agent. These were the "soldiers." The agent employed certain men from each band who acted for him in agency-directed affairs. In 1874, Good Buffalo, a Pitahawirata, was appointed to fill a vacancy.[26] He and others received small salaries as long as they "faithfully served" in their assigned duties.[27] These duties were not the traditional responsibilities of acting as village or hunt police but were an extension of the agent as enforcers of agency rules and promoters of "civilization" programs.

One of their principal duties was to see that children attended school. In the spring of 1873, the soldiers were told that if they saw any of the school's scholars in the village, they were to send or take them to the school immediately. The day schools were to be kept full. To fill the quota, five children were to be brought from each band—". . . one half of these to be good sized girls." The girls were to do laundry, housecleaning and other chores. The agent gave the soldiers four days to carry out this order.[28]

Other responsibilities were to keep livestock off the agency farm fields, to act as runners or messengers, and to report each morning to the council house to see what their assignments were for the day. A head soldier, selected by the agent, was in charge of seeing that work was performed. Agreement to do as the agent directed put them under his control, since their tenure and salary was dependent upon his approval of their behavior. Money had become important as a means of purchase of food and other necessities in these difficult times. For this reason, the soldiers' close ties to the agent and agency could cause a division of their loyalties among the agent, their chiefs, and the people, especially when an assignment was in conflict with tribal opinion.

A shift in the Pawnee traditional governing structure was illustrated by an increased sense of power by some agent-appointed soldiers. In a June 1871 council meeting, the chief Chaui soldier challenged the chief's authority saying, "I think we soldiers have as much to say as anybody. Our Head Soldier says one thing and Pitaresaru another. We will leave it with him [the Head Soldier]."[29] The chiefs would not have tolerated this situation in former times. When it did happen, with silent agent approval, it tended to lessen the band chiefs' authority because those soldiers ambitious to curry agent favor pressed their advantage. In his

1872 annual report, Agent Troth revealed the strain that had developed and the subjection that had occurred, saying, "The Pawnee have entirely abandoned the war path, are subject alike to the protection and restraints of civil law and the complete control of their agent, and their chiefs and soldiers vie with each other in supporting and aiding me in the administration of their affairs." [30]

The Chiefs' Resistance to Total Acceptance of Civilization Programs

In spite of the agent attempts to break the chief's power, the chiefs were not totally noncommital or accepting of all the new ideas introduced in the "civilization" program. They often spoke their minds and rejected proposals offered by the agent. Employees, including the agent, teachers, farmers, and physicians were closely watched, and over the years the Pawnee chiefs sometimes sharply criticized them in and outside of council.

In 1871, Pitaresaru complained about an agency farmer. Before this one came, he said, the previous one always had flour ready for the people when they returned from the hunt. "We could see that the other farmer did something for us. We can't see what this farmer does for us, or that he tries to do anything. I have been walking around the farmhouse and can't see anything he has done except a little handful of wheat. I can't ask you for flour, for I know you have no wheat raised. I would like a better farmer." Concurring, Sky Chief added, "That man tells the truth. I don't believe any chief will say the farmer does anything for them. I don't think he has sense. If he was any benefit to us we would not mind his using our mowing machines. * Some of the mules are dead and others nearly starved. If he had any sense he would take pains to show us something, but he doesn't know himself." [31]

At other times, the chiefs complained about the agency physician and the trader, seeking to have them removed. In this manner, the chiefs tried to exert authority and demand the services

---

* Sky Chief called the mowing machines "ours" because Pawnee funds paid for them. Individual Pawnees did not use them and they stayed on the agency farm.

that they believed should be rendered them as the government's obligation through treaty. Many agency employees were not successful because they were there for purposes other than to help educate the Indian or set examples of "civilized" behavior. Much has been said about the feathering of agency employees' nests at the expense of the Indian, and probably no agency, even during the Quaker years, escaped completely the lazy, incompetent, and greedy individual. For some, it was an easy way to make a living, and many did not leave government service as poor as when they entered.

The Chiefs Face Allotment and Houses and Other Contrivances of Civilization

I want you to build houses and the right way is to get your agent to draw up a paper for you to sign it and send it to me.
                                    —Supt. Barclay White, June 11, 1872

The Pawnee chiefs recognized the benefits to be gained by accepting some aspects of civilization. Originally, trade items like guns, kettles, and cloth in the forms of wool strouding, calico, and later canvas for tipis were adopted. Now more complex items, such as houses, were introduced. This interest in non-Indian dwelling types did not originate with the Pawnees but was the result of government planning. Getting the Pawnees and other tribes onto individual farms was one goal of the Northern Superintendency Quaker administration. On August 20, 1870, shortly after Quaker entrance into Indian affairs, Supt. Samuel Janney called together agents under his direction, including Pawnee Agent Troth. According to an Omaha newspaper, the purpose was to discuss the "civilization and moral improvement" of the Indian and how such improvements could be funded. "The policy of the United States government is to secure them permanent individual houses on allotments in severalty in order to promote civilization."[32] Behind the aim of placing each Indian and his family in a dwelling on a land allotment was the desire to break down the tribal solidarity found in close-knit village life. As soon as families were separated on farms, then, it was believed, each would learn to be independent of other tribal members and become a self-sufficient farm family in the pioneer American mold.

After the 1871 winter hunt, when the tribe was once again home in its villages, the agent brought this matter to the attention of the chiefs. He opened the April 3 council meeting by saying the chiefs had asked him to divide their lands and have houses built on them. He intended to visit the superintendent at Omaha and wanted to know their latest thoughts on the matter. Pitaresaru spoke first:

> I told you to build houses for me. I don't know now whether or not to build here. I don't want to build here because we have no wood. We have plenty of land. We are not poor in that way. . . . I am willing to settle down and have ground cultivated. Tell the Supt. my band have not enough wagons to move us up. Maybe the Sioux will not trouble us anymore.[33]

Pitaresaru's remark about the Sioux reflected the fear that dispersal of the people into areas distant from one another would drastically reduce their ability to defend themselves. Since the Quakers discouraged the acquisition of guns for protection or any purpose, it seems strange that such a course of dispersal could be urged in the face of ongoing hostility of the Sioux. The agent was well aware of the perilous situation, but the establishment of farmsteads was policy and was pursued, regardless of its impracticality and dangerousness at this point.

In order to pay for surveying the land to make individual farms, the chiefs were urged to sell some of their land or take money from their annuity. The agent knew how dear the annuity money was to the tribe and that the chiefs would have to choose to sell land rather than decrease the annuity any further. Money was needed to purchase necessities and to pay their debts to the traders. Terrecowah declared that they would sell some of their land but that the government did not always pay for it what it was worth. They wanted a fair price. Troth's rejoinder was that it would sell for what it would bring and who would pay the most for it, which was not exactly the case.[34]

Sky Chief said they were willing to sell the land in the direction of the railroad, but not toward the river. They would keep that. Eagle Chief, a Skidi, added that he wanted the most money that could be obtained for the land and wanted the farmstead land ploughed so it would be ready for planting. He had been interested in the new ideas and implements for farming for some time.* In conclusion, Pitaresaru told Troth to tell the superintendent that he would select a place for his band, but he would not consider moving if there was an insufficient wood supply.[35]

Troth transmitted the thoughts of the Pawnee chiefs to Superintendent Janney, who then informed Indian Com. Ely Parker that they had stated their wish that their lands

> along the north bank of the Loup Fork and in the eastern part of their reservation be divided among them and land broken and houses built for them. However, they did not want allotments in severalty like those laid off for the Omahas, Winnebagoes and Santees, but merely a division of land among themselves, giving to each person or head of family a farm subject to their regulations as promised in Article 5 [actually Article 6] of their treaty, September 24, 1857.

Janney continued that if the commissioner consented, then he would give Troth permission to divide the land into individual plots and assist the tribal members in fencing and breaking the land and building houses. As if to lend encouragement to the proposition, he said the tribe had shown greater interest in industrial pursuits than ever before.[36]

At the June 1, 1871, meeting, the chiefs wanted permission to go on the hunt. Superintendent Janney, who was in attendance, again told them to look forward to the time when there would be no buffalo and that they should think of other ways to live. He assured them that Spotted Tail had said that his people would not disturb them and they should not fear them. Lone Chief, Skidi, replied that he was not afraid of the Sioux. As if responding to the superintendent's suggestion that other ways of living should be considered, he said that he wanted the land divided so that "we can take care of our wood." Agreeing to move away from their present location into other areas may not have been so

---

* The Skidis, even now, will jokingly say they were more advanced in those days than the South Bands. A Skidi cousin speaking to Garland Blaine said, "Oh, you Rats [Pitahawirata] you were *just* backward."

much to fulfill the government's plans for them to disperse to individual farms as it was a measure to protect their scarce timber sources by moving closer to them to prevent their being stolen by the whites.[37]

Pitaresaru said his Chaui Band wanted to be near the first timber, at a location near the Pitahawirata Band. Eagle Chief the Skidi said he was glad to hear the land had been surveyed. He and his men were not afraid of the Sioux (if he should resettle) and he and his men would run them off and steal their horses. More thoughtfully, Terrecowah, the old Pitahawirata chief said, "Sometimes we do things we would afterwards do differently, but I am satisfied now as they are decided." This perhaps indicated a certain misgiving about the land division and relocation of the tribe.[38]

Except for the Skidis, who were more accepting of change, in each of the foregoing statements made by the other band chiefs, there is a positive, but not heartfelt, response to moving onto individual farms. But requests most deeply concerning the tribe are made in the same breath, so to speak. The hunt, the Sioux, timber theft, and annuity distribution were of greater importance. But they felt they must make token acceptance of the new ideas in hopes that in turn the government would assent to their requests. But Pitaresaru's last statement on the subject reveals a hardening stance against some of the proposals.

> I am the leader, I want my payments this year and the goods. The other chiefs can do as they please. I suppose they have settled it that way. Then I will make up my mind. I don't want to divide the farms for we want to be together. When we had a talk [before] I know I told you to build houses for me. Then I wanted to go further up again. Now I want it done as I say.[39]

Here the principal spokesman for the tribe, realizing the danger in the allotment idea, fires a parting shot saying that he does not want to divide the tribe and he wants the government to do as he says. Sky Chief added that he had selected a village site for his band where they could be together. "I don't think that it is necessary to survey our lands. We can pick them out. . . ." Terrecowah reinforced the others by saying that they themselves could divide their land into four parts, not individual allotments, and he wanted their annuity goods soon to take on the summer hunt.[40]

It becomes apparent here that although the agent and superintendent were thinking individual allotments, the chiefs had reconsidered and now preferred to settle in new village sites on undivided lands. This was not a new practice and had been done over the centuries when conditions warranted it.

The July council minutes make no reference to houses or resettlement. The reason for this may well have been that on June 7, the Sioux came and attacked again, despite Janney's prediction.[41] During the balance of July and August, the people were on the hunt.

The September 7 council discussed other subjects, but the records contain no mention of the matter. But on September 25, the subject is brought up. Agent Troth announced that last spring the chiefs had agreed to give their entire cash annuity to break land and build houses, but that then the Sioux had come down, and thereafter, at another council, the Pawnee chiefs would not agree to it. However, the survey had been contracted for and completed, and the land was measured off "for your use as farms." He wanted them to agree to appropriate enough money to finish paying for the survey and to complete work on the mill. The total would be about $3,000.

The chiefs replied to this, always adding a sentence or two referring to their real concerns. Pitaresaru said, "We want you to spend $3,000 for these purposes. We see the mill is not yet finished and you need the money to go on the work. We like you to let us know when you have not enough money. * We want you to have money to pay for the surveying. We want you to hurry up the superintendent for we want our guns to defend ourselves."[42]

Baptiste Bayhylle, the mixed-blood interpreter, who seemingly accepted the ideas of the agent and government for changes, added, "I am not giving up my idea of building houses, but not this year. Some other year we will try to appropriate the money

---

* It must be kept in mind that all the quotations of the Pawnees were written down by the agent or assistant and that there is definite question that the *words* were always accurately given, especially if the agent needed agreement.

to build. I am sorry we did not succeed this year. If we do not do this, there is no use in trying to be civilized."[43] The agent must have been pleased with these words, but considering the interpreter's job depended on following the current policy line and not disputing the agent, his words are understandable.

In his 1871 annual report, Agent Troth summed up the year's efforts at "civilizing" the Pawnees with less than accurate statements. He said that most of the tribe seemed to be impressed with the necessity of providing their food by other means than by going on the hunt. "Other means" meant farming, but he neglected to say that for many years a large portion of their sustenance came from traditionally successful crop raising methods.

Troth continued, less than accurately, that they were eager to live on small farms in houses. For this, the Pawnees had requested the survey and division of six hundred ten-acre plots. However, at this time, the tribe did not consider it safe to move to them because of the Sioux danger. He gave the number of recent Pawnee deaths from Sioux attacks, adding with a singular lack of compassion, "We have the satisfaction of believing they were prepared for the sad change."[44]

After this year, and with the continued attacks by the well-armed Sioux, the Pawnees were adamant in not wanting to leave the safety of village life, which provided the possibility of instant response by numerous warriors when attack came. The Quaker agents seemed to have given up at last on the foolhardy plan to scatter all the Pawnees across the land on snug little ten-acre farms. In 1872, it was claimed that eighty Pawnees were living in houses.[45] However, this account did not say how many houses or how many Pawnees per house.

Civilization Through Educating the Young

One important goal of the civilization program was to educate the Indian and to remove from him the cloak of ignorance as defined by the white man. The value of schooling was apparent to the Pawnee chiefs, and if accurate, council remarks of the 1870s reflect this. In a March 1871 meeting, Pitaresaru said, "Yes, we are glad our children are learning to read and write, and when the trader [Samuel B. Walton] doesn't do right, we will get them to write to Washington to our Great Father."[46] In another meeting, Eagle Chief observed that the whites knew that the Pawnees could not read or write, so they made claims against the tribe hoping to gain from their ignorance.[47]

Pawnee interest in the white man's educational system was of varying intensity. Samuel Allis, Skidi Band teacher, told about his first log school that he built in 1845. The missionary said that Skidi chiefs would send their heralds into the villages to call the children. Then Allis would see two or three warriors, "leading a band of some 150 children to his schoolhouse." Not more than fifty could crowd into the room at one time, so he would teach them for a time, then send them out and another group would file in to be taught. But, he added, if not harangued to send their children, the Pawnees would never send more than thirty or forty to the school. He blamed the children's absences on their attendance at hunts and other tribal activities. He added that those who did attend regularly forgot much of what they had learned in those intervals away from school.[48]

Elvira Platt was on the scene when the Quaker administration at the Pawnee Agency began in 1869. As early as 1844, she and her husband, Lester, were hired to teach the South Bands' children. She claimed she replaced Allis, who had only two Skidi students at that time.[49]

Some time later, agency dissension caused the pair to leave government employ. In 1862, records show she was hired again to teach. At this time, in spite of treaty stipulations, the government had built no school for the Pawnees. She held classes in inadequate quarters, and the sixteen mostly mixed-blood children attending were boarded in a dilapitated old cabin.[50]

Her philosophy of education was that no success could be achieved unless the children were completely separated from their families in the villages. In order to do this, she discouraged and prohibited parental visits. She also asked for a fence high enough to keep the children in the school area and their families out. She believed in keeping the children at school during the entire year in order to keep them away from what she called the debilitating influence of their traditions.[51] She also tried to drastically mask the Indian appearance of the students by cutting the boys' hair short and putting everyone into clothes donated by the

Pawnee Indian reservation school in Nebraska. Agent Jacob Troth had it built starting in 1872, to fulfill U.S. government treaty obligations. Photo by John Carbutt. Courtesy of Pamela Oestriecher Collection.

Society of Friends or made at the school. One child who went to school for the first time was handed some clothing to wear. He put it on and appeared in class. The teacher looked at him as he stood there and ridiculed him before the others because he had put the trousers on backwards. Deeply shamed, he turned and ran out of the room and back to the village, and as he said, he never set foot in the hated place again. In later years, he said that it had seemed most reasonable to him that the buttons should go down the back of the trousers.[52]

Platt was also determined that boys should become farmers, and each day they were sent into the school garden or to the agency farm fields to pull weeds, hoe, harvest, or do whatever was needed. This behavior was much against all Pawnee precepts, in which crop planting and field tending belonged to the woman, who was giver of life as was Mother Earth. It was a traumatic time for the children, who sometimes ran away, and for their parents. They reluctantly sent their children to school under the request or demand of the chiefs, who in treaty councils had agreed that certain numbers be sent.

Elvira Platt was determined to keep the government's part of the bargain, and there is little doubt that in her way she cared about the Pawnees. In certain ways, she was trusted by them as a reliable white person, even though her methods of educating their children were not always accepted. Sometime before his death, she said that Two Chiefs entrusted to her keeping one of his most sacred belongings, a red pipestone tablet. He told her no "common eye should fall upon it, and I could not know what wonderful things he saw when he looked down upon it in ceremonies." After his death, a Pawnee came to claim it and she returned it. * [53]

In remembering the school in Nebraska, Wichita Blaine talked about some who attended it and why they did so in the 1860s and 1870s. [54]

> The feeling of "we" the family was very strong. Each famiy cared for its members as well as it could no matter how hard the times were. But if it couldn't, it would pick out a young son and take him to a warrior and good hunter and request that he care for him. At a public gathering the father or uncle with the boy at his side addressed the warrior. I am too poor. He is a good boy. I have respect for you. I will give you this boy. Then the man accepted the child and raised him as his own. The boy always knew who his folks were and was told to go help them whenever he could as he grew older. This is how the South Bands did. We took care of our poor children and taught them as best we could. But I think that the Skidis did not do this, but sent poor children off to government schools. But even the South Bands had to send their orphans sometimes, if there was no one able to feed or care for them. But they held onto them as long as they could. During those days there were lots of orphans. I was one, but my uncles took care of me.
>
> One young boy who was living with his old grandmother used

* A Lashapitko (Resaru pitku) or (Two Chiefs) signed the 1848 treaty as a Tappage (Pitahawirata) Band chief.

to watch the school and its boys at a distance. He saw they had warm clothes and shoes in winter. They sang songs they had learned and carried hard tack and brown sugar in their pockets. One day he was very hungry and he went from the village to the school and had a meal there and he liked it. So much food. That night he thought about it and made up his mind to go and try it out. He went to class. The teacher got up and stood in front of the class. He said, I did not understand that white learning was a long process. You sat down. Then you stood up. You sang. After all day, I didn't learn anything. They did not take us outside to learn anything in the old way. At the end of the day he went back to the mudlodge and told his grandmother about his disappointment. She said, they have different ways. I'm old and need you here, but maybe you'd better go and learn their ways. No, Grandma, I'm going to stay with you. I never did go back.[55]

In this Pawnee comment, reasons for sending children to school included the inability of the family to care for their young children or orphans. They were sent to the school to obtain food and warm clothing and to learn "white ways" in order to understand or cope with them, as the old grandmother inferred. Many children in school then were the children that the tribe could not care for in the "starving times" in the 1870s. They were not necessarily eager to learn to write or read but wanted to have enough to eat.

Just how successful the government educational efforts were is undeterminable. There had been twenty-five years of attempting to teach the Pawnees when the Quakers came to the reservation in 1869. Then, it was claimed, few could write and very little English was spoken after ten years of treaty-funded programs. Many thousands of dollars had been spent on schooling, buildings, and agricultural items, but there was little to show for it, although agents had claimed a steady increase in "civilization" among the Pawnees.[56] Before the Quakers arrived, an agent's 1867 annual report claimed that the school was "flourishing." Average attendance was said to be around seventy, and all except four of the younger children could read. However, attempts to make the larger boys "industrious" were not successful.[57] Success was equated with working willingly in the fields. Young men, hoping to be warriors, saw this activity as onerous. It was woman's work as set forth by sacred sanctions and not part of their proper role behavior.

During the Quaker years after 1869, there was increased emphasis on the manual labor system that the 1857 treaty had described and the philosophy of Indian education of the day demanded. Larger boys spent three months in class and the rest of the time had to work on the agency farm. Younger boys spent ten months in class. At what·age they were deemed old enough to be apprenticed to the miller, engineer, tinsmith, and carpenter is not indicated. In 1872, the school boys were the main laborers of the 210-acre farm. The girls were largely employed as cooks, laundresses, and seamstresses and were used to clean the school facilities. It was said that this was to train them to be good wives and mothers in the "civilized" sense, but those who went through the system often felt it was demeaning and that they were treated as servants. None of the tasks they performed in the school setting were applicable to the reality of their future lives in the earth lodges of the village.

It was claimed that classroom subjects were taught with success. These included grammar, writing, geography, and arithmetic. It is not known how much learning was simply rote, since English was also being learned concurrently with other subjects. Platt learned to speak Pawnee, so it is assumed she must have used it and English in order to explain new concepts to the children. One of the favorite stories remembered by little boys in later years was about a warrior, who came from far across the eastern water to help the white men fight the evil Sioux-like English. His name was Lady Fat.[58]

Agent Troth eventually repaired and built better school quarters and obtained furnishings to replace those items that had long been inadequate or nonexistent. Elvira Platt, after continual requests, finally got the fence she had wanted. Each year, it was said that more children attended: fifty-one in 1869, seventy-seven in 1870, and eighty in 1872.*[59] In 1874, tribal unrest made

---

* There were 1,062 Pawnee children in the 1872 census. Of the eighty children in school, twenty of them were there because of treaty requirements. The lack of overall Pawnee interest and belief in formal school learning seems indicated.

it difficult to keep the students in school, and no figures were given for that year.

During the Quaker years, it is apparent that many students were there to fill the treaty quota, which the agent insisted on, threatening to withhold annuity funds for noncompliance. Mixed-blood children with a white parent often attended because there was not always total acceptance of them by the tribe. Because they were part white, it was thought that they particularly should learn "white ways." Since the mothers had often been abandoned by the father, they also needed assistance as needy children. One South Band source claimed, perhaps erroneously, that there were more mixed-blood children among the Skidis and that was why they were more interested in the white man's education.[60]

Civilization Through Manual Labor

Article 4 of the Pawnee 1857 treaty stated that the Pawnees were to be furnished two blacksmiths, one of whom would be a gun and tinsmith. Each man was to have two Pawnees working for him as apprentices. They were to be paid for their labor. A miller and an engineer were to be hired, and they, too, would have apprentices. In Article 7, the government agreed to hire six laborers for three years, and these men were to teach the Pawnees how to care for stock and to use farm implements. Specifically, for every laborer furnished by the United States, the tribe would furnish three men to work with them under the direction of the agent. By such procedures, it was hoped that the skills needed to be a successful farmer would be learned and imitated by other tribal members.

As the years went by, the majority of the apprentices seemed to have been agency school boys, instead of men, especially after the period passed in which the government agreed to pay for non-Pawnee labor. An 1871 report noted that school boys were apprenticed to the tinsmith and blacksmith, and four others were listed as farm laborers. Consequently, they were not in classes in the day school.[61]

After the Quakers reached the agency, they began the repair

of dilapidated buildings and the construction of new ones. The gristmill was an innovation and Indian funds and labor were employed in digging the race, building the dam, and altering the building itself.[62] School boys were used on the agency farm and in construction of agency buildings. In 1872, it was proposed to build a new school building. It was to be constructed by the agency carpenter, Wallace Mannington, with "a sufficient force of Indian boys to complete it."[63] In the *Report of Employees, 1st Quarter of 1870*, not counting the agent or the clerk, ten of twenty-nine employees were Indians, who were listed as a farm hand, ox driver, and assistants.[64]

In the spring of 1871, Agent Troth reported that Pawnee men came regularly to the office to apply for work, but he was unable to hire them for "want of funds to pay them for their labor."[65] Here the civilization program bogged down. The idea to teach the Pawnees the skills to work as the white man did for wages began to succeed. But now that some individuals were ready to apply their knowledge and seek employment, there were no funds to pay them. Again in 1873, Agent Burgess noted that many young men wanted to work for compensation but that there were no funds or any scheme being developed that could aid them. Significantly he added that, "In assuming the habits of civilized life, they feel helpless, and while they may see others reaping the rewards of their labors in gathering plentiful crops, they feel like initiates in a new life."[66]

The 1872 annual report stated that the 210-acre agency farm produced 1,900 bushels of oats; 4,000 bushels of corn; and 1,500 bushels of potatoes; in addition, 15 acres produced vegetables of many varieties. These crops were grown and harvested mainly by the labor of Indians, principally the boys at the school, who also cut and hauled all the fuel for the agency and school. It is assumed, since they were students, they were not paid for this tremendous amount of labor. Who received these crops is not specified. Whether they were consumed by agency personnel or students, or sold for profit is undetermined. There is no evidence that the Pawnees who were impoverished at this time were issued any of them. It will be recalled that in the next year, Agent Troth said in response to the Pawnee chiefs' plea for food that he would get each band two sacks of flour. The farm this year is said to have produced 1,100 bushels of oats, 312 bushels of rye, and 760 bushels of wheat. According to the agent, "Our heaviest crop is corn and the yield promises to be fair."[67] He also added that he saw no reason that the farm should not be self-sustaining and "at the same time aid the school and other departments of the agency materially in the carting of supplies, provision, and fuel."[68]

In 1874, funds from the Pawnee annuity were to be used to hire Indian men and their horses to do spring plowing. A number of day laborers paid "at a reasonable rate" were to be hired to till and plant the agency farm crops. However, the Indians' horses were not strong enough to break the new prairie sod, so the agent hired it done by outsiders. It was well known that Indian ponies were usually in poor condition in the spring due to poor winter forage. This must have been apparent to the agent, so promising to hire Pawnees may only have been a hopeful gesture. The annuity funds set aside for this purpose were therefore used for wages for outsiders.

In order to turn buffalo-hunting, "squaw patch" Pawnees into farmers under the civilization scheme promoted by the government, it was necessary to train individuals and convince them to perform new roles. It became apparent that the main emphasis must be to instill new values in the school-age tribal members in a controlled school situation. With a few exceptions, older men and women could not be so easily convinced of the wisdom or practicality of the new ways. The Pawnees had agreed in treaty to supply children for the school room and men to learn the trades of farmer, smith, and miller. When the funds supplied by the government were terminated, according to treaty agreement, the "civilization" process, if it were to succeed, had to use funds from the Pawnee annuity. The chiefs often reluctantly consented to such expenditures in hopes that the agent in return would accede to requests they made, which to them were of greater need.

In the mid-seventies a few men did farm work, but much of the labor supplied to run the agency farm came from the school boys who did not have to be paid. And there were no funds to pay those men who had learned skills and wanted to work.

The planned conversion of large numbers of the population to learn new manual training skills and settle on individual farms had not occurred. One of the reasons was that individual farms and male-dominated farming were antithetical to male-female cultural roles dictated by tradition, religion, and the social needs for a close, extended family in village life. Other reasons were the fear of Sioux attack on individual farmstead families; a suspicion of the government's goals and its means of attaining them; a reluctance to cooperate with government programs, which still outweighed the obvious fact that the old ways were changing with the loss of the buffalo herds and the freedom to pursue them; and, overall, a general malaise resulting from the deculturating effects of reservation life.

Pawnee Traditional Medicine and White Man's Diseases

The crying voice
That cries at intervals.
This was one of the songs sung by a Chaui doctor, Rawawahku. It was symbolic of the pains of childbirth that come at intervals.
—Garland J. Blaine

All cultures have their medical practitioners whose knowledge has evolved through generations. Much is known about the ability of the Pawnee doctors to cure various illnesses, set broken bones, remove projectile points, prevent and cure infections in wounds, and alleviate certain psychological ailments. Among other abilities, they also assisted at both normal and difficult births and could perform some forms of surgery.[69]

This Pawnee account of medicine and doctoring was given:

If you were sick or felt ill, or depressed, or were wounded or hurt, so that you felt the need for a doctor, you went to one, or he would come to you. He would look at your face and say, Rawa [Good], tike [son] or tsupat [woman], or whatever your relationship name, tell me about yourself. What makes you most comfortable? What makes you most uncomfortable? And you would explain, I'm uncomfortable in warm places, etc. Then he might ask you about how you felt about the women members in your family and the men, your brothers and sisters. Do you argue and so forth. What age do you feel sorry for little children? What age do you feel you don't have to feel protective about them and so forth. When do you feel protective again, say at fifty?

If you went to the doctor's you would stay there four days and he would be watching you and talking to you. Then he would talk to you and say, You are a wolf or you are a buffalo or a bear and you must do these things. He said that because there were different animals that individuals esteemed.* They felt a link between God, the animal and themselves. It was not passed from father to son. It was an entirely different animal depending on the individual's dream or vision. When a man was wounded badly, sometimes his true nature came out. One man who was shot began to act like a horse. He bucked up and down wildly and made the noises of a horse. The doctors roped him, whipped him across the back and sang Horse Songs as they drove him to the village. There they doctored him.

If it was a wound, a doctor might doctor you. If it was a fever or other illness, he might say, I can't help you. You will have to go to a doctor with a buffalo or bear or horse Sacred Bundle. He himself was a wolf doctor, say, and would doctor only those who were wolves or had been identified as being under the protection or spirit of that animal.

All of my uncle's life it was thought he was a bear. When he got very sick, it was found out that he was a horse. He dreamed of it. A horse said to him, I am going to try to help you. If I make it out of this ditch we are in, we will make it and you'll live. The horse ran and tried and tried and tried and couldn't get up out of the ditch. At this time my uncle was making the motions and noises of the horse and his mother knew he was a horse and not a bear. He came out of the coma for awhile and told his family, I am not going to make it and I will die. Soon after he did.[70]

For some doctors, they had the expression "they unraveled him." They cure emotional conditions. They would talk to you to find out what was wrong with you. They would listen to you and then tell you to do something that you might have difficulty in doing. For instance, he might say that you should visit or relate to those relatives you might not associate with in the normal course

---

* Garland J. Blaine said that it was possible that the idea that the Pawnee had clans at one time may have derived from early observations that different men were members of different societies belonging to the horse, bear, buffalo, deer, and others. Different members of the same family would not necessarily belong to the same society. It would depend on whether a man had a vision or dream and the animal that appeared to him in it.

of events or with whom you had failed to keep up communication. He had his reasons for suggesting this or something else, and if you refused he would say that you had been told how to feel better and if you did not, he had said what he believed was the cure. This type of treatment cut out certain types of dreams and anxieties [you had]. One thing that was suggested was to find new acquaintances at that time because they are stimulating and bring a change.

Ideally, except in an emergency, a doctor would fast one day before treating a patient. Then on the second day he would open his Sacred Bundle. He would look at his medicines. When Wichita Blaine opened his Bundle, he had medicine in little bags made of canvas, handkerchiefs and skin. He was blind so he could tell what they were by the way they were wrapped and by the knots tying them shut. Sometimes he would ask me, does this look like this? After he had inspected the Bundle contents he would take his pipe and tobacco. We would then go out to our corn field, pull up a stalk and get dirt from under the roots. This was usually after the corn had been cut and the stalk was dry. The corn was sacred to us and the Mother Earth it grew in was also sacred. He got a wash pan, put this dirt in it and coals and made a fireplace. He would make certain kinds of smoke to use on the ill person. Sometimes they inhaled it, other times they just smelled it. He made the blessing motion by cupping his hands in the smoke and passing them down over his body. I should also mention that sometimes the dirt under Mother Corn was used as medicine itself. * [71]

Some Pawnee doctors used mouth, tongue and teeth. Grandfather chewed medicine, then put his mouth over the spot and sucked and blew. You could hear the sounds. He would spit in a can as he went along. I recall when I was about eight to ten years of age, Robert Taylor, my little cousin, who was three, was very ill. His mother, father and sister came to our house. Grandfather had me take him to the corn field. We took some dirt from under a corn plant and went back to the house. He took his Buffalo Bundle and opened it. He spread the corn field dirt upon his face and put on black moccasins and a dark blanket around him. He faced the boy toward the South and gave prayers and sang songs for about fifteen to twenty minutes. He placed his mouth on the

* Wichita Blaine was a Buffalo Society doctor.

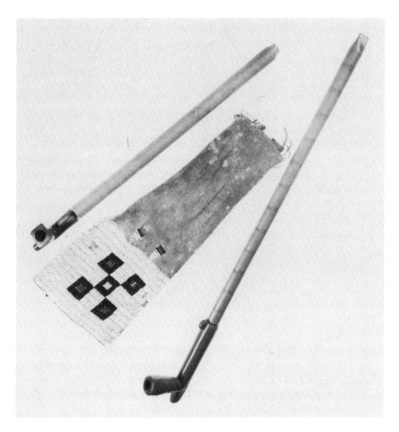

Pipes, pipe stems, and pipe bag belonging to Wichita Blaine. The beadwork is white, green, black, and yellow. Photo by Dr. R. E. Venk. The Blaine Collection.

vital places near the navel and sucked there. There was a green discharge. The boy began to move. Then my Grandfather asked Hawk Norman, who was also a doctor, to pray and he did. More songs were sung. All at once Robert sat up and screamed. Grandfather said, "Let him be. Let him cry. Let him be what he wants to be. For the next few days let him go where he wants to go." This was done. Their family stayed with us for two weeks. Robert and his father went to the outhouse one day. Coming back they saw

Uncle Louis, who had been dead for awhile.* They came back and told Grandfather and Hawk Norman. They got cedar and went outside, smoked and talked to Uncle Louis. He was, they discovered, the cause of the illness. After they had talked to him, everything was alright. Robert and his family went back to their house.[72]

There was a man with cataracts. The doctor told his protégé to go to a nursing woman and tell her to come to where he was if she felt sorry for them. Tell her, he said, that you are doing this for the tribe and feel sorry for this man. She consented and other women got her milk in a little horn. Then the doctor poured the milk in the man's eyes three or four times. He took a white cloth, wrapped around a bullet. He then carefully scraped the eye, then used his mouth, tongue and suction to remove the cataract.[73]

Doctors sang certain songs before doctoring, and during intervals in the song, they would doctor. Sometimes they used their hands on the body. During childbirth, for instance. A midwife and other women were also there. The doctor would sit by the mother's head or shoulder. He would begin praying. He would tell the mother-to-be to think this or do this by the relationship term he called her. He would say, "Tirawahut did these things. These things we suffer. We must have faith. It is not easy to produce our tribe, but think deeply. It is Tirawahut's way. Think in your mind and He will grant it." He talked like this to her. Sometimes as he sang, he held her legs, or her side, wherever he felt it was necessary to help in the birth. All of this knowledge came from his sacred vision, where to touch each patient and what to say.

We do not tell people what we know about doctoring unless

---

* To the Pawnees, the return of the dead in connection with illness is not unusual. Mary (May) Lockley Good Eagle told Garland and Martha Blaine that she had been sick recently, but knew she wouldn't die. One evening as she was getting ready for bed, she heard a knock on the door. She sat there awhile not wanting to open the door and said, "Can I help you?" Then a man said, "Aunt May?" and she recognized it was Henry Murie. She said, "Why Henry, it's you, but you are dead." "Yes, Aunt May, but I came to tell you you are going to be sick, but you will get well." There was further talk, and Aunt May asked Henry if he would come in. He said, "No, I don't live here [on earth]." She closed the door soon after. Sometime later, as she was walking to church, things began to get dark. She went to the hospital and fainted. When she awoke there, she remembered what Henry had said. She told us that she may have dreamed Henry's visit, or imagined it, but if this happens, she added, whatever they say will happen. At this time in 1974, Aunt May was ninety-one years old.

Medicine packets, roots, red ochre, white chalklike substance, a Harahey flint knife, and other objects from a Sacred Bundle used in the curing practices of a Pawnee doctor. The knife is four and one-half inches long. Photo by Dr. R. E. Venk. The Blaine Collection.

they are sincere. If you tell anybody then they will use it, but not sincerely, and it will lose its effectiveness. "They will be playing with it" is our expression, and it is too sacred to play with.[74]

For healing ailments that required internally or externally applied medicines the Pawnee had a varied pharmacopoeia derived from the plants found in the woods, fields, and along stream banks. One of the medicines was sumac. It had several uses, one of which was on the battlefield. If a man got a bad wound, and there was nothing else available, a doctor, or someone else if a doctor was not in the group, would clean out the wound, then urinate on it. The wound was then closed and a poultice of chewed sumac leaves placed over the wound. A large leaf or leaves would be placed on top of this and secured by whatever tying material was available. This served to stop bleeding and keep insects out of the wound.[75]

Melvin R. Gilmore, in his important work, *Uses of Plants by the Indians of the Missouri River Region,* described many of the plants used by the Pawnees. Sumac, he reported, was used as indicated above, to stop hemorrhaging. The berries and other parts of the cedar were used in various ways for coughs, colds, nervousness, and bad dreams. *Typha latifolia L.*, or cattail, was used for dressing burns and scalds and to alleviate infant chafing. It was also utilized as a diapering material. The corm of *Arisaima triphyllum L.*, or Jack-in-the-pulpit, was powdered and applied as a counterirritant for rheumatic and other aches. *Acorus calamus L.*, or sweet flag or calamus, was an all-around medicine. Its roots were chewed or ground, and an infusion was made that relieved colds, coughs, and toothache. *Laciaria scariosa L.*, or blazing star, cured diarrhea in children. *Silphium aciniatum L.*, called pilot plant, compass plant, or gum or rosin weed, was used as a tonic to cure general debility. *Heliantus annuus L.*, or sunflower seed, combined with a root (unnamed by Gilmore) was chewed by nursing mothers who were pregnant to safeguard the suckling infant.[76]

The Acceptance of Some of the White Man's Medicine

All of the above-mentioned plants, plus many others were gathered and utilized by the Pawnee doctors as age-old remedies for most of the afflictions that beset their people. But contact with the whites brought new illnesses for which they had no cures. Smallpox, diphtheria, tuberculosis, venereal diseases, and others for the most part resisted all their known curing techniques, and the tribe saw great numbers die in the nineteenth century. The realization that white man's medicine should cure white man's diseases was logically apparent to the Pawnees and they accepted such innovations as vaccination. In 1870, Dr. George L. Simpson, a local physician, was hired by Agent Troth to vaccinate the tribe. He reported that 661 showed evidence of previous vaccination and 629 showed no evidence and were vaccinated.[77]

Eventually an agency physician was hired, and the chiefs requested that money from their annuity be set aside for medicine.[78] Not all Indian agency doctors were qualified, nor were they all sympathetic to the Indians or eager to perform stipulated duties. In 1874, the Pawnee chiefs complained about Dr. D. L. Davis and said they would not have him because he did not give them proper attention.[79]

Agent Troth had little faith in the Pawnee medicine men. In one council, he told the chiefs that it was wrong to kill people and it had come to his notice that this had been done by "some of your people," referring to the tribal doctors. Pitaresaru emphatically denied it and nothing more was said.[80] In 1874, Agent Burgess declared, "Pawnee medicine men exerted a great deal of influence and retard our work and will prevent any but the best physician from doing what he might to cure their illnesses and improve their sanitary condition."[81]

This aspect of so-called civilization, that is, the introduction of modern medical techniques, medicine, and practitioners, received a mixed reaction from the Pawnees. Most Pawnees never sought the new doctors, while a few others utilized the skills of both cultures, depending on circumstances. Major Frank North told of Pawnee Scouts whose various ailments had not been cured by Army doctors but whose own medicine men treated them and effected cures in them all.[82] In the main, the people preferred the medical practices of their own doctors, based on knowledge gained through sacred visions, experience, and holistic techniques.

In 1873, during his stay at the Pawnee Agency, Wilhelm A. Dinesen, a Danish visitor, observed the government's efforts to "civilize" the people.

The Indians do not now suffer harm because they are not Christian, but it is demanded that they have the same ideas as we have or at least claim to have. The white man can see that the Indian cannot resist his civilization and he destroys the Indians mercilessly. But the white man will not understand that the Indian cannot *adopt* his civilization and in this regard the white man is unreasonable in his judgment of the red man. We give him a few days to acquire that which took us thousands of years. But he cannot, he will not submit like the Negro; the Indian dies when robbed of freedom and independence.[83]

By the 1870s, the Pawnees had been under the influence of the larger society's "civilization" programs for several decades. Few of the new ideas or changes sought by the U.S. government were embraced heartily or completely in the educational, medical, or economic spheres or any other aspects of culture not discussed here. But the long term effects of contact with a "civilized society" had devastating results. By the early 1900s, there were less than seven hundred Pawnees alive, living on a reservation far from their homelands.

✝✝✝
7
The Pawnees and the Annuity

A Power Struggle

> Pitaresaru: *"I want to know if my soldiers are to distribute the goods?"*
> Agent Troth: *"I have only to help the Sup't., he and the Commissioner have decided that $3,000 is not to be given the Chiefs and soldiers unless he [Superintendent] distributes the goods as last year."*
> Pitaresaru: *"We want to distribute the goods."*
>   —*Pawnee council, September 16, 1872*

"Annuity" is defined as an annual payment of money that con-tinues for a given number of years or for life. The American In-dian was introduced to the concept and experience early in his relations with the United States. In 1791, a treaty with the Cher-okees to extinguish all title to certain lands included the provi-sion that the United States would deliver "certain valuable goods" immediately to the Indian treaty signers for the Cherokee people. Also, an annuity of $1,000 would be paid them.[1]

There were several views as to how Indian annuity funds should be spent. In 1816, Lewis Cass reflected a view of his time, saying that without annuities some Indians could not feed or clothe themselves, and the United States had a moral obligation to pay them, considering that the Indians' signing away of their lands removed their hunting grounds and farming locations.[2] In 1818, Secretary of War James C. Calhoun stated that annuities would be useful if spent in establishing Indian schools.[3] In saying this, he mirrored the opinion of many that such monies should be uti-lized in "civilizing" the Indians by teaching them the basic skills of literacy. Another idea was to purchase farm animals and tools and teach agriculture as the non-Indian citizen practiced it.

In time, annuities were used for purposes other than to provide items of sustenance or to promote civilization. Under the provisions of the 1834 Trade and Intercourse Act, valid claims against Indian tribes could be paid to the debtees from annuity funds *before* the remainder was distributed to the tribe. Profligate use of the provision began soon thereafter, with claims sometimes fabricated in order to share the annual windfall, as it came to be seen by the unscrupulous.[4]

Promises of annuity payment could be used by the U.S. government to influence Indian behavior when it seemed expedient. Records indicate that the government offered some Indian treaty signers substantial individual payments and future annuities in exchange for agreeing to sign land cession treaties.[5] Control of tribal behavior could be gained by threatening to withhold or actually withholding annuity funds. In 1851, the Chippewas were told not to return to the homeland they had ceded. If they did so, their annuities would cease.

In many treaties, articles were included by the government commissioners stating that if the designated tribes warred against other tribes or took part in depredations on white citizens, their annuities would be terminated or be used to pay for the damages incurred. As an example, in 1862, after Siouan hostilities in Minnesota, it was decided to take annuity funds due the tribes to pay for non-Indian deaths and damages.

A somewhat similar but more massive loss of annuity came after the Civil War. The U.S. government claimed that by entering into treaties with and joining the Confederate military forces, the Cherokees, Creeks, Chickasaws, Seminoles, Choctaws, and some other tribes of Indian Territory and Kansas had forfeited their treaty rights, including the payment of annuities due them. In each tribe, there were actively loyal Union factions, but their actions and loyalty did not prevent their loss of annuity.[6] Due to their Confederate connection, these tribes were also forced to make further land cessions in 1866.

A flagrant example of government withholding annuity goods and money came after the passage of the Dawes Act in 1887, which provided for allotment of Indian land in severalty. Indian tribes strenuously resisted this act and refused to give up any more land or to be moved again. In certain tribes, resistance to signing allotment agreements or to selecting land for individuals was met with strong response. The government threatened that if an individual or family did not choose, accept, and take up residence on an allotment, or if they should leave it, their annuity would be withheld.[7]

The decision as to who were to be the direct tribal annuity recipients became a source of contention between Indian tribes and the government. In 1834, the reorganization of the Indian Service included an act in which the payment of annuity was regularized. Chiefs of an Indian tribe were to be the primary recipients of any treaty-dictated funds.[8] Because the government and its representatives had dealt with tribal leaders up to this time, it seemed efficient for the chiefs to distribute annuity good and money.

Later, when it became necessary to contain and eliminate vestiges of tribal autonomy, it was realized that by their controlling the annuity and its distribution, the chiefs also maintained power and influence in their traditional roles as distributors of wealth. In 1847, regulations were changed so that payment was made to heads of families rather than to the chiefs. It was thought that this would also contribute to a more equitable distribution of goods.

Among many tribes, this switch in procedure brought anger, protests, and attempts to change the regulation. Even before this date, Ioway tribal annuities had been distributed to individual families. The chiefs had strenuously objected. Speaking for the chiefs before the agent, Walking Rain said, "When you spoke of this matter of paying money to heads of families, we thought it was for one year. We have talked this over and think our plan best. We have some serious objection to this manner of paying annuities. Many times we are compelled to make national debts and give presents to our friends. Our chiefs would not be able to gain credit or give presents." White Cloud, the traditional head chief, had even threatened to take the annuity money away from the agent at the time of payment, if the agent tried to distribute it to families.[9]

Pawnee Treaty Provisions

In the 1857 Pawnee treaty with the U.S. government, there are four articles that refer to the annuity. Article 2 states that in consideration for land ceded by the tribe, $40,000 a year for five years would be paid to the tribe. After that, there would be $30,000 a year paid as perpetual annuity at the discretion of the president. At least one half of this amount was to be paid in goods. In Articles 3, 4, and 5, certain conditions were imposed on the Pawnees if they were to receive the payment due them. In the third article, it was stipulated that children between seven and eighteen must be kept in school nine months of the year. If parents or guardians did not see that their children attended the school provided, there would be deducted from the parental annuities an "amount equal to the value in time, of the tuition thus lost." In Article 4, there were additional strings. If any Pawnee should steal, injure, or destroy any item supplied to the tribe by the government, such as houses, shops, machinery, stock, or farm implements, the cost of such articles would be deducted from the annuity. In Article 5, the Pawnees promised to commit no depredations on either white or Indian "at peace with the United States." If any property should be stolen from the above, it must be returned, or if destroyed the government would compensate the owners with funds from the tribal annuity.[10]

Although there were probably others, one recorded threat to withhold annuity for school nonattendance happened in June 1873. The chiefs were told that the school must be filled or flour, a part of the annuity purchases, would be withheld. In September, the chiefs were again reminded to send five children from each of the four bands to the Pawnee Manual Labor School to fill the quota.[11] There was hunger in the villages. The summer hunt had failed and food caches were nearly empty. The urgent need for flour was recognized and used by the agent to obtain conformity to his regulations.

Provisions calling for withholding Pawnee annuity were adhered to. However, the government was not consistent or so rigorous in maintaining its annuity commitments to the Pawnees, such as furnishing annuity goods requested and needed, or get-

ting them to the tribe on time. Late arrival of much-needed supplies and funds became common, as more and more tribes were
brought into the annuity system. The Pawnee chiefs on more
than one occasion repeatedly had to ask the agent when the
grievously needed annuity supplies would arrive.

An annuity payroll consisting of a tribal census had to be made
before the annuity could be requested. In December 1875, after
the arrival of part of the Pawnees at their new agency in Indian
Territory, the agent said the annuity could not be paid because
not all of the people had arrived.[12] Pawnees still on the journey,
and those at the new agency, were left without badly needed supplies at a time when there were no crops yet planted or caches of
dried food to feed them.

Annuity Distribution

In 1871 in the Northern Superintendency, annuity goods were
purchased by the direction of the commissioner of Indian Affairs
and shipped and charged to the superintendent. He was held accountable for them until he had procured vouchers showing that
the goods had been distributed to the tribe. The information was
included in his quarterly report to the commissioner. To determine the amount of money to be paid per capita, a census was
taken annually. Four copies were made of the payroll, one each
for the agency office, the superintendent's office, the commissioner of Indian Affairs, and the second auditor of the U.S. Treasury. Payment time called for definite procedures. Present were
the superintendent, agent, clerk, interpreter, and an officer of
the army, if there were an army post within sixty miles of the
agency or place of distribution. If no officer were present, then
two disinterested citizens must be present. At a typical distribution, when the payment table was ready, an Indian herald at the
door called out the name of the chief of the first band or group to
be paid. The superintendent then called out the amount due him
and his family, counted the money, and handed it to his clerk.
The clerk recounted it, and if correct, he handed it to the Indian
who then touched the pen, an act that signified or stood for his
signature. When all payment had been completed, the signatures

were witnessed by the clerk, superintendent, agent, interpreter, military officer, or citizens. Each of them signed the certificate stating that the annuity payment had been completed.[13]

The Pawnee chiefs, like the Ioway chiefs, were opposed to the white man's control of the distribution of money and goods. Preston Holder commenting on the traditional flow of wealth within a tribe said,

> This reassortment of wealth was probably sanctioned and as rigidly enforced as the opposite principle, the lowest contributed their best and received the least. In order to maintain their position, the upper ranks had to control enough wealth to validate that position since their primary economic function was to control the flow of wealth and redistribution of goods.[14]

This became increasingly true for the Pawnee leaders after annuity payments became the main source of incoming wealth, when traditional means of acquiring wealth, such as buffalo robe selling and horse stealing, were curtailed and governmental control of tribal and individual rights and freedoms increased.

The government's plans to control annuity distribution intensified. In the fall of 1870, Supt. Samuel Janney went to the Pawnee Agency to distribute goods and money. After traditional greetings, he offered to divide the goods among the families, "but the chiefs would not consent. They preferred to divide them among their bands and the result was as usual, the poor and aged got little or nothing," he observed.[15] The chiefs believed, as is true in other stratified societies, that there is not usually an even distribution of wealth among the privileged and the poor. But Barclay White, when he became superintendent, was determined to change this situation and described his experience the next year at the 1871 distribution. When he arrived, the chiefs expressed satisfaction with the $3,000 that was to be divided as "salary" among them and the leading soldiers or warriors. However, they declared that the annuity goods were theirs, and they had always divided them and desired to continue. Barclay wrote in his journal,

> I read to them the resolutions adopted by them in council with Supt. Janney, and told them plainly, I was there to distribute the

goods and intended to do so. I asked them in what proportions they desired the money paid, and they said they would leave that to me. I told them I would not take the responsibility, and they must apportion it themselves. They then asked that the Council be adjourned until an hour in the afternoon in order that they might confer together and decide upon the apportionment. . . . When we next assembled, the Interpreter said, "These men have been four hours dividing three thousand grains of corn representing dollars. They do not know whether they have it right and want you to tell them. They have agreed that eighty dollars to be paid to each of the chiefs, sixty dollars be paid to each of twenty-four soldiers and two hundred and eighty dollars to the interpreter. Does that take all of the $3,000?" Taking paper and pencil from my pocket, after a minute's calculation I informed him the amounts were correct. Instantly from every part of the council came the exclamations of surprize, "Ugh! Ugh! Ugh!".* They evidently concluded that a "little learning is not a dangerous thing," and school instruction might be good for Indians.[16]

White then paid the above amounts to the chiefs and warriors, and afterwards he insisted he would divide and distribute the goods carefully. After this was done he noted that "the poor and aged women expressed their gratitude and satisfaction, as they received more and better goods than on any previous distribution."[17]

Early in 1872, the chiefs in council complained again about the method of distributing annuity goods. Apparently women teachers at the school had been involved in dividing and dispersing the goods at the last distribution mentioned above. Pitaresaru disagreed with the practice in a discussion with the agent. In a June meeting, Sky Chief repeated their objections, saying he did not want "Mother who teaches the children to distribute their goods again."[18] To allow a woman to have this privilege was demeaning to the chiefs and made them and the people more aware of their subordinate position and declining authority—which could be said to be one government objective.

Among the Pawnees there was a strong sense of band autonomy traceable to their history of separate villages often isolated by great distance. After their villages were together on the reser-

* The Pawnee declaration of surprise or amazement is not "Ugh" but "Wuh."

Pawnee Indians receiving their annuity payment in the early 1870s. To re-ceive payment each Pawnee touched the pen and then an X was placed by the individual's name. Photo by John Carbutt. Courtesy of Pamela Oestreicher Collection.

vation, the government treated them more or less without indi-viduality. Each band chief realized decreased authority in dealing with the government. He became one of many, rather than being dealt with as the head chief of his band. To offset or minimize this, Pitaresaru said the chiefs wanted the money divided by bands. Eagle Chief, of the Skidi Band, and other chiefs agreed. Sky Chief remarked that if this were done, then each band could do what it wished with its share.[19]

For the most part, in council the chiefs acted in support of one another against the outsiders' group represented by the agent or others. In many other aspects of tribal life, such as annuity distribution, they considered themselves separate bands or "tribes," as they once were called.

In June 1872, the Baltimore Friends Committee came to observe Pawnee advancement under their aegis. In the usual council, the chiefs brought up before the visitors the issue of annuity goods and cash distribution. Pitaresaru became more explicit in the presence of those he thought might override the superintendent's decision. He told the Friends that, when he was in Washington to make a treaty, each band was promised $5,000, and "if we don't get but $15,000, we want $5,000 more as promised. We know we can do what we please with our money." He continued that now there were so many minds that "we cannot think alike."[20] Whether he was referring to the contradictions between the goals of the chiefs and the agent and superintendent or to the sometimes dissenting opinions of the "soldiers" paid by the agent, or to other differences of opinion is not stated. But increasing difficulty in reaching traditional consensus among tribal leaders seems to be indicated.

Sky Chief, recalling his memories of the Washington treaty talks, added that they had been told they were to receive that money only for five years. When they learned how to take care of money, then they could have all their annuity in money. He seemed to be reasoning that now it was some time after the five-year period, and the Pawnees felt able to handle their own money without the interference and control of the government. He added that many people had died so there should be more money for individuals.[21]

Barclay White disagreed, saying that the treaty called for only $15,000. And, he went on, it would be distributed the same this year as last year. The chiefs and soldiers would get salaries if the commissioner of Indian Affairs approved them, and *if*, he emphasized, he himself distributed the goods. He ended by stating that money taken out of the annuity for salaries lessened the amount that other tribal individuals received. He did not mention that the continual use of annuity funds for farm implements and other less than useful items (from the Pawnee standpoint), depleted the annual individual annuity sum even further. Pitare-saru responded that, as for the superintendent's previous oversee-ing of the so-called equitable distribution of goods, that the su-perintendent may have thought he was being fair, but some families got only two blankets.[22]

In September, the chiefs continued their efforts to regain con-trol of the coming distribution of annuity goods. At this time, the chiefs restated their position forcefully, and the agent re-peated they would receive their salaries only if the superinten-dent was in charge of goods' distribution. Pitaresaru replied that it looked as if the chiefs had no sense—not to be allowed to do what they should do that is, distribute the annuity goods. With less than tact, Agent Jacob Troth broke in, saying that the rea-son why the superintendent wanted to distribute the goods was that he was better educated and could divide them more fairly. He then fell back on the evasive technique of saying he would write to the superintendent giving him the Pawnee views. The chiefs countered that he, the agent, had been sent to represent the superintendent and the commissioner; and they wanted him, the agent, to take hold of this matter. Their insistence was futile, and a letter was drawn stating that the chiefs wanted to distribute the goods in the coming annuity payment.[23] Everyone knew what the answer would be.

In late September, Superintendent White arrived at the agency and distributed the goods, although Pitaresaru informed him that he wanted his soldiers to undertake the task. Terrecowah said to White, "We want you to see us distribute the goods once and see that we are fair." Sky Chief earnestly stated that they wanted to do what was right. They could not count the money, it was true, but they could distribute the goods.

White told them flatly, "There is but one way of doing busi-ness and that is to do it right. . . . I want you to watch me, and if anyone doesn't get what is right, tell me."[24] With that, the issue was settled, and the chiefs stood back aware of their defeat once again. Although it might seem that the government had the in-dividual Pawnee's interest at heart, its control of annuity distri-bution became a part of the continued effort to erode the power and position of the chiefs among their people.

Annuity Goods Ordered and Received

European goods were originally introduced to the American Indian as trade items in the seventeenth to nineteenth centuries, when at different times and places he brought his furs to exchange for non-Indian produced objects. Objects accepted were generally combinations of two main types: items that were entirely new in the cultural experience, such as handkerchiefs, glass beads, or mirrors, or items that became substitutions for older traditionally made articles, such as metal kettles for pottery vessels; cloth for skin clothing; and guns, which were better weapons in some ways than were bows, arrows, and spears. After the programs to civilize the Indians began, a third type of annuity good appeared: items that were not entirely wanted by, but selected for, the Indians, such as plows, garden seeds, domesticated animals, paper, books, and pencils.

The 1871, the Pawnee annuity goods list contained mostly items of the second and third types. These included sheeting, calico, muslin, red flannel, blue drill (a coarse cotton or linen cloth), and Conestoga ticking (possibly used for tipi covers since Terrecowah once said that buffalo were scarce and the people did not have enough skins to make tents and moccasins).[25] Ready-to-wear clothing included 300 red shirts; 50 military coats and pairs of pants; 100 cassimer (a twilled woolen cloth) coats; 200 pearl wool and black wool hats; 240 handkerchiefs; and 700 plaid, wool shawls.

Steel knives replaced flaked stone knives in the first years of Spanish and French colonial contact. Now, 96 pocket knives, 120 axes, and 480 butcher knives were ordered. The knives were used principally in meat and hide preparation, although the traditional bone hide flesher was still used. Fifty metal kettles were part of the replacement of the older tradition of Pawnee pottery making, but wooden bowls continued to be made. At the agent's urging, the chiefs consented to request also 100 scythes, 20 spades, and 20 shovels.

Not all goods requested and approved by the chiefs and listed on the requisition order sent by the agent were received at the time of distribution. The 1871 order included forty Spencer rifles,

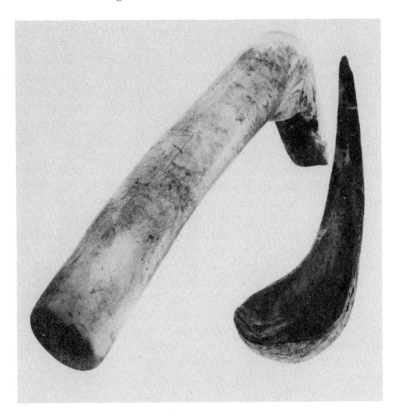

Pawnee hide flesher and bison horn spoon. These objects were brought to Indian Territory from Nebraska. There the Pawnees continued to use them. This flesher is twelve and one-half inches long. It had a metal blade attached with sinew to the top. Note the designs carved in the side. A horn spoon is used today in the Pawnee food blessing ceremony. Photo by Dr. R. E. Venk. The Blaine Collection.

sixteen kegs of powder, twenty double-barreled shotguns, and two hundred pounds of lead. None were received.* Nineteen cases were empty when the shipment arrived and it was not

* Wilhelm A. Dinesen described annuity distribution graft as he learned of it in his 1872–74 visit to the Pawnee Agency and other agencies.

All Indians under the jurisdiction of the government and agent are, as I mentioned, to receive one blanket a year. This is the procedure: a shipment of crates

Pawnee camp scene in Indian Territory. The woman is using a flesher to scrape excess flesh from the hide. Nearby stand a mortar and pestle. The canvas covered rounded structure made of bent saplings at one time had a cover of hides and served as a temporary shelter on the hunt. It was also used in winter in wooded, sheltered places along streams. Photo by W. S. Prettyman. Courtesy of Archives and Manuscripts Division of the Oklahoma Historical Society.

stated whether they were supposed to have contained the above-mentioned arms or other articles. The value of the goods received and delivered was $6,307.02, although the estimate order

with or without blankets is sent to agent A and receipts for rail-freight charges, delivery, etc. are included with the accounts of disbursements to Indians. But the crates are sent back to Washington, unopened, and from there they go to Agent B and so on. The Indians get no blankets, they could not protest with any hope of redress, because the agents and the bureau in Washington are in collusion.

He did not name any specific agency where this was supposed to have happened, if it did.

Pawnee wooden bowls. Wooden and pottery containers were replaced by metal and ceramic vessels after European and American trading relationships developed. The bowls shown here had ceremonial uses. The largest one is slightly over six inches in diameter. Courtesy Thomas Gilcrease Institute of American History and Art, Tulsa, Oklahoma.

including the guns was $15,000.[26] Somewhere more than half the value of the Pawnee annuity goods had disappeared, or had not been approved of by the Indian Office, or had not been available by suppliers, or had gotten into other hands.

Guns, We Need Guns

We were always told by the old men born in Nebraska, that the government wanted to get rid of us to get our good Nebraska land. They would not give us guns so that the Sioux could attack us and kill us and we

*could not defend ourselves with just the few guns that we had. That was
the government's plan at the end.*
—*Garland J. Blaine, 1969*

A man's need to have a gun became increasingly apparent to the
Pawnees after the Sioux and other enemy tribes had guns and
used them against them. The well-armed Sioux increased their
hostile efforts against Quaker-dominated tribes in the nineteenth
century. The Quakers seeking peace between peoples often turned
a deaf ear to tribal requests for arms to use in defense against
neighboring tribes having superior fire power.

There were limited ways to obtain guns. In the seventeenth
and eighteenth centuries of European and American Indian trade,
furs and skins were exchanged for guns, which then were often
used by the Indians against their enemies.[27] As early as the 1670s,
the Sioux sought to obtain guns from the French to combat the
gun-possessing Crees. In 1672, the Ottawas and Hurons exchanged all their furs in Montreal for guns and ammunition to
war against the Sioux.[28]

Beaver trading tribes had greater access to guns than did the
buffalo hunting Pawnees and other tribes west of the Missouri in
the eighteenth century. These tribes had little access to the
woodlands and lake areas that produced the beaver and other
more desirable and valuable furs needed for the European market. The Sioux bands of the Minnesota region in this period had
access to good fur bearing animal sources and could trade them
for guns.

In the reservation peiod, there was some trade in buffalo robes
and hides with the Pawnee traders, and some guns were purchased in this way by those who had enough funds or credit to
purchase them. But this means was inadequate, and repeatedly
the Pawnee chiefs asked the agent to buy guns for them with
their annuity funds.

In his first annual report in 1869, the Pawnees' first Quaker
agent, Jacob Troth, said that the Pawnees no longer wanted their
annuity money spent on guns, pistols, and hunting knives. It is
suspected that this idea originated in Troth's Quaker philosophy
and was not the opinion of Pawnee warriors.

The next year, on November 14, 1870, he held a council to determine what the Pawnees wanted in their next year's list of annuity requests. Pitaresaru, the first to speak, requested Spencer rifles. Eagle Chief, of the Skidi Band, said that twenty repeating rifles were badly needed. Sky Chief did not want white man's pants or coats. Guns and materials for tipis were what he wanted placed on the list. He wanted enough Spencer rifles for the chiefs and soliders. If the chiefs had no guns or old or unworkable weapons, it would indicate the Pawnees were poorly armed indeed.[29]

On June 9, 1871, a short council entry states that the chiefs asked for delivery of their rifles and annuity goods to be hurried up. The next month, Superintendent Janney came to the agency. The goods had not yet arrived, and when the chiefs asked about the guns, he dissembled and said that he had not been informed whether the guns were included. The chiefs wanted Janney to complain to Washington about this. They emphatically stated that they wanted *all* the goods on their original list, including the guns, sent to them. They said the most important and necessary items (guns) had been omitted previously.[30] Pitaresaru, speaking directly to Janney, insisted that the missing goods be sent to them and they must have guns to defend themselves against the repeated Sioux attacks.

The next day, the council met again and talk concerning the annuity continued. Sky Chief said they would have to borrow gunpowder for the tribe to take on the hunt because they had none. He stated it would be returned when the annuity goods came.[31]

After the tribe returned from the hunt in September, the agent told the chiefs that the annuity goods were at Omaha and would come by train to Columbus soon. Terrecowah, looking forward to this, told him, "We want our guns, and to build our houses." The agent did not reply to this, according to the minutes, but changed the subject to the mill and his need for money from the annuity to repair and complete it.

On September 25, another council was held, and Sky Chief brought up the subject of guns again. "We want you to hurry up the Supt. for we want our guns to defend ourselves." Good Chief repeated this and added as an incentive to procuring them, that they were willing to give up $3,000 of their annuity to finish the mill. Later in the meeting, Pitaresaru repeated that they wanted their guns very soon, and they also wanted hay rakes.[32]

In the above statements and others throughout the minutes of their councils, the chiefs framed their statements about annuity requests to include the items most important to them, such as guns or "salary money," followed by a request for items that they knew the agent wanted them to have or wanted to have, such as hay rakes, houses, or mill repairs. In these years, the chiefs used a pattern or system of trade-offs, which were attempts to get what they really needed and wanted by compromising with the agent and accepting articles that were not required as part of their real world. By asking for houses, they hoped to please the agent so that he would reciprocate and request what would please them. There was always compromise on their part but not much on the agent's or superintendent's part. For example, as mentioned, the chiefs received small, badly needed annual sums, called salaries, but to acquire them, they lost their control of goods distribution.

However, after the advent of the Quaker authorities, compromise and bargaining for guns may have been futile. It is suspected that most Pawnee arms came from their own expenditures in the public market, a circumstance that accounts for the small number owned. They did not have the means to buy all that were needed.

In 1874, the chiefs continued bargaining, requesting that $5,000 of the annuity be spent for agricultural implements, and the balance of their money be distributed as cash. This request was refused, and it was recommended that the money be spent on food instead.[33] This countering measure could not be refused because of the urgent need for sustenance.

In February, the agent wanted to purchase hay for the agency horses, but the chiefs objected. Sioux attacks and depredations continued and they declared they wanted that money spent for guns. They requested that the agent "take measures to procure them sixty guns to a band." But the agent informed the chiefs that such a request could not be made and was impossible, as the government did not furnish guns to any Indians or allow the agent to do it. They could buy them if they had the means to purchase them elsewhere. In the agent's minutes appears this statement, "They feared attack by the Sioux this Spring."[34]

A Changing View of Annuity

In March 1874, in a resolution instigated and written by the agent, the tribal leaders signed for a most unusual expenditure of their $15,000 annuity. No blankets, cloth, kettles, or guns were included. Instead, $10,000 was requested for purchase of seeds, breaking of prairie sod, the purchase and repairs of agricultural implements, sheds, and so forth.

Significantly, the resolution included payment of Indian labor for plowing "those parts of the Reservation not worked exclusively by Indians as hithertofore." This is of interest because appearances indicate that the Indian and agency farm fields in production already were as large as the predominately Indian work force could handle. Added to this was the consideration that some lands lay fallow because of fear of Sioux attack on women workers. How was all this land to be used?

The amount of $4,250 was to be spent for Indian labor to open the new acreage. In other words, Pawnees were expected to work for this sum that was already owed them as annuity under their treaty. None of the chiefs' comments were written down in response to this innovation.

Of the balance of the $15,000, $4,000 was to be set aside for chiefs' and soldiers' salaries "while they faithfully serve in the performance of their duties respectively assigned."[35] Perhaps, the usual amount of $3,000 had been augmented to assist them to agree to the above expenditures.

An evolving concept of annuity payments and the related use of Indian labor is expressed by Com. of Indian Affairs Edward P. Smith, who said in his annual report of 1874:

> Many of the appropriations, in accordance with treaty stipulations, provide that annuities should be paid cash in hand or in goods distributed per capita to be accounted for to the Government on the receipts of the chief. All bounty of the Government bestowed in this form is worse than wasted, tending to produce perpetual poverty by providing idleness and unthrift.[36]

In proposing that Congress pass legislation that would encourage individual Indian "improvement," he suggested that, "wherever per capita distribution provided by treaty has proved injurious or without benefit to its recipients, a distribution of the same may, in the discretion of the President, be made only in return for labor of some sort."[37] There was a question of the legality of demanding labor be performed for treaty-derived annuities. Such monies were not "bounty," but government obligations due for Indian lands ceded.

Official frustration is evident in the foregoing statements. The U.S. government "civilization" efforts were not showing the results that had been hoped for because they were ill-conceived, unacceptable, and rejected by many tribal populations. They ran counter to basic Indian society values and traditional behaviors.

Some instances indicate that the government would not allow the "civilization" process to work even if there were indications of its success. Whenever the Pawnees wanted to handle their own annuity money, and thus establish patterns that the "civilized" man had, they were not allowed to do so. When they went independently to the agent and asked for work, there were no funds set aside to promote this desire to become self-sustaining. Idleness often attributed to the Indian, and called laziness, was not the result of annuity payments "given" by the government as the commissioner described them. It was caused by the restrictions of reservation life and removal of means for attaining the status of a successful man in the traditional and most culturally valued ways.

In a few years, the idea of working for annuity payments became established and was described by former Superintendent Barclay White, who was no longer in active government service, after a visit to the Pawnee Agency in 1877.

> The agent held a council this morning with all the leading men of the tribe, and notified them, that the able bodied men must perform labor for their share of the cash annuities before receiving them. This new rule and order is in accordance with a recent law of Congress enacted to encourage industry in the tribe.[*]
>
> Being compulsory industry for money which is properly their due for payment of interest on government bonds, placed to their

[*] Indian Appropriations Act of March 3, 1875. U.S. Statutes at Large, vol. 18, Sec. 3, p. 449.

credit as a consideration for lands under treaty stipulations, the law is not honest or just, even if intended for a good purpose, and is a measure very difficult for the Indian to understand or appreciate, and for the Agent to carry out in practice without distrust and general unpopularity.[38]

In summary, annuity payments to the Pawnee and other American Indian tribes resulted from their signing treaties with the United States, in which they ceded their lands. From the beginning, the government was able to control the use of the annuity to a large extent. The agent could approve or disapprove of goods wanted by the Indians or the methods of distribution of cash and goods. Withholding the annuity was provided for in some treaty articles in order to control behavior deemed unsuitable in relation to others and to the accomplishment of acculturation programs in force in the nineteenth century.

After the Pawnees received annuity payments, there were many changes in the way they acquired what they needed to feed and clothe themselves. Since hunting was curtailed and animal hides were not available in sufficient quantities, they found it necessary to purchase certain articles such as shirts, calico, blankets, and canvas for tipis. Also, food items such as flour, sugar, coffee, and beef had to be purchased. Many items were new to their cultural inventory, and others, such as guns and ammunition, were necessary to compete with other tribes in hunting and warfare. The Quakers who came to the Pawnee Agency after 1869 frowned upon firearms and discouraged use of annuity money for their purchase in spite of the desperate Pawnee need for the means to defend their people from ongoing Sioux attacks.

A large amount of Pawnee annuity funds in the 1870s was channeled into the schools and agricultural "civilization" programs. Seeds, new types of farm implements, and wages to teach a few Pawnee men new skills were paid from the annuity after the treaty period during which the government had agreed to pay for such expenditures. At times, the agent in some way convinced the Pawnee chiefs to agree to spend two-thirds of the annuity for such items. This was done even in the face of the continual hunger that haunted the tribe. So convinced were the Quakers that new farming methods and life on dispersed farmsteads would

"civilize" and save the tribe that they ignored other circumstances, such as hunger, loss of incentive, depredation and murder by enemy tribes. These factors made such use of annuity
money senseless and costly.

With the annuity came loss of choice. The Pawnee learned to
bargain with the purveyor, not over price of goods, but over what
goods they could have and how they were to be distributed and
divided. The annuity payment was anticipated long before it arrived, because for many persons that was the only time when
needed supplies could be obtained.* For the chiefs and leading
men, the small amount of money paid them could be used to try
to maintain status while also attempting to pay off debts with the
trader.

Pawnee leadership patterns changed as a result of the chiefs'
relations with the U.S. representatives in authority. From an assumption of equality, as first maintained in treaty negotiations,
they were forced to assume a polite obsequiousness, which became covert hostility. This attitude was punctuated with strong
but usually futile arguments with governmental authority figures,
as the chiefs' position as leaders of tribal affairs was threatened
and gradually eroded.

Such statements as "we want to be like white men" were made
by a few, perhaps sincerely but more likely facetiously, to please
the agent or superintendent or the visiting Society of Friends
committees. The Pawnee leaders had hopes of gaining approval
and obtaining what was needed to sustain their people. Annuity payments that began as inducements to treaty signing often
ended by demeaning a proud people who were forced to learn to
stand in line at a payment table.

---

* Interest in the annual annuity payment continues. The following comment
in "Pawnee Village News," a column containing news of Pawnee activities by
Beatrice Eppler, appeared in the *Pawnee Chief*, the local newspaper, on January
25, 1990. It said, "Right now the tribe has been wondering and asking, 'When's
Annuity?'" The payment usually averages less than twenty dollars per capita.

†††
8
Our Mother the Earth

Loss of a Country

Yonder they are coming,
Although strange misfortunes have befallen me
Yet it is mine this country wide.
                                      —Pawnee song

From the beginning, one purpose of New World colonization and settlement was acquisition of land for establishment of town-sites, ports, roads, farms, and later railroads. Individuals who had no land of their own in the Old World, or who had owned land, wanted to possess it on the American continent. This and other motivations and subsequent actions came at the expense of the original users and owners, the Native Americans, or Indians. Treaties of friendship, followed closely by requests for purchase and cession of Indian land, began in the seventeenth century. The land coveted extended from the Atlantic Coast to the Pacific Ocean.

Acquisition of a continent was not made without coercion and military force, used when necessary as one tribe after another resisted the westward push of the strangers into their homelands. At the end of the nineteenth century, very few Indian tribes remained on their aboriginal lands with access to their villages, hunting grounds, cemeteries, and sacred places.

Treaties were initiated by the United States to espouse peace and friendship and to make U.S. and tribal government relationships possible and legal. The Pawnee relationship with the United

States followed this path. The first treaties began on June 18, 1818, with the "chiefs and warriors of the Grand Pawnee [Chaui] tribe," with the "chiefs and warriors of the Pitavirate Noisy Pawnee [Pitahawirata] tribe" on June 19, with "the chiefs and warriors of the Pawnee Republic [Kitkahahki] on June 20, and with the "chiefs and warriors of the Pawnee Marhar [Skidi] tribe" on June 22.[1]

Thereafter, as the pattern emerged, treaty commissioners would appear with requests for land cessions. The next U.S.-Pawnee contact culminated in the treaty of October 9, 1833, with the four confederated Pawnee bands, as they were called. In this agreement, 7,060,694 acres south of the Platte River were relinquished. The amount paid for this sizable amount of land was $4,600 in goods annually for twelve years. Items such as farming tools and instruction were also promised.[2]

On August 6, 1848, Lt. Col. Ludwell E. Powell met with the chiefs of the four bands and gained their consent to cede 110,419 acres north of the Platte River near Grand Island.[3] The treaty was signed at Fort Childs, soon to be renamed Fort Kearny. The pioneer movement toward the Northwest had begun, and this post stood near the Oregon Trail, a wide dusty gouge through Pawnee country along the Platte.[4] The military post was deemed an important site for protecting the settlers moving slowly westward, and thus the United States' effort to acquire the Indian land that surrounded it. For this relinquishment, the tribe was promised $2,000 in goods.

A decade later, on September 24, 1857, the bulk of the remaining Pawnee lands, 14,722,560 acres north of the Platte River, were ceded for $40,000 per annum to be paid for five years, then $30,000 annually with the President's assent.[5] What was left of the Pawnee territory, which once covered much of present-day Kansas and Nebraska, was 285,440 acres designated as a reservation in what is now called Nance County, Nebraska. Then, not unexpectedly, this remaining bit of land became a target for settlers' and speculators' greed, as the surge for removal of all Indians from Kansas and Nebraska began in the 1860s and continued into the next decade.

A sale of part of their reservation was proposed in an April 3, 1871, council meeting. The agent began by discussing the possi-

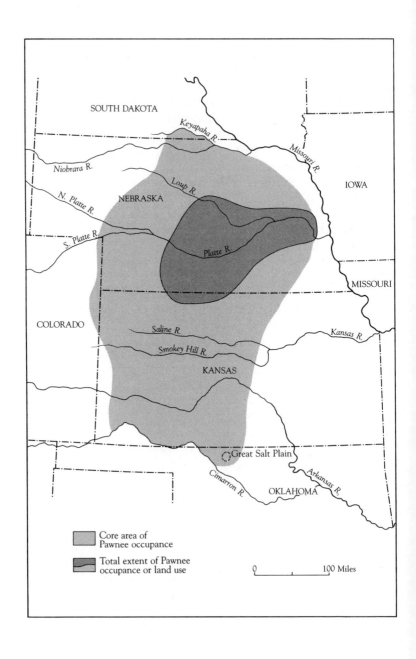

SOUTH DAKOTA

Keyapaha R.

Niobrara R.

Missouri R.

IOWA

N. Platte R.

Loup R.

NEBRASKA

S. Platte R.

Platte R.

COLORADO

MISSOURI

Saline R.

Kansas R.

Smokey Hill R.

KANSAS

Great Salt Plain

Cimarron R.

OKLAHOMA

Arkansas R.

Core area of
Pawnee occupance

Total extent of Pawnee
occupance or land use

0   100 Miles

bility of individual families living on farms or allotments as provided for in their 1857 treaty. He added that to meet the expenses of surveying the land and building houses, it would be
necessary to use some of the annuity money. Then, obliquely, he
said if the Pawnees would rather, they could sell some of their
land to pay for these expenses. There was a discussion about this,
and Sky Chief is reported to have said that they wanted to sell
their land near the railroad and not in the vicinity of the river.
Other chiefs agreed with him. * 6

By October 1871, surveyors were in the field to determine the
reservation boundary lines. A telegram dated October 10 from
Silver Creek Station, a town on the railroad near the southeast
corner of the reservation, noted that a prairie fire had burned all
the stakes in place and it would be necessary to survey again to
find the corners.7 In a council called on November 15, the sale of
land was brought up again by the agent. Sky Chief informed
him, "We said we wanted to sell land south of the Platte river."
Eagle Chief said that he was anxious to sell on the other side of
the river. Others declared their agreement to sell, and Pitaresaru
said to sell the land south of the Platte.8 This land south of the
Platte was part of Cession 191, ceded by the tribe in 1833.

Did the chiefs believe that this, instead of the land south of
the Loup, which was part of the reservation, was still theirs to
sell? It is certain that the agent did not mean the land south of
the Platte but the land located south of the Loup. The Loup
River emptied into the Platte from the north. The chiefs may
not have understood or have had fully explained to them that the
1833 cession removed the land south of the Platte from their
control and ownership. It is known that some bands continued
to live in villages south of the Platte for many years on the ceded
lands, until their reservation was created north of the Loup
River. The tribe wanted the reservation to be south of the Platte
because that was a traditional place of residence for the three
south bands. Also, Sioux enmity had increased, and living south
of the Platte gave some defensive advantage. Their request to

---

* Unless the chiefs had been asked to think about this before council, it
seems unlikely that a decision of this importance would have been made so
readily without extended discussion among themselves beforehand.

live there was not granted because in the 1857 treaty there was a stipulation that the tribe must move north of the Platte onto the new reservation within a year. Movement into new villages there began in 1859.[9]

From the government's point of view, a reservation located south of the Platte would have placed the Pawnees directly in the path of westward-bound settlers and of a railroad line that was planned to be built along the river. However, in 1871, it seems there must have been a tribal misconception about Pawnee rights in the land south of the Platte, since the chiefs indicated they wanted it sold and desired to keep the reservation timber land on the north side.[10]

News and rumor traveled fast, and in the spring of 1872, the agent received queries from outsiders about the sale of Pawnee land. He replied that a bill authorizing the sale of some 50,000 acres south of the Loup was in Congress but stated, "I do not know if it has passed."[11]

On June 10, 1872, in "An Act for the Relief of Certain Tribes in the Northern Superintendency" Congress approved the survey, appraisement, and land sale designated above.[12] After the conclusion of these former two actions, the secretary of the Interior would authorize public sale and the proceeds would be placed in the U.S. Treasury to bear interest of 5 percent payable semiannually, "except if a portion shall be deemed necessary to be used for Pawnee immediate use."[13] Since tribal approval of this Act had to be gained, this phrase was added as an enticement for the needy Pawnees.

The Pawnees were not the only ones who were to obtain "relief" by being relieved of their land. In this same Act, the Omahas were urged to permit sale of 50,000 acres; the Otoes and Missourias, who did not assent to the Act, 80,000 acres; and the Sac and Fox of the Missouri, 16,000 acres from their very small holdings in southeast Nebraska.[14] This attempt to take so much land simultaneously from Nebraska tribes resulted largely from pressure exerted over the years by state officials and the public, eager for land.

A committee of Friends visited the Pawnee Agency about this time. In councils with the chiefs and leading men on June 11 and 14, no mention was made of the land sale, or at least it was not recorded in the minutes. However, much advice was given on sending children to school and learning proper farming methods. The chiefs, although gracious in their responses, replied that the people were hungry and that the amount of the annuity was not correct.[15]

Unaware of the land sale bill's passage, the tribe left on their hunt in early July. As the Act stipulated, it was necessary that their consent to the sale be obtained, so Agent Jacob Troth set off to overtake them at Grand Island.[16] It is not known whether the Pawnees knew at the time that the land to be sold was part of their reservation, or whether they still thought the land to be sold was south of the Platte.

On July 15, 1872, Troth and the chiefs met, and after the explanation of the Act's provisions, the chiefs expressed dissatisfaction with the deposition of the land sale proceeds. They argued that they agreed to sell land so that certain purchases could be made and improvements accomplished as soon as possible. They were led to believe, they said, that these purchases would be made when the agent had touted the land sale in the November council. They did not want the money spent in the East but wanted it kept here and spent here.[17] They remembered that money collected for timber thefts had been deposited in the treasury in the East, and they had not been able to claim it or use it as needed.

It must have been obvious now to the Pawnees that any of their funds from any source were under the control of the government and not theirs, except in an attenuated sense. Troth explained what the money was to be used for, according to the congressional Act, and that the money was to draw interest until it was used. He said Congress believed that money would be expended to better advantage for them in four years rather than one or two.[18]

The Pawnees were frustrated that their agreement to sell land was not to bring soon the funds that were needed urgently, which the agent had earlier said would be available. One could ask if, in order to expedite their consent to sell, he neglected to inform them earlier that their money would go to the treasury in Washington, where it would be relinquished by Congress at the time and in the amounts decided by it and other decision makers there.

The agent then told the Pawnees that the land could not be sold unless they would agree to the Act as it had been passed by Congress. Overdue on their start for the hunting grounds, the Pawnees gave in and signed the following statement on July 15, 1872, which was to be sent to Supt. Barclay White, then to Indian Com. F. A. Walker:

An Act for the relief of certain tribes of Indians in the Northern Superintendancy [sic] No. 129 was submitted to the Pawnee Tribe in open council and read and explained to them. When it was resolved by them viz., Resolved, That the Secretary of the Interior be authorized and requested to sell our lands as provided in the bill No. 129 and although we prefer to expend our money in one or two years, we consent to one fourth of the proceeds of such sale being expended each year for four years.

Signed by the Chiefs in open council at Grand Island, 7 mo. 15th 1872.[19]

On October 9, 1872, contract was let for the survey of the 50,000 acres south of the Loup Fork. The land was to be surveyed and subdivided into tracts. The surveyors were A. V. and William A. Richards of Nebraska.[20] They went about their business, and on December 14, another contract was signed by them whose purpose was to "Reestablish the Out Boundaries of the Pawnee Reservation." Supposedly this came about because settlers on the boundaries were in disagreement with the previous survey boundary locations. As the survey proceeded, the Indian commissioner appointed George H. Thummell, an attorney at Grand Island, and Warren Green to be appraisers. The Pawnees were to select the third commissioner, and they chose their agent, Jacob Troth.[21]

In doing their work, the surveyors found a discrepancy. After carefully checking their points and distances, they informed Supt. Barclay White that the reservation was not thirty miles long as stipulated by treaty, but only twenty-nine and one-half miles long. By calculation, it was discovered that the Pawnees had not received the 4,800 acres they were entitled to have.

Superintendent White informed the commissioner that the land in question was already settled and very fertile. As if to dispose of the matter quietly, he said the Pawnees already had an excess of land, and "there appears to be no occasion for interfering with the settlement." He suggested that a reasonable amount of money be paid the tribe and that it be "expended only in such a manner as will advance the tribe in civilization."[22]

Yet, by 1875, the tribe had not yet been compensated according to the Estimate of Funds, Third Quarter, of that year, in which is found the statement, "To indemnify the Pawnee Indians for 4,800 acres. . . ." The amount was to be expended for payment of Indian labor on the agency farm and for general beneficial purposes in establishing the Indians on a new reservation.[23]

By November 7, 1873, the appraisers' work was completed; the data entered in the journal; and that and other reports forwarded by Thummell to the Indian commissioner, along with a list of expenses.[24] A year later, no sale of the land had been authorized, and in council, on October 8, 1874, the chiefs requested that as soon as possible action be taken to sell their present reservation, which was not part of the approximately 50,000 acres recently surveyed and appraised.[25] In addition to this, the Pawnees insisted that they be paid for the 4,800 acres. The commissioner said the price of $1.25 per acre was fair and that Congress should consider appropriating money for it.[26] In the 1875 agency estimate of funds needed, the sum of $6,000 was requested.

During the year of 1875, the Pawnees' major concern was their continuing deprivation and also the problems of removal and separation of the tribe on three reservations. A major focus of the Nebraska legislature was to pressure for removal of the Pawnees and the Otoes, and also to attempt to extinguish the tribal land titles. On February 19, 1875, the legislature urgently appealed to Congress to act upon their request.[27]

Although permission had been granted in 1874 by the Pawnee chiefs for the sale of the Nebraska reservation and legislation was proposed to do this, Congress took no action during the session ending in March 1875.[28] But Nebraska state officials were satisfied to hear that on April 10, 1876, "An Act to Authorize the Sale of the Pawnee Reservation" passed in Congress. It repealed the Act of June 10, 1872, authorizing the sale of the 48,424 acres, adding that land to the acres of the remaining reservation land. The total of 224,775 reservation acres would be appraised in 160-acre tracts and sold in no larger amounts.

The improvements on any of the lands were to be appraised separately. When this was completed, a public sale was to be advertised for three months in one newspaper in each of the cities of Chicago, New York, Washington, Saint Louis, and Omaha and Columbus in Nebraska. The land was to be auctioned at appropriate places near the reservation. None was to be sold for less than the appraised value of $2.50 an acre. Payment was to be made one-third cash in hand, with two equal remaining payments to be made later.[29]

Section 2 of the Act stated that $300,000 was to be appropriated before the sale. No more than $150,000 was to be used to pay for expenses already incurred. The balance was to be used first to pay for expenses connected with the appraisement and sale of the Pawnee reservation. Second, it would go for subsistence and immediate needs of the Pawnees until they became self-sustaining in their new Indian Territory reservation. Third, it would be used for purchasing the items needed to continue the "civilization programs," such as agricultural implements, livestock, schools, and other such expenses, through June 30, 1876.

All expenses for sale of the Nebraska land, subsistence of the people, and purchase of their new reservation were to be repaid to the United States by the Pawnees from proceeds of sale of their Nebraska lands. If there were any surplus funds left, then the money would be deposited to the credit of the Pawnees in the U.S. Treasury.[30]

The seventh section of the act established the boundaries of the Pawnee reservation in Indian Territory between the forks of the Arkansas and Cimarron rivers. This land had been ceded to the United States by the Cherokee and Creek tribes in treaties on July 19, 1866, and on June 14, 1866. The acreages from each of them were given as 230,014 from the former and 53,006 from the latter—a total of 283,020.[31] (See chap. 9 for a description of the negotiations between Agent William Burgess and the Cherokee leaders.)

The last section of the Act provided for 160-acre allotments for those Pawnees who would care to take them. No mention was

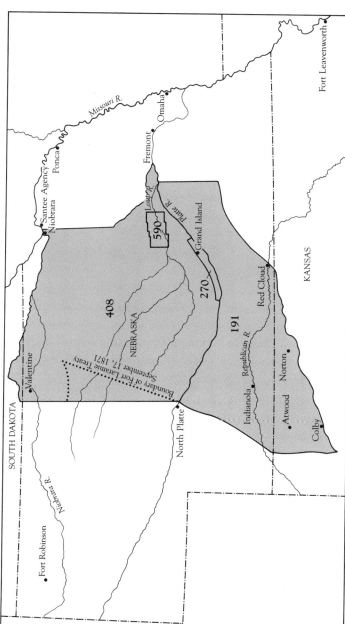

Source: Charles C. Royce, Comp. Indian Land Cessions in the United States, Bureau of American Ethnology, 18th Annual Report, Part 2, 1899.

made of the surplus land that eventually would result if all Pawnees decided to participate in the allotment program.*

In Nebraska, the years following 1876 were economically difficult, and few farmers could raise the one-third cash payment required for Pawnee land purchase. Much of the land was sold to speculators for $2.50 an acre. The first auction sale was on July 15–16, 1878, at Central City, Nebraska. There were few purchasers. The highest bid was $6.00 an acre, and 5,983 acres were sold. After this event, applicants went to the U.S. Land Office at Grand Island and paid no less than $2.50 an acre. Between 1878 and 1884, 156,638 acres of the 278,837.20 listed acres of reservation were sold to eighty-four individuals. Speculators who had means to purchase 1,000 acres or more each acquired a total of 138,761 acres. This left 120,194.2 acres available for settlers, who bought less than 640 acres.

The cry for land for pioneers' settlement had been raised prior to Pawnee land relinquishment, but in the end the speculator gained the bulk of it and later sold it for between $10 and $100 an acre. By 1910, the total Nebraska acres sold were 287,462.56 for a total of $779,586.81.[32]

The 23,512,343 total acres in Table 5 can only be an estimate. The amount of Pawnee and other tribal land holding claims is uncertain because of overlapping claims and cessions made by other adjacent tribes, such as the Omaha, Otoe and Missouri, Kansa, and various Dakota bands.

Bearing on this point, archaeological evidence indicates a long-time Pawnee residence in a great portion of Nebraska. Some other tribes were more recent inhabitants displaced from cessions of their lands in other regions or migrations of warring tribes into their territory. The Fort Laramie Treaty of September 17, 1851, between the United States and the Sioux, Northern Cheyennes, Arapahoes, and other tribes, set the boundary in Nebraska between the Pawnees and Sioux without the Pawnees being present

---

*Even at this time, the possibility that this would not be a voluntary but rather a compulsory action grew as the idea of universal allotment of individual farms to tribal members gathered favor across the United States. When allotment in severalty became an Act of Congress in the next decade and was later implemented, millions of acres of reservation land not allotted were taken and purchased by the United States, and the Indian land base diminished once again.

Table 5
Pawnee Land Losses in Acres, 1833–93 *

	Treaties			Allotment Agreement	Total
1833	1848	1857	1876	1893	
13,074,000	110,419	9,878,000	278,837.2	171,088 (surplus)	23,512,343

* The figures are those given in Pawnee Docket 10, The Pawnee Indian Tribe of Oklahoma vs. United States. Indian Claims Commission, Findings (July 14, 1950; June 17, 1957; June 14, 1960; January 31, 1961). The 1893 surplus acres were Pawnee Indian Territory reservation lands remaining after allotment. They were later opened and sold for settlement.

or being consulted. The land east of the treaty boundary line drawn across Nebraska was considered by the treaty parties present to be Pawnee land, and land west to be Siouan. But at one time the Pawnees claimed their range to be as far west as Devils Tower in Wyoming. It was said, "When the warriors came this far they knew that other tribes' lands lay beyond." [33] Thus, tribal claims and U.S. government description of specific tribal land possessions could differ and result in inaccurate title.

Like other Native American inhabitants of the United States, the Pawnees lost their village sites, crop fields, hunting lands, sacred places, and the graves of their ancestors. For the Pawnee people, this systematic land taking by treaty by the United States occurred in a sixty-year period between 1833 and 1893. Only a small fraction of Mother Earth could be called their own after allotment in Indian Territory in the latter year. Later, as the years passed, the majority of Pawnee allotments in Oklahoma were sold for various reasons, mostly economic. Only in tribal memory could the words of a song sung by Wichita Blaine be true,

> Yonder they are coming
> Although strange misfortunes have befallen me,
> Yet it is mine, this country wide. [34]

9
The Last Days

Pawnee Removal from Nebraska

Full history of the plot to eject the Pawnees from their home may never be recorded, for there are few men alive who know the facts. If it should be written there would be disclosed a carefully planned and successfully carried out conspiracy to rob this people of their lands.
　　　　　—George B. Grinnell in Pawnee Hero Stories

Whenever the whole tribe gets tired and wants to go away we will ask the authorities to help them.
　　　　　—Barclay White to the Pawnee chiefs, October 18, 1873

I do not want to leave this place, God gave us these lands.
　　　　　—Terrecowah, Pawnee chief to Barclay White, October 18, 1873

The idea of moving the Pawnees and other tribes away from Nebraska was an old one. As early as 1849, Com. of Indian Affairs Orlando Brown suggested that smaller frontier tribes, such as the Sac and Foxes, Otoes, Missourias, Poncas and Omahas, and if "possible the Pawnees would be moved down among the tribes of our southern colony."[1] He was referring to the region called Indian Territory, recently occupied by the Five Civilized Tribes removed from the East, including the Cherokees, Creeks, and others. It was realized that settlement of regions beyond the Mississippi and Missouri rivers was difficult as long as tribes such as the Pawnees resided and claimed lands there.

However, the Civil War put aside such plans. After it was over, the Five Civilized Tribes were forced to make amends for some tribal factions' support of the Confederacy. Treaties instigated by the United States forced them to relinquish western lands assigned to them in former treaties. In those agreements they had given up homelands in the East that had been wanted by state and federal governments for settlement and exploitation by their own citizens. Now the government wanted them to give up more land in Indian Territory for eventual settlement of other tribes from other parts of the country who were in the way of western expansion by settlers, railroads, and other interests.

In the 1870s, the idea for removal of the Nebraska tribes surfaced again. Com. J. Q. Smith believed that reservations should be consolidated in Indian Territory lying south of Kansas and in several other major areas. He confessed that Indian sentiment was opposed to such removal, but he recalled there had been obstacles to overcome among the tribes who had come from the East but, he claimed, were now thriving in Indian Territory. "With a fair amount of persistence, the removal thither of others can also be secured," he argued.[2]

Among the Pawnees there were opposing opinions about leaving their homeland. For years the Pawnees had visited the Wichitas after the winter hunt, if both agents approved and the stay was not too long. Some tribal members had attempted to stay and live among their friends.* But there was official ambivalence about such visits, sometimes seen as being detrimental to the efforts to "civilize" the tribes. After an unauthorized visit of 485 tribesmen to the Wichitas, Supt. Barclay White, in council on October 18, 1873, harangued the chiefs for allowing this visit and threatened to remove them from office if they could not control their bands.

In order to indicate that this group did not represent the views of the entire tribe, the old Pitahawirata chief, Terrecowah, arose and said, "I do not want to leave this place. God gave us these lands." Lone Chief, who the missionary John Dunbar said was opposed to removal to Indian Territory, "as were all well-informed men of the tribe," said, "I have made up my mind to stay here on my land. I am not going where I have nothing." Of opposing view, Good Chief, of the Kitkahahki Band, said his people had made up their minds to go south and live.

---

* In March 1873, a Pawnee tribal faction took advantage of their annual visit to the Wichitas to visit the Kiowa camp of Kicking Bird on Cache Creek on the nearby Kiowa reservation. Their purpose was to make peace with former enemies in the event that they should come to live permanently near their friends, the Wichitas. The council was successful, and the hosts gave horses to the Pawnees, who in turn put blankets and shawls on the Kiowas' shoulders. (Mooney, *Calendar History of the Kiowa Indians*, pp. 333–35).

Sky Chief, Terrecowah (Arusa wetarurekahwah ahu, Brings Horses Out to Show from His Herds Near the Village), and Curly Chief (center), prominent Pawnee chiefs in Nebraska. Sky Chief died in 1873, killed by the Sioux. The others made the trek from Nebraska to a new reservation in Indian Territory. Courtesy Smithsonian Institution, Bureau of Ethnology.

After hearing other voices, White said, "Whenever the whole Pawnee tribe gets tired and want to go away we will ask the authorities to help them."[3] This statement seems to indicate that the idea of removing the Pawnees was well established as an action to be undertaken at some date. Maj. Frank J. North, who seemed to have had first-hand information, mentioned the requests of Big Spotted Horse and Frank White to take their families and permanently remove from the tribe. North said that the chiefs arose one by one and denounced as frauds these two warriors and claimed they were trying to deceive the people. The chiefs, North claimed, were bitterly opposed to the move, but the people now showed enthusiasm, "although there was not an acknowledge chief in favor of it."[4] After the October 8 council, the tribal leaders spent much time discussing the problems facing their tribe by weighing the arguments for and against staying or removing to Indian Territory. In the November 15, 1873, council with the agent, Pitaresaru and several other chiefs and soldiers requested permission to go to Washington and talk to the President about going south to live. They said they were willing to pay their own expenses. The agent agreed to relay their request.[5] It would seem there was little chance that it would be honored and an invitation was never received. The wording in the council minutes does not indicate that the chiefs intended to request removal, but implies that the tribal leaders wanted to discuss their general situation, including tribal hunger, the continuing Sioux attacks, and other serious concerns. Significantly, even before the council meeting, the commissioner of Indian Affairs had written on November 7 to Wichita Agent Jonathan Richards, seeking his opinion about the removal of the Pawnee tribe to the Wichita Agency.

Another letter on the same subject was written on November 29.[6] After receiving these communications, Richards called a council of the chiefs and headmen of the tribes at the agency: the Wichitas, Delawares, Caddoes, Ionies, and Wacos. He wanted to go through the formality of obtaining their consent for the placement of the Pawnees at the agency. After deliberating, the leaders, including Black Beaver, the Delaware, agreed that the Pawnees should be allowed to live at this agency, if they so desired. But there would be certain conditions that they must agree to before final approval could be given. They would live in an area set apart from the others so that there would be no conflict or interference with the affairs of those peoples already residing there. They would continue to follow the road toward "civilization" by farming, stock raising, and other such labors. Their children would be enrolled in school. (One hears the words of the government rather than those of the Indians present.) They would also agree to transfer all property belonging to them, or the income thereof, such as annuities, to be used in the support of the Wichita Agency schools, "or those to be established for the Wichitas and Affiliated Bands, including the Pawnees, and such general use for the benefit of these united bands, as may be desirable."[7]

Permission was granted, and in January 1874, twenty-seven lodges of Pawnees, about three hundred people, arrived at the agency and their leaders went before the chiefs of the above tribes and requested that they be allowed to make their homes among them. It was decided to grant their request and to ask that they be provided for in the same manner as were the tribes already in residence.[8] Although the Pawnees had not been informed at this time, in late 1873 and early 1874, it was already planned that all of their people should leave Nebraska and that more of them would be sent to stay at the Wichita Agency.

The winter months of 1874 in Nebraska were cruel. The hunt was unsuccessful, and hunger visited each lodge in turn. Uncle, the Wind, blew through the Pawnees' worn clothing, and visitors to the villages remarked that children were seen outside naked in the cold. The expected Sioux raids were the heated subject of discussion in the councils, where the chiefs asked for the protection they always claimed was due them according to their memories and understanding of treaty agreements. Their demand for guns went unanswered, except for the agent's remark that, if they wanted guns, they would have to buy them with their own money.[9]

To White, Agent William Burgess indicated concern, but it mostly centered on the deleterious effect tribal fears and unrest had on the "civilization" program's advancement and continuance. "It is next to impossible to crowd out of their minds [these concerns] and for them to have aspirations for a higher life and a better mode of living," he commented. In the February 16 council, he told the chiefs that some changes were to come, but he was indefinite as to their nature. In making such radical changes, he told White, he expected opposition from the Pawnees, and said that he wished "to be sustained from headquarters in all changes and orders which may be considered peremptory."[10]

On March 18, 1874, the chiefs signed a resolution framed by the agent that stated they would allow $10,000 of their annuity to be used for seed, livestock, wagons, the repair of sheds, and the breaking of five hundred acres of prairie sod, as well as the payment for the use of Indian teams and labor. Considering that there were strong possibilities that the government had serious plans for the removal of the tribe, this request seems unusual.[11] Why break five hundred acres for planting in the coming year of 1875 if no tribesmen were to be there?

By late spring, the agent reported that many tribesmen were much discouraged and that they had "turned their backs on improvement and progress."[12] Unbeknownst to the agent, the chiefs turned their backs on him; and with the encouragement of Lester Platt, the local trader, dictated an appeal to the commissioner of Indian Affairs on May 20, stating a need to visit him and requesting that steps be taken to sell their Nebraska reservation and initiate the search for land in Indian Territory for a new home. Platt had come to the reservation in 1844, and now felt animosity toward the Quakers for discharging his wife from her long-held teaching position. The letter to the commisioner said:

> Peter resara says, "Tell our Great Father [the President] that we want to go and see him very much, that we may arrange with him to dispose of this land which is surrounded by whites and get other land south."
>
> Terrecowah who has been chief over 30 years says, "Tell our Great Father that I agree with Peter Leshuro, head chief of the Pawnees and all of the chiefs, that we must go and see our Great Father face to face that we may talk straight and understand each other and try and improve our condition. The agent does not want us to go. He talks a plenty, but does nothing—we are poor and in a sad condition and the agent is afraid to have our wants

made known and forbids our going to Washington lest we talk of his misusing our money."

Then comes a statement evidently added or suggested by the trader to enhance his position.

Tell our Great Father that we have full confidence in you [Platt]; that you understand our wants having been with us 30 years, and have been acquainted with all of our Great Chiefs that are laid low, and you and Terrekowah stand as the Representatives of the past.

An Indian Sitting [sic] by Says [sic]: "The fact that the Government changes Agents so often is because they have no confidence in them their agents."

Nesharu Turaha [Good Chief] Head chief of the Kithahas, says: "It is good that I hear now that you are going to see our great Father and tell him of our great wish to see him. . . . [B]ut we are all of one mind to see our Great Father and arrange to dispose of this land which is surrounded by whites and go where we can get a living." Others reinforced these thoughts and said that eight of the chiefs want to go to Washington, "and we are very urgent in this matter."[13]

A change in opinion in leaving Nebraska is made quite clear in this message, and one wonders how much of the document was Platt's contriving for purposes of self-interest. The chiefs involved had no way of reading what was written or sent in its final form; and most sources, other than government records, indicate that Pitaresaru seems to have strongly resisted removal. Good Chief, on the other hand, seems to have been a strong advocate of living with the Wichitas.

Lester Platt had his own motivations in playing an unofficial role in this advocacy. It is difficult to know how close he was to the Pawnee chiefs at this time. He had made a bad beginning in 1844, when he came to the agency hoping to be appointed a teacher. His brother-in-law was already an agency farmer. He did not get the job and seems to have stayed around. He soon became an object of dislike by the Pawnees for his acts of violence against them; in one cited case, for example, he hit a man with a coal shovel. In a tribal meeting in October of that year, a

Pitahawirata chief and others complained bitterly of Platt's whipping tribesmen. They asked that he and other violent employees be removed. The agent rejected the chiefs' request, according to the Presbyterian missionaries who became the objects of agency and employee dislike for their criticism of such behavior.[14] In 1846, Platt was appointed a teacher, which drew a comment from Reverend Timothy E. Ranney that the Pawnees had less confidence in him than any other white man. The year before, Platt was a trader, "not by government, but by his own account. He is very obnoxious to Pawnees, so much that they have threatened to take his life."[15] Although time may have softened his views and behavior and brought about some degree of acceptance by the Pawnees, his advising the chiefs to send such a letter to Washington seems to have resulted less from concern for Pawnee welfare than from self-interest that would become more apparent in months to come.

In 1873, a majority of the chiefs had declared that they did not want to remove from their homeland. All evidence seems to point to an obdurate stand on the matter. However, increasing hunger and starvation had been a part of the Pawnees' lives since then, and desperation may have led to opinion changes by some. In the summer of 1874, they had been told that they could not go on a hunt. So during a visit of representatives of the Board of Indian Commissioners, the chiefs requested that the board intercede with the authorities to see if permission could be gained to hunt, so badly did they need food.[16]

In August, the Kitkahahki Band requested permission to go south toward the Wichitas. The agent refused permission, explaining that the conditions in that part of the country were unsettled, and it would be unsafe. In the spring and summer of that year, Comanche and then Cheyenne and Kiowa resentment of government policies and treatment had increased, with resulting hostility at the Wichita Agency and raids across the Red River into Texas. To warn the Pawnees in case any had thoughts of leaving without permission, the agent said that force would be used to return any persons who should decide to go on their own. Some time before this, Good Chief had been given a pass to take Comanche Wife to visit her people, but instead of a few men, he had allowed a large group to accompany him, and the agent reminded him of this transgression.[17] During this same meeting, a resolution, proposed by the agent and signed by the chiefs, stated that all funds for "teachers, millers, tinners or other mechanics" whose services could be dispensed with, should be spent instead on food and other necessary articles of comfort for the tribe." While this measure may have been derived from necessity to gain funds to feed the hungry people, it also may have been part of a plan to end the employment of those who could not be employed at a new agency where there would be few facilities in its early months of operation. It will be recalled that earlier in the year, the chiefs had signed a resolution asking that $10,000 be set aside for breaking five hundred acres of land and for other agricultural items. There seem to be contradictions between the two requests; one indicates a possible closing down of the agency, and the other an expansion of the "civilization" program by converting more acres to farmland for future use.

Sometime after this unsatisfactory council, the Pawnee chiefs circumvented the agent and superintendent and sent another petition, dated August 21, to the commissioner of Indian Affairs. This time the letter writer was B. F. Spooner. According to John Williamson, an agency employee at the time, Spooner had arrived in 1872 and was a quarter-blood Sac and Fox. Williamson considered him very intelligent and well-educated. Spooner soon became a "waiter" for one of the chiefs. This was a traditional method of gaining acceptance. He took care of the chief's horses, did other errands, and lived among the Pawnees as one of them. In less than two years, he could speak the language well enough and became a confidant and adviser to the chiefs. When Big Spotted Horse had returned from his visit to the Wichitas with their invitation to come and live with them, Williamson said that Spooner advised them not to tell the agent about this. Spooner also told them that the reason the agent did not want them to move to Indian Territory was that the agency employees would lose their jobs. At least, Williamson thought Spooner had told the chiefs this.[18]

In August, chiefs of the Kitkahahki and one Pitahawirata, Fighting Bear, sent a message to the commissioner of Indian Affairs, with Spooner penning their requests. This would seem to indicate that the other chiefs were not asked to be present, or did not concur with the requests that are stated therein, or perhaps, did not think it wise to be involved in this unofficial effort.

Pawnee Village, Platte Co., Nebraska
Aug. 21, 1874

Hon. Commissioner of Indian Affairs,

I herewith present the petition of the Kitkahhars Chiefs and of Fighting Bear head soldier of Petowhowerat Band * of the Pawnee Indians praying that you permit them to make a visit to the Indian Territory for the purpose of selecting land upon which their tribe might settle in case they could get permission from Congress to remove. I would state that they have recieved [sic] invitations from a joint meeting of several of the more civilized tribes of that territory asking them to remove. The large majority of the tribe have been asking for a removal for a year at least, but the Agent and superintendant [sic] are determined that they shall not be heard at Washington and refuse to give them a proper hearing upon this subject. Having been thwarted in all endeavor to get a hearing at Washington they tell the Agent that they are going. Not comprehending that an Indian has no right to travel on a journey for the benefit of his tribe which might hurt the feelings of the Hicksite Quakers from Penn. to Neb. and cause joy to the Orthodox Quakers of the South, they are determined to go on their mission of Peace and benefit to their tribe. Please consider their petition as coming from men well disposed and I am assured you will not be biased by the interests of eclesastical cliques [sic].†

The permit would ensure them safety while I know they are bound to go, and they say to the threatening of their Agent that if their Great Father sends his soldiers to kill them or drive them back they are ready and willing to die in defence of their enterprise. . . . Knowing their leader to be a man of great spirit and daring, while at the same time the most consistent friend of the

---

* Capt. Luther North called Fighting Bear, a Pawnee Scout, a Pitahawirata chief in his references to him. (Danker, *Man of the Plains*, pp. 47, 139.)

† Somewhere Spooner had acquired the notion that rivalry existed between branches of the Society of Friends concerning the Indian agencies under their care. He seems to assume that the Hicksite-controlled Northern Superintendency did not want any tribes under its jurisdiction to remove and be under the Orthodox Quakers, who controlled the agencies of the Central Superintendency in Indian Territory.

whiteman, I make this appeal on their behalf trusting that you will interpose your power for the protection of the Indian.

I, the writer, can talk Pawnee some and understand it wholly, was formerly interpreter for the Chippeways of Swan Creek Black River, etc. of Michigan, and for references would refer you to G. I. Betts their Agent, Hon. David H. Jerome of Saginaw, Hon. James Birney of Bay City, Mich or Hon. George T. Williams of Saginaw City, Michigan. I would here state also that the head Chiefs of this tribe have sought permission four times to visit their Great Father, but find it impossible to get further than Omaha. Their whole object being to get permission to exchange their reserve for one in the Indian Territory. Now as the President has expressed his view of this matter in his two last annual messages to Congress * and as the wishes of the Pawnee nation meets this view of the President, it hard to know that interests wholly eclesastical [sic] should labor to defeat both the wisdom of the President and the well being of these Indians.

Written on Behalf of Lasharo Turahay, Take ta sah currie, Arulaysharlocos, Kitkahhars Band of Pawnees, Cur rux ta puc or Fighting Bear, Petowhawerat Band.

B. F. Spooner[19]

Whether Spooner's motivation for taking up the cause of the Pawnees and writing to the authorities was altruistic or otherwise cannot be decided with the records now at hand.

Undoubtedly both Agent William Burgess and Supt. Barclay White were made aware of the complaints voiced for the Pawnees by Spooner and Platt. The bureaucracy tended to alert its own when outsiders criticized policy and suggested that all was not well at a given agency. Platt had been heard from before in 1871 and 1872, when he and others signed complaints against Agent Jacob Troth, although his wife had denied his complicity in the former year.[20]

Now Platt sat down to write again in September 1874. He wrote to Commissioner Smith with "sad feelings" at the plight of

---

* Spooner was correct in this statement. In both his 1872 and 1873 annual messages to Congress, Pres. Ullyses S. Grant spoke about the use of Indian Territory as a place where friendly tribes could be removed and said that efforts would be made to do so. He said that Indian Territory "is sufficient in area and agricultural resources to support all the Indians east of the Rocky Mountains." (Richardson, *Messages and Papers of the Presidents*, vol. VII, pp. 200, 252.)

the suffering Pawnees. He sought help for them and explained some reasons for their straitened conditions, which other evidence suggests he did not exaggerate. Serious accusations were made about the use of Pawnee annuity funds. He said that four hundred acres of prairie had been broken, and white men had been paid $3.00 per acre for plowing, but the Pawnees were charged $4.00 per acre for having it done. Only $5,000 was left of the $15,000 that was supposed to be distributed as annuity goods, and the former sum was to be spent only on flour. The interpreter had revealed to Platt that there "was not $1.00 coming to them per capita" from their cash annuity. He explained that they had already spent the money as credit at the trader's. "The agent pays in tickets and the trader discounts them largely [illegible] and then takes them to the agency and gets the money. A gentleman says one told him they did not regard the treaty, but did what they thought best." He ended his letter by asking that the Pawnees be allowed to leave Nebraska and go where they could find food.[21]

Platt made some serious accusations in this letter. He claimed that the Pawnees paid more for the plowing done on four hundred acres than was actually paid for the labor of having the work done. If this were true, then where did the extra $1.00 an acre go? Funds were requested for plowing five hundred acres of land, and Platt said that four hundred were done. Of the annuity, $10,000 had been requested for this work and for purchasing agricultural items. From his other accusations, it would appear that misuse of Pawnee funds was a possibility. The statement that the trader claimed the bulk of the annuity money, and the Pawnees received none, is possibly true. In some agencies Indians paid high prices and the trader made excessive profits. In some instances the Indians were never out of debt. Sometimes agents and traders were in collusion for profit, and the Indians received little or no annuity cash payment.

It is interesting that Platt should mention trading practices, for he himself was involved in trading at this time, according to a Danish visitor, Wilhelm Dinesen, who lived with him. Dinesen said that Platt lived on the border of the reservation about a fifteen-minute walk from the Pawnee villages. He "owned a piece of land, did some farming and cattle raising, maintained an inn for travelers and a store that was always filled with Indians who traded buffalo hides, furs, buffalo meat and Indian curios—in addition to the blankets they received from the government—for food, sugar, tea and cloth." * [22]

With Platt's letter went a petition from a majority of the chiefs but not Pitaresaru, who may have been dead at this time. It was an appeal for recompense for Platt, who it was claimed had been of assistance to them over the years. Three examples were given. First, he had raised a large crop of corn and potatoes, which he gave them when they were needy. Second, he also taught their children and fed and clothed them "without help from the government." (He had ten to twelve children in his 1846 school.) Third, in 1861 he supplied nearly four hundred [illegible] of flour when there was no way to get provisions due to the deep snow. For all of this Platt said he had never been compensated, and "for which we are still indebted to him." The chiefs then asked that he be given land adjoining the reservation and his own that would make a full section. [23]

Exactly how Platt convinced the chiefs to make this latter request on his behalf is not known. He may have suggested that he would write the letter to get help for them if they in turn would sign the petition. On the petition, there are thirteen names, but no X's, indicating that the signatures had not been attested to by the men named. It would seem that here was a man who had not performed these few acts of charity out of the goodness of his heart but who had toted up the obligations over the years while running a profitable trading establishment.

September was usually the month when the harvested corn was roasted in its husks in fragrant, smokey pits tended to by women and children. Thoughts of cache pits filled with the dried corn, beans, pumpkins, and buffalo meat satisfied the workers who knew that the people would be sustained through another cold winter. Soon hard work would be accompanied by the round of ceremonial dances in which marvelous feats of magic were enacted, feasts were prepared, and songs and dances of thanks-

* Dinesen did not have a good impression of the management of Indian affairs. He said, "America is the scene of many and great frauds, but none such as occur in the Indian Department since it passed from military to 'Christian' hands."

giving performed. All of this ritual gave the people a sense of time and continuance and a place in the annual earth cycle created by Tirawahut.

But September of 1874 was not like that. There were few fields of corn that had escaped the grasshopper hordes, and the hunt had been a failure. There was not enough to eat and there had not been for a long time. Just how many ceremonies were performed that fall is unknown. There may have been an intensity of effort in order to try to rectify the relationship between themselves and the Supernatural Beings; for it is certain that the world in which the Pawnees lived was difficult and unpredictable. Their thoughts of moving to be near the Wichitas were perhaps a last effort to try to control their lives away from the destructive Sioux, the timber stealing whites, and other hardships that were intensified by hunger and the inability to act independently and rectify the problems that overwhelmed them. Just how many of the people gave voice to the idea of removal is unknown.

But the agent's annual report, dated September 1, noted that for some time a portion of the people had been looking forward to moving to Indian Territory, and that some were so anxious to go that they wanted to leave without permission, even before there was a place for them to settle. He added that nearby white settlers and others eager for a chance to gain land in this fertile country spurred the Pawnees to insist on removal. "They do not see why we do not let them go," he added. Traders talked to the people and urged them to sell what they would not need or want to take with them, and speculated on any property that might be sold. In order to facilitate a quick sale, the traders undoubtedly assured the Pawnees that they had heard the tribe would soon be moving. It also was true that the Pawnee need for guns and food contributed greatly to the sale of their belongings aside from the considerations of removal.

In council on September 8, Burgess warned the chiefs that the Pawnees should not tear down their lodges and sell the timber in them. Some had been selling the poles and crotches that held up the large roof beams to settlers, who used the timber to build sheds and other things.[24] This sale of valuable timbers had gone so far that it was reported that "they have been persuaded to utterly destroy three of their four mud-lodge villages."[25] Agent Burgess defined the difference between personal property and property belonging to the tribe. Tribal property was that purchased with government monies or annuity funds such as farm wagons, horse gear, and such.[26]

By this time, individuals involved in selling property were quite certain that some time soon they would be leaving the reservation. The Skidi leaders sided with the agent and said they would do whatever he wished and stay in their homes. Some Chaui and Pitahawirata chiefs remained uncommitted, either to the agent or to the voices demanding immediate removal, although they said they would leave sometime. The Kitkahahki, however, said they intended to do whatever they pleased with their property and were now, this very day, preparing to go south. A heated discussion ensued, and a leading Kitkahahki warrior, resenting interpreter Baptiste Bayhylle's remarks, argued and scuffled with him saying that he was working against them. The latter, who was part Skidi, sided with his band chiefs and also with the agent, who gave him his salary. After this, the Kitkahahki chiefs said they were going and if the soldiers followed and shot at them, they did not care. They intended to do what they believed was right for their people.[27]

John Williamson, an agency employee who spoke Pawnee, claimed he was asked by the agent if he would go speak to the chiefs and try to persuade them not to leave. He said that some of them claimed that the "medicine men" had talked to the Great Spirit, and He did not want them to live among white men any longer. He had sent hot winds and grasshoppers, which proved that he wanted them to leave that place.[28]

In traditional times before U.S. intervention and disruption of tribal life, it was not unusual for a Pawnee band to move from time to time to a new location and establish a new village with proper ritual. There were various reasons that this was done and among them may have been the belief that Tirawahut had indicated that it should happen. If there were any time in their history when it would be probable that this belief would be activated, it would have been now.[29]

After the council, Burgess wrote a letter and sent a telegram to Supt. Barclay White informing him of the Kitkahahki's imminent departure. In his letter, he blamed Lester Platt, the trader, for agitating the tribe and "having upset our calculations." As a partial solution to the problem, he suggested that perhaps a compromise could be made by dividing the reservation's future sale proceeds. The three South Bands could receive part and leave the reservation, while the Skidis could receive part and remain in Nebraska.[30] In the agent's opinion, the Skidis had made much progress in adopting government ideas and would continue to do so in the future.[31]

Two days later, Burgess claimed the Kitkahahki chief and leaders came to him and told him they regretted their defiance, and they would not leave until after the annuity was paid and they could talk to Barclay White.[32] The reason for their change of mind is not explained. It may have been that the need for food and goods was so great that it was imperative to obtain these necessities before departing. A substantiation of this possibility came later in the month when the agent declared that hunger "was driving them almost desperate" and the Pawnees wanted to go. The question can be asked, Was this situation allowed to develop so as to increase the entire tribe's need for flight? It would appear that emergency measures could have been taken after so many months to alleviate such dire conditions.

During September, accusations against Burgess began to appear in state newspapers such as the *Omaha Republican*. This served to keep the pot boiling at the reservation, and public opinion focused on it. Nevertheless, the Skidi Band chiefs continued to state their preference to remain in Nebraska as late as September 28.[33] Although the government gave the Pawnees no inkling in September that removal was possible, in October it was ready to set the wheels in motion to expel the tribe from its homeland.

In Washington, plans had been completed that would allow a search for a new reservation in Indian Territory. The pros and cons of allowing the tribe to stay or to send them away had been weighed. Nebraska public and official opinion that inveighed against the Pawnees' remaining in the state contributed finally to the U.S. government's consenting to the tribe's removal. Tribal petitions to leave gave an overt reason for permitting the tribe to go, as if the government thought only of the Pawnees' wishes.

Knowledge that the Skidis and others in the Chaui, Pitahawirata, and Kitkahahki bands did not want to leave carried no weight when the decision was made to pursue the 1849 idea of consolidating the tribes of Nebraska and Kansas in Indian Territory.

Official notification came to Superintendent White in a September 22 letter from the Commissioner of Indian Affairs Smith. In it, he said that if by act of council the Pawnees requested to move to Indian Territory that it would be approved. White was to go to the agency and discuss this with the chiefs and to tell them that if they approved, plans would be made to select a reservation for them. Funds from the sale of their Nebraska lands would be needed to pay for a new reservation in Indian Territory through congressional legislation.[34] He was also to tell them that they would probably be located in the eastern part of Indian Territory, not near the buffalo hunting regions. They should not delay their decision in order that Congress could act on the entire matter.[35]

In his journal White recalled the time:

The Pawnees had been restless during the year and were very anxious to remove their homes from Nebraska to Indian Territory. Many causes had occurred to make them dissatisfied with their present reservation. Buffalo had been destroyed by the whites, their timber was being taken by white settlers, the Sioux were continuously making murderous raids upon them, lately the locusts had eaten their crops. Indian tribes whom they claimed as relations and had been in the practice of visiting were removed to the Indian Territory. White settlers were making homes all around them confining them more closely to the reservation than before. They had petitioned the authorities at Washington to permit them to select a home in the I.T. and to remove there, and I had received instructions to now carry to them permission to appoint a delegation to represent the tribe and accompany their agent to the I.T. with the view of selecting one out of two tracts of land there, which the Commissioner of Indian Affairs had named in my letter of instruction.[36]

Although the above statement reads as if the Pawnee removal was a logical outcome of the conditions that surrounded them, closer study reveals that while some Pawnees were "anxious" to leave their reservations for the reasons White indicates, not all were, especially the leaders whose opposition has been quoted previously. In studying causes given for Pawnee removal, it is apparent that some were due directly to lack of commitment by the government to honor its promises to protect the tribe against both Indian and white depredations and intrusions.

Confinement to the reservation, a policy pursued vigorously by Superintendent White, was in part to reduce white complaints and fears of so-called hostile Indians, even though the Pawnees did not seem to be involved in the many depredation claims pressed against them. As for the May council request by the chiefs to have a reservation selected for them in Indian Territory, there is no record of that council in the minutes usually taken, so it is not known exactly the circumstances that brought about that decision or just how much compliance was agent motivated and pressured.

Now with the arrival of the commissioner's instructions, pressure was about to be applied again to those leaders who did not want to leave Nebraska to do so. Two meetings were held at the Pawnee council house, one on October 5 for which there is no record in the Pawnee council minutes. However, B. Rush Roberts, visiting the Northern Superintendency agencies as a member of the Board of Indian Commissioners, reported on the meeting, saying that "the subject of removal was strongly urged on them."

Reasons given for this pressuring were that grasshoppers had destroyed their crops, and that they had been invited "by their relations, the Wichitas, to go and live with them."[37] They were not told that reservation locations under consideration were in the eastern part of Indian Territory and not near the Wichitas but instead were mislead by the suggestion that their new homes would be near them.

At the October 8 council, Roberts, White, and Burgess were principal government representatives. An already prepared set of resolutions pertaining to removal and other pertinent matters were read to the Indian leaders. According to Burgess, the document had all the force of a treaty after the chiefs agreed to and signed it.[38] The plan made no exceptions. All tribal bands and members were to remove eventually.

The chiefs listened to the plan. When the council was over, they left to discuss the matter among themselves. Whether public tribal band meetings were called is not known. But in cases of this great importance, it was traditional to send heralds through the villages announcing that the people must come together and hear the chiefs tell them about the matter at hand.[39] Because of the gravity of this encounter with the government and its already prepared plan for removal, it is assumed that each band and its chiefs and leaders met to discuss what was to be done, whether to accept, reject or try to modify the plan.

The manner in which it had been brought before them left no question as to the inevitability of their removal from their homeland. In two days, the chiefs met again with the government representatives, and Agent Burgess said "though not quite to their wishes, finding they could not modify it, they finally acquiesced, and the resolutions were signed by all the chiefs and headmen of the tribe." This statement indicates that although the chiefs disagreed with portions of the plan, pressure was exerted to bring their acquiescence. The exact points of difference were not disclosed.[40]

The resolutions as written in the council minutes and signed by the tribal leaders, Supt. Barclay White and Agent William Burgess included the following summarized articles: Resolution 1. The Pawnees requested that their present reservation and the improvements it contained be sold at the earliest time possible for its full market value. Resolution 2. They asked that the government set aside, as soon as possible, a reservation of approximately three hundred square miles of well-watered, arable, timbered land in Indian Territory in a healthful location, away from wild tribes, which would be satisfactory in all respects to the tribal members. This reservation would "be allotted in severalty, 160 acres to each head of family and 80 acres to each unmarried person over 18 years of age." Resolution 3. They requested those improvements necessary and agricultural stock and implements needed, to be supplied and paid for from the proceeds from the sale of the Nebraska reservation. Resolution 4. The Pawnees asked that no congressional appropriation be made for the cost of removal, that "we be allowed to move ourselves to the new reservation accompanied by agency employees, paid out of their regular salaries." Resolution 5. They stated that if Congress and the Indian Department approve of the above, that when the tribe has removed to Indian Territory, it agrees to abandon the hunt and to provide itself a living from herding and tilling the soil. Resolution 6. This article gave the names of forty men, ten from each band, who would represent the tribe in the selection of the new reservation under the direction of a person or persons appointed by the commissioner of Indian Affairs.

A supplemental list of resolutions was made in the same council. The first resolution stated that the chiefs and headmen who were selected to remain in Nebraska had the approval of the others to act in their interests in matters affecting the local situation but, in matters pertaining to the entire tribe, the consent of all chiefs must be obtained. The second resolution stated "that outside traders and other white persons, near our present reservation having taken advantage of our necessities and received by purchase, in trade, or pawn, our government wagons, gov't. plows, and poles of our winter lodges, we have by request that none of these parasites, or any white squaw men, be permitted to remove, or settle among us there. We have suffered from them in the past, we desire to be rid of them in the future. The third resolution stated that any funds appropriated be placed in the agent's trust. Any that are not needed for specified purposes should be "deviated" for use in supplying provisions for the tribe and any contingent expenses that may be needed for removal.[41]

So, under duress and manipulation, tribal leaders agreed to leave Nebraska. Conditions described before—continual hunger, harassment by settlers, pressure from so-called friends to go and leave all their problems behind—increased cultural dissolution. All may have been allowed to develop and continue so as to wear away the will to remain. Perhaps the government did not force the Pawnees to leave, but it programmed the outcome by allowing devastating conditions to exist. When it was ready to suggest removal if, as it was sanctimoniously said, the Pawnees wanted it, the people felt they had little choice.

The councils were carefully planned as to what would be said and the resolutions, which supposedly were requests by the tribal leaders, were already written down and in Superintendent White's pocket when he entered the council room. Even so, B. Rush

Roberts claimed that the Society of Friends was not altogether convinced that removal was advantageous. For one reason, Pawnee advancement in "civilization" would be slowed by it.[42] Just how much argument the Quakers put forth against it in the commissioner's office or among congressional delegates is unknown. Whether the Pawnee cultural imperative to remain in their ancestral and God-given home was even considered is not known. It is certain that the Quakers' goals in Indian affairs in Nebraska were undermined by state and national government representatives. Indian removal was favored by these officials, as has been said before.

Once the Pawnee tribe had been told that removal was at hand, no time was lost in beginning the process. On the very same day as the council, October 8, a pass was written for the advance party of forty men and their families to go south to the Wichitas, as agreed upon in resolution and council. Resaruturi, or Good Chief of the Kitkahahkis, is the only named individual, and the usual admonition for good behavior was included.[43] Another pass was issued to Joseph Esau, a Skidi Band member and agency blacksmith's apprentice. He was to act as interpreter for the party and explain its mission to anyone encountered who would need to know.[44]

Agent Burgess was not yet through the day's letter writing. He also wrote to tell Wichita Agent Jonathan Richards that the advance group would soon be on its way and what its purpose was. The group would travel to his agency and stay there until some authorized person came to take the group "to show them the unoccupied country where the government desires them to locate."[45] The Pawnees may have understood that they were to have a hand in selection of their new home, which they believed would be near the Wichitas, but this last phrase indicates that their role was simply to be taken and shown what the government had selected, whether they approved of it or not.

It did not take long for news to travel that the Pawnees were going to leave their Nebraska homeland. One of the first to be informed was Lester Platt. Apparently his request for land as payment for his past "charities" to the tribe had not been honored, although the suggestion by him and others in the nearby communities that the tribe be removed had probably weighed in the official approval.

On October 10, acting as a spokesman, he wrote another letter, this time for three Pitahawirata members—Fighting Bear and Big George, who carried the following message from the old Pitahawirata chief, Terrecowah:

> Terrecowah, chief 40 years says that all the chiefs ask for Keatskatoos, L. W. Platt, to go with them to their new reservation— further along time ago I received Keatskatoos in my village and he has been like a brother to me.—and now my Great Father, I desire that he may be our agent at our new home in the South as he understands our language and our ways, and has skill and judgment in farming and managing our young men, and Mrs. Platt is very skillful in educating our children, and so forth.
>
> Terrecowah, by his messenger, Big George and His head soldier, Fighting Bear says the same.[46]

This request may well have been a valid request, because by now hunger and other serious conditions that existed had frustrated and angered the tribal leaders. Weighing the value of Burgess and Platt against each other, Terrecowah may have decided that there was more to gain, or less to lose, if Platt could be the agent. But again, it cannot be known how much of the message was inspired by Platt himself.

Platt was not through yet with his appeals to the Great Father, and the next one in the form of a petition from the chiefs would seem to have been suggested by him. He knew of the resolutions signed by the chiefs in council a few days before. The one that galled him was the one that stated that "none of these parasites . . . be permitted to remove or settle among us there. We have suffered from them in the past, we desire to be rid of them in the future." This referred to the white traders and squaw men, who had traded unfairly for government property, lodge poles, and other items. Apparently, Platt was considered among the group. The response, as it appeared in the petition he formed, said:

> We the undersigned chiefs of the several Bands of Pawnee Indians understanding from our [illegible] and who was present at the

Council that in the resolution drawn up on the 8th of Oct. inst. by Barclay White there was one in which he indulged his personal spite reflecting on our old friend, Keatskatoos, L. W. Platt, which was not interpreted so that we understood it. We therefore ask our Great Father the Commissioner of Indian Affairs to strike out that resolution and give no heed to it.[47]

The petition continued by saying that the Platts had done more good for the Pawnees than others had done and that the Indians wanted him for their agent and wanted Mrs. Platt to manage the education of their children in their new home. Twelve chiefs names are affixed to the document. They are the same names, in the same order, as those in the August petition. Whether any favor of response to this request was received by the chiefs directly from Washington is doubtful.

The Platts' long experience with the Pawnees had both positive and negative aspects. Just how much profit was made in the Platt trading post is not known, but it may have been considerable. Now some Pawnees and the Platts seemed to believe there was something yet to be gained by promoting further contact, even after the tribe's removal. Quaker officials did not want Platt, who had influence with the chiefs and could and had made public his perception of government shortcomings, to continue his association with the tribe. As it turned out, the Platts remained in Nebraska.

The constant and great need for food was still the Pawnees' main concern, and on October 16, Burgess issued food supplies to six hundred inhabitants.[48] In less than a week, he notified the commissioner that food and other supplies would also be issued to the second group of tribal members before their removal.[49] Hunger stalked the village, and so did the Sioux. On October 23, they raided and successfully captured horses, six of which belonged to Eagle Chief, who angrily demanded that the government provide protection for those who would remain on the reservation. Burgess thought it possible that the raiders could have been white men.[50]

The second party that was prepared to leave waited until the authorized persons who would accompany them were appointed and approved. The two men selected were John W. Williamson and A. L. Alexander, agency employees. Their instructions informed them that approximately 250 persons would be in the party, and it was planned that they make a buffalo hunt while on the way to provide themselves with meat and robes.

The men were charged with caring for any reasonable needs and requests and reporting to Burgess as often as reasonable while on the journey south. In case they should encounter the advance party, Williamson was instructed to ask that they choose about ten men from each band who would act as representatives of the entire tribe to "select" their new home. He was to order this group to continue their journey immediately and directly to the Wichita Agency, where Burgess said that he would soon be waiting to take them to show them their new reservation. Williamson was to inform the Indians that they could not settle where they pleased and that the government would do all it could to please them and place them in an area "sufficiently remote from other tribes" on land that did not conflict with any preceding claims by other tribes.[51]

The Pawnee leaders still did not know that their reservation was not yet selected and that it would be some distance from their Wichita relatives and friends. Living near the Wichitas had been a most important factor in their considering their future. The record does not indicate that they were ever informed before removal that they would not be living close to the Wichitas. The surrounding areas were already occupied by Cheyennes, Arapahoes, Kiowas, and others on reservations.

Instructing Williamson to tell the Pawnees that they were not to settle down any place they chose seems to indicate that they were being prepared for the news that living near the Wichitas was not a certainty and living where they wanted to or thought they were going to live was not their choice. A lack of choice had not been in *their* original plans. Allowing the tribe to believe that they were going south to live near the Wichitas may have served as an inducement and have been a means of gaining their consent for removal.

In later years, John Williamson wrote an account of the removal journey as he recalled its events. The route the tribe followed and major events along the way are described and excerpts from it are included here. There are differences between his account and the official records. This may be explained by the fact that he wrote his memories many years after the event. His numbers of migrants differ from those of the official count. He reported that there were many more Pawnees than the estimated number at the starting point, over 1,400 in all. He added that the agent came, and they conferred about the matter and concluded to allow this number to go.[52]

Williamson also claimed erroneously that the commissioner of Indian Affairs attended the October council in which the Pawnees were informed that they would be removed to Indian Territory. It is presumed that he meant B. Rush Roberts, a member of the Board of Indian Commissioners. It was decided there to have Williamson accompany a group of forty warriors, who would go to inspect the new reservation that would be selected for the Pawnees.

In the official record, this party departed on approximately October 11, but the pass for Williamson and Alexander was dated October 30, with the indication that they were to accompany the second larger group. Agent Burgess reported that the second party of Pawnees left the agency in early November. Williamson said he and Alexander went to nearby Columbus to purchase a complete camping outfit, and on the second day of November "we left Genoa with a light covered wagon, drawn by a team of mules and our outfit also included a pair of good saddle horses. Arrangements were made for the forty Indians to go to Grand Island and meet us at a place on the Platte River, where many bridges cross the stream."[53]

Apparently, in recalling all these events much later in his life, Williamson intertwined the details concerning the advance group with those about the second larger group. In any event, he was not expecting the large number that did arrive at the Grand Island location. His comment that the agent came and tried to convince all but the forty (who were already well on their way south) to return to the agency is puzzling. The conference in Williamson's tent in which the agent decided to let the entire 1,400 go is not recorded in the official record.

The season was late, and although food had been issued, it would probably not last the entire journey. It was decided to travel southwest, toward western Kansas, where buffalo might be found. About November 7, 1874, the long trek began. Although wagons and teams carried many people and their belongings, others rode horseback, and still others carried packs on their backs and walked. They could only walk about twelve to fourteen miles a day, a rate that set the pace for the entire group.

The first place named on the Pawnee migration route after leaving Grand Island is Red Cloud, Nebraska. Passing this town, the Pawnees moved on, crossed the Republican River and camped.

It was not long before claim seekers began to appear. Williamson and Alexander went into Red Cloud to purchase some supplies. While there, Williamson was confronted by a law officer, who asked him if he was in charge of the large group of Indians that had passed by. When he said that he was, he was put under arrest. The officer explained a horse had been stolen, and since he was in charge of the Pawnees, he was responsible. Williamson told him that earlier in the day, while passing a farmstead, a horse tethered there had become frightened by the large group passing by. He had seen it break its rope and run off. He told the officer he was welcome to come to the Pawnee camp, and they could look to see if it was there.

The next morning the officer and owner arrived and searched but the horse was not among the Pawnee stock.[54] Even without proof, the assumption had been that the Indians had taken the horse. Both men left the camp. Later, it was heard that the man had found his horse some place else.

It was not long before another claimant came to camp insisting that the Pawnees had stolen some of his wheat stored in a small sod house. Williamson investigated and found that the man never had any wheat and was hoping to make a little money off the Indians. Williamson had been instructed that anyone making a valid claim was to be told to make an estimate of the loss and, with Williamson's signature attached, send it to Agent Burgess. In this case, the man was told to write to the agent and tell him about his loss; but without Williamson's signature, Burgess would assume that it was a false claim.

The Pawnees rested all that Sunday, and the next day they repacked their belongings on wagons and horse or human back. They then took up the march in a southerly direction, hoping for sign of buffalo. The Solomon River came into view; and the horses and wagons, and those afoot, crossed it as they had always done in the days when they had passed this way on their way to hunt or to return from visiting the Wichitas, or from stealing horses. Only this time, it was known that this was probably the last time that the river would flow over horses' hoofs or human feet in a land that no one could remember as not having been theirs to use since time began.

Williamson said they crossed the river about eight miles west of Cawker City, Kansas. There he requested that the Pawnees camp while he went to nearby Beloit to visit friends. He asked them to remain there while he was away, but when he returned— his account does not say how long he was absent—the Pawnees were gone.

He seemed to believe he was a tribal favorite when he claimed the chiefs selected him to accompany them. If that were the case, it may not have been for the reasons he thought. He was twenty-four years old, and his abilities and knowledge were minimal compared to the maturity and life experiences of the chiefs. He was probably viewed as a minor annoyance, but one that they could cope with under the circumstances. The compelling need to search out a bison herd for food far outweighed any commitment they may have made to stay and wait for Williamson while he visited with friends in Beloit. *

The young man found himself trying to follow the trail of his "charges." There was no town nearby, he said, where anyone could tell him if they had seen the people. All day he rode, scanning the horizon and searching the ground for signs. At dusk, he came upon a log dugout house in the bank of a canyon. An unfriendly woman refused him food, information, or the use of a nearby haystack to sleep in. She finally consented to the latter request, if he would keep alert and leave if he heard anything. During the night, he awoke suddenly to hear a horse whinnying and the sounds of a herd. He quickly got up and left quietly,

---

* Apparently, the chiefs had made an estimate of his character in 1873 at Massacre Canyon. In later years, they accused him of deserting them when the Sioux attacked. (Blaine, G. and M., "The Hunters Who Were Massacred," *Nebraska History*, p. 356.)

thinking that the place must have been the headquarters of a band of horse thieves who were abundant in the state at that time.

The next day he rode on, ascending a bluff that overlooked a valley. In the distance, he saw the Pawnee camp and rode to it. When he demanded to know why they had gone on without him, he said that the Pawnees thought that he did not intend to return and had gone to get soldiers. Apparently, their conclusion was reached at Red Cloud, where he had threatened to do this because the tribal members had wanted to stay there and beg because they were hungry, and he refused to allow them to do so.[55]

The route continued southward, crossing Wolf Creek near the present town of Luray. There a large group of white men rode into camp and told Williamson to get his Indians out of there as fast as he could. A school teacher and children had been killed by some Indians, and they thought that these were those Indians. Williamson said he denied that the Pawnees could be culpable because they were friendly and on their to a new home.

None of Williamson's arguments seemed to have had an effect on the aroused posse, who threatened to open fire. Williamson told them that would be foolish to do this since there were fourteen hundred Indians, including four hundred armed warriors. They were also carrying the United States flag, he pointed out.

At this time, Spotted Horse and an interpreter, Harry Coons, came up and the situation was explained to them. Spotted Horse calmly told the intruders that his people would not leave until they were ready and assured the men that it was not his people who committed the crime. One of the men, a Dr. Spillman, said that he believed him. Spotted Horse then invited him to eat supper with him and he accepted. The mood of the group seemed to change. Perhaps, wisdom had overcome impetuosity at the sight of fourteen hundred friendly "hostiles." Since they were a great distance from any settlement, they stayed all night and departed in the morning, Williamson said, in an entirely different frame of mind.[56]

As far as is known, Williamson wrote the only eyewitness description of the Pawnee "trail of tears." * Unfortunately, he rarely

---

* In the nineteenth century, U.S. Government policy forced Indian tribes to sign land cession treaties, abandon their lands, and migrate to distant areas un-

gives a description of camp life or what the Pawnees said or did on that 1874 November and December journey. No where can one read of any contemplation or consideration of what the up-rooting of the people meant and what their reactions were. Occasionally, there is a superficial description that indicates a certain lack of understanding or compassion. One example follows in Williamson's own words: "Many amusing incidents happened while we were enroute. When a rabbit showed himself the Indians and their dogs would surround and so bewilder him that escape was impossible and it was amusing to watch them catch it." [57] What could have been so amusing about watching hungry Indians make certain that even such a small prey as a rabbit did not escape?

Williamson also found it diverting to watch the Indians and their dogs fording a stream. He commented that the Pawnees had several hundred dogs with them, animals that he said were a crossbreed of dog and wolf. When these animals attempted to swim across the stream, they would get swept along. "I have enjoyed a good many laughs as I watched their attempts to go in a straight line if the current was swift and would be obliged to swim diagonally and would set up such a yelping and barking." [58]

Problems with overburdened ponies attracted his attention. Their backs became sore with the weight of their packs, to which was often added the weight of a hungry woman worn out from day after day of walking and leading the horse. When the horse became tired of the weight, it would buck and throw the woman

---

populated by whites. The ceded Indian lands then became available for white settlement and exploitation. The horrendous hardships suffered by the Cherokees, Choctaws, Creeks, Chickasaws, and Seminoles gave the enforced marches the name, Trail of Tears. Death by starvation, exposure, and disease occurred to thousands of poorly clad individuals herded westward from their abandoned farms and villages in the South and East. But these tribes were not the only ones to suffer. Any tribe that was forced to remove from its lands had its own tragic story to tell. Indian Territory and Oklahoma Territory (that later were joined to become the state of Oklahoma) contained over sixty-five tribes or tribal remants on reservations by the end of the century. Included were the above-mentioned tribes, as well as Senecas, Delawares, Sacs, Foxes, Osages, Apaches, Cheyennes, and Pawnees, among many others. Some tribes, such as the Modocs and Nez Perce, were removed from as far as the Northwest and California.

off, then buck again, and often succeed in ridding itself of the chafing load. The woman, sore from walking and being thrown, would begin to cry. Then other women would come and help her reload her pony.

The death of Spotted Horse sobered Williamson. When the Pawnees arrived near Bunker Hill, Kansas, Spotted Horse went to Williamson and asked if the group could camp near Spring Creek. Near there his brother had been killed some years before by the Sioux, and Spotted Horse wanted to go to his grave and mourn. He said, "I may never come this way again," and seemed to be very depressed. The weather was cold and damp and he was urged not to do this because he might become ill. He said it was not important and spent the night at the grave. When Williamson talked to him the next morning, he sounded hoarse. In the afternoon, Williamson was asked to come to his tipi, where he found him lying ill on a pile of buffalo robes. Around him, Pawnee doctors were dancing, shaking gourds, singing curing songs, and applying hot irons to his chest in an attempt to rid him of the illness.

He was ill for three or four days, and Williamson visited him each day. The Pawnees were apparently an object of curiosity to some residents from Bunker Hill. A minister, and his wife and daughter came to visit, and when the man learned that Spotted Horse was ill, he offered to go to his tipi and pray for him. Williamson permitted this and concluded after the visit that there was every reason to believe that the ill man had accepted the "white man's faith." Why he came to this questionable conclusion is not given.

Several more days passed, and after midnight one night, Williamson was summoned to Spotted Horse's tipi. He obviously was extremely ill and spoke to Williamson in a whisper, "Now Brother, in a little while, I will be dead and gone and I want to be buried in the white man's cemetery and have a coffin and have the man who prayed with me to preach my funeral sermon. I want you to get the Big Father in Washington to put up a stone where I am buried. On the stone I want my name written, also the words that I was a friend of the white man."

There is only Williamson's account of the event, but it is probable that Spotted Horse, a believer in his religious traditions, would have preferred a Pawnee burial but was not sure that it would have been allowed in soil not belonging to the tribe. He may have preferred to lie beside his brother, but that unmarked grave lay on the prairie, perhaps on land now owned by the whites. He may have decided that it would be better to have his grave in a place where his people would know where it was, and it would not be disturbed. A white man's cemetery was the best choice.

Of Spotted Horse, Williamson said, "He was about thirty-five years of age at the time of his death. He was a fine looking Indian of a very mild and gentle disposition, always courteous and pleasant to those he met and with his passing away, we lost one of the finest specimens of Indian manhood. I believe that when the great day arrives, Spotted Horse will be there with some of his white brothers."[59]

The weather was turning colder. The illness and death of Spotted Horse had delayed the southward journey a "week or ten" days. About a week's travel from Great Bend, Kansas, the need for food was becoming so acute that Williamson wrote to Supt. Barclay White informing him of the situation and asking him to write to him at the Great Bend Post Office. White replied that there was no money but sent him a voucher for $1,800 to buy flour, soda, sugar, and coffee. That was all, no meat or other foods. The post office was in the back of a local store, and Williamson walked to the front and asked the merchant if he would sell him the food and accept the voucher. The man seemed reluctant to accept it, even though it was explained that it was good, and he had only to send it to Washington to get his money.

Williamson noticed a man near the door motioning to him, so he walked with him outside where the man told Williamson that he was a local merchant and that he would accept the voucher. He had a carload of flour "which is not just up to the mark, and rather than return it, I will sell it to you cheap."[60] Precisely what was wrong with the flour, whether it was full of insects, or moldy or bad for some other reason, is not said. Williamson accepted his offer, believing, perhaps, that as hungry as the Pawnees were, any food was acceptable regardless of condition.

The Pawnees camped along the Arkansas River, and Williamson sent word to them to come into town to the place where the freight car stood. "In a short time the streets were filled with Indians and a great many curious white people." The chiefs had been put in charge of dividing the flour among the four bands. Long lines of women trudged from the car to the camp, each carrying a sack of flour on her back. Proud of himself, Williamson said that "to show their appreciation," that night they held a little celebration and invited him to share coffee and Pawnee bread. *

The next morning, camp was broken and they headed in a southwesterly direction from Great Bend. One foggy night soon thereafter, white men sneaked into the encampment and ran off about one hundred horses. When this was discovered the next morning, many of the men and Williamson pursued the white men to try to find the animals, which were an absolute necessity for continuing the journey. Fortunately it was sandy country and the trail was easily followed. While riding along the ridges, some of the party sighted a group of men trying to get a herd of horses across a fast-flowing stream. When they looked up and saw the Pawnees coming down upon them at full gallop, they hastily abandoned the stolen herd, which was rounded up and driven back to the camp.[61]

The next problem that faced them was crossing a wide stretch of burned, blackened prairie. The horses depended on prairie grasses for food. The situation became so serious that it was necessary to use the bark from cottonwood trees for fodder. The women did the hard work of hacking down "enormous trees." The horses then stripped off and ate the bark, leaving each tree looking like "a huge white skeleton." This food was not adequate, and it took a long time at each stop for the animals to consume enough to satisfy their hunger. Even then, the horses became weakened, and travel became slow.

At last, the tribe reached the Medicine Lodge River, near a place called Sun City. There they found good stands of winter rye grass, an excellent feed for the horses. The people crossed the

---

* This bread is made of flour, salt, soda, and water mixed and patted into flat cakes and fried in hot grease until brown on the outside. It is called fry bread, and it is still made by the Pawnees and other Indians.

river and camped in a wooded area on the south side. During the night a blizzard struck. The Pawnees had wisely camped in a protected place and were sheltered in their tipis. However, a great many wagon freighters lost their lives in the storm, and one of the mules Williamson used for his wagon was found frozen to death in the morning.

Far across the snowy fields, a small town could be seen. Williamson went to it and asked if there was a "booze joint" there. There was, and it plied its trade among the cowboys and cattlemen that came up the cattle trail nearby. Williamson took it upon himself to warn the proprietor not to sell whiskey, should any Pawnees ask for it. He warned him of the danger to the entire place if the Indians should get whiskey. In his opinion, the Pawnees while sober were, as he put it, docile, but unmanageable when under the influence. He said that they could kill each other in that condition.[62] His opinion, if true, must have been caused by a late development among a people who punished severely any incidence of drunkenness by public whipping and who usually were described as a sober people. The hard and stressful conditions of their recent lives may have contributed to a change.

The blizzard and resulting deep snow prevented the tribe from moving for some time. Again hunger became the immediate problem, and the chiefs went to Williamson, repeatedly asking him what he was going to do about getting food for the people. No buffalo herds and little other game had been sighted over the entire distance of the journey. Part of the government's negligent and irresponsible planning for the trip had included planning to supply tribal food from the hunt after the insufficient food supplies were consumed.

As hunger increased, Williamson said the people believed that they had done something to offend the Great Spirit and began to hold religious ceremonies. One of the "sacred advisors" had had a dream in which one of the Sacred Bundles had not been cared for adequately. He said the ear of Sacred Corn it contained was broken. A chief came to Williamson and told him about the dream and said that there was to be a ceremony to open the sacred bundle. He invited Williamson to come, since he was sceptical about such things, and the chief wanted him to see that the dream was true.

As predicted, the ear of corn was broken, "but whether this was known to them before the bundle was opened I do not know," Williamson said, still doubting. Unfortunately, he gave no details of the ceremony, only commenting that they began to repent, as he interpreted it, and tore blankets and calico into strips and hung them on the trees to whip in the wind. Because they had no blankets to spare, he asked why they did this. They were sacrificing the blankets to the Great Spirit to make amends for not caring for the Sacred Bundle as it should have been, allowing Sacred (Mother) Corn to become broken, it was explained.[63] Mother Corn was one of the most sacred objects in the Pawnee belief system, and for this to have happened was disastrous. The personal feelings of the people were those of despair, because day by day as they traveled farther and farther from their homeland, the number of misfortunes increased.

Soon after, Williamson went up the Medicine Lodge River to hunt alone. He encountered a man, whom he told of "the starving and pitiful condition of the Indians" in his charge and of his not being able to secure food for them. The man told Williamson that he had a large herd of cattle in the valley and that he had sold cattle previously to starving Indians and that he would be glad to do so at this time. Williamson explained that it would take a long time to get permission or authority from the Indian Office for the purchase. The man said that it was not necessary. All he required was Williamson's signature on a statement, saying that there was dire need for the Pawnees to have cattle for food and stating how many head of cattle he had purchased. The price as $14.00 a head, and Williamson asked for one hundred head. The man did not seem apprehensive, saying that the government had always sent him money for such requests.

When Williamson got back to camp, he gave the chiefs the good news and asked that some of them and their men go with him to round up and slaughter the cattle in the rancher's corrals. Then the chiefs could divide the meat. The heralds went throughout the camp giving out the good news, and "it caused great rejoicing."

The next morning they found the cattle to be longhorn Texas cattle in only fair condition. They picked out a hundred head, butchered them, and carried the meat back to camp. Feasts were held that day with an offering made to the Great Spirit with the acknowledgment that they had grieved Him, but he had forgiven them and sent them food. At least this is how Williamson interpreted the outcome of the day.[64]

In a few days the journey southward began again. Leaving behind the last town in Kansas, they approached the state's southern boundary and the northern edge of Indian Territory. Williamson's and Alexander's food supply began to run low. Although not certain of its exact location, they knew that the Cheyenne and Arapahoe Agency was their next stop according to Williamson's orders. They decided to leave the slow moving Pawnees and ride on ahead and find it and procure food.

They counciled with the chiefs, telling them of their plans. The next morning, the two men, Harry Coons, and Brave Chief and his son (Kitkahahki) left the camp, taking their remaining food and some meat provided by Brave Chief. They traveled on horse, averaging about twenty miles a day. Their journey was comparatively uneventful until the fourth day. At that time they sighted a band of seven Indians identified as Cheyennes, six men and a woman, who appeared to be hostile. They thought that the seven might try to capture them and steal their outfit.

They were not overly concerned because they had a defensible position in the edge of a narrow strip of woods. As the Cheyennes came nearer, Brave Chief walked out into the open a short distance and made signs that they intended to fight back if attacked. At this, the Cheyennes quickly turned and went out of sight beyond the woods.

Brave Chief, the most experienced in warfare, said the party must move along the edge of the timber to where there were some fallen trees, the timber was thinner, and there would be a better view. They followed his advice, and when they arrived there they listened and heard voices.

The Cheyennes were returning, but they would have to go through a narrow opening in the woods one at a time. It was decided to stand in a straight line and fire as they came through. It was thought that they would not expect the Pawnee party to have moved to this spot and the latter would have the advantage of surprise.[65] The first man through seemed to be a chief, who later was identifed as Medicine Arrow. He was a fine-looking, middle-aged man, dressed in "full war costume," painted, and with a large silver medal hanging on his chest. As he came to where the men were waiting, Williamson raised his rifle, and Medicine Arrow, startled to see them, dropped his rifle and put up his hands. Brave Chief called out for Williamson not to shoot, then Medicine Arrow motioned his men back. Brave Chief was instructed to tell him in sign language to dismount. When he did this, Williamson held the rifle steady while Brave Chief searched Medicine Arrow for other weapons and picked up the rifle he had dropped. The other Cheyennes also obeyed these instructions and soon all were disarmed.

After their capture the Cheyennes begged for food. It was decided to take them down to a little creek and prepare some provisions.* The Cheyennes walked ahead, and the others followed with guns ready. Once there, they were told to sit on a long log. Brave Chief talked to Medicine Arrow in sign language. What the subject of their conversation was is not known, but after awhile, Brave Chief asked Williamson if it would not be wise to smoke the pipe with the Cheyennes since they had always been enemies.

Both Brave Chief and Medicine Arrow may have participated in battles between their tribes. In the 1830s, the Pawnees stole the Cheyennes' Sacred Arrow Bundle in battle, and in the 1850s several serious encounters occurred, in one of which the great Cheyenne chief, Alights on the Cloud was killed. In the 1860s, warfare continued, and in the 1870s, Pawnee Scouts were in engagements with the U.S. military against the Cheyennes.[66] Now that the Pawnees were moving to this country, Brave Chief believed it wise to change their relationship. He stated also that if they were turned loose (without smoking the pipe, a sacred act), they would find other Cheyennes and bring them back. Williamson agreed, and Brave Chief brought forth his pipe, and tobacco

---

* Men leading a war party were not allowed to ask for food and water, and were expected to go hungry if sustenance was not offered (Grinnell, *The Cheyenne Indians*, vol. II, p. 193). Since the Pawnees were the enemy, and therefore outside the Cheyenne social system, this rule apparently did not follow.

Pawnee enemies. Sioux and Cheyenne chiefs and warriors at Fort Laramie in 1868. They are identified as Spotted Tail, Brulé Sioux (far left); then Roman Nose, Cheyenne; Old Man Afraid of His Horses, Sioux; Lone Horn, Sioux; Whistling Elk and Pipe. The last man is unidentified. Courtesy of Western History Collections, University of Oklahoma Library.

was brought from the wagon. He took a burning ember from the fire, lighted the pipe, and carried it to Medicine Arrow. *

He offered it to him in the traditional way. Medicine Arrow did not refuse it, but he did not smoke it and handed it back to Brave Chief with the gesture to smoke it. Brave Chief did so, taking a few puffs, and then following ritual, handed it back to the Cheyenne, who instead of smoking handed it to the man next to him on the log, who smoked it and handed it on to the next man. The last Cheyenne offered it to Harry Coons and then

---

* The pipe played an important role in both Cheyenne and Pawnee religious, economic, and political affairs as well as in preparation for warfare. According to Cheyenne belief, in some circumstances, if a man was offered the pipe it indicated that the offerer had a request that should not be refused. Therefore, it behooved a man to consider seriously the acceptance of the offer to smoke. On the other hand, in some instances there could be serious consequences if the pipe was not accepted and smoked when offered. (Grinnell, *The Cheyenne Indians*, vol. II, pp. 8, 10, 11, 128.)

Brave Chief's son, who both smoked the pipe. It was then taken to Alexander and Williamson. What ensued is told in Williamson's words, full of bravado and ignorance.

> We thought we would be as stubborn as the Cheyenne and therefore refused to smoke. Brave Chief came over and talked to us and tried to persuade us to smoke. This so enraged Mr. Alexander and myself to think that after going to the trouble to cook coffee for them and then have the Chief refuse to smoke that pipe that we concluded we would shoot the whole eight of them. This would guard us against their spreading the news to other Indians that we were in the country.[67]

He told Coons and the others what he planned to do, but Brave Chief urged him not to do this. He may have thought that Medicine Arrow might smoke the pipe eventually, since he had allowed his men to do so and that it might have been Cheyenne protocol to wait until all others had smoked before he did so. Whether he told this to the brash Williamson is not known, but he advocated letting the Cheyennes go and returning their guns to them without ammunition. He had found that the agencies were nearby and thought it was improbable that this party of Cheyennes would give them any more trouble. Williamson, apparently realizing that Brave Chief knew more than he did about such situations, backed down and supper preparations continued. Coffee and "homemade camp bread" were given to the prisoners before they were given their freedom. They stood and pleaded for their ammunition, but this was denied them. Williamson did not say whether Medicine Arrow smoked the pipe or not.

After the Cheyennes left, the others ate their supper and decided to continue the journey, traveling until late that night. In time, they came to the Canadian River, near which the Cheyenne and Arapaho agency was located at Darlington, north of the present site of El Reno, Oklahoma. Williamson was relieved to see the U.S. flag flying over the new army post, later named Fort Reno, located near the Indian agency. They arrived at the agency at three o'clock in the afternoon, seven days after leaving the main party. There they were greeted by Agent John D. Miles. He was not surprised to see them and had been looking for their arrival since the Indian Department had notified him of their coming. Williamson told him the rest of the group would be arriving later.

After the horses were taken care of and the men had had some food, Williamson visited with Miles. He was asked if the party had met any hostile Indians en route. Williamson told him of their encounter with Medicine Arrow's party and how they had captured then released them. Agent Miles then took him to the military camp's headquarters where he told his story to the commanding officer. He added that he had wanted to kill the Cheyennes instead of releasing them and asked what the government would have done if he had done so. The general replied, "I wish you had killed them and I would have seen that you received a medal for it."[68]

He went on to explain that "this chief, Medicine Arrow or sometimes called Medicine Water, was an escaped Cheyenne from prison and was a very bad Indian and was causing a lot of trouble." If Medicine Arrow was Medicine Water, he had become a notorious person.* His notoriety or bad reputation with non-Indians came from his response to the conditions in which he and his tribesmen found themselves at this time. The southern Cheyennes faced hunger and starvation. Between 1872 and 1874, it is estimated that over 7,500,000 buffalo were killed by white buffalo hunters. The Cheyennes had complained of this activity and had been promised, they thought, that the government would do something to prevent the decimation. But they could not see that the situation had changed. Unlicensed whiskey dealers sneaked into their camps and drunkenness became a problem. Bands of horse thieves preyed on their herds, and there seemed to be no help from the government in the prevention or cure for these afflictions.[69]

By June 1874, just a few months before preparations were

---

* It is doubtful that Medicine Water and Medicine Arrow were the same man as Williamson claims one officer said. Karen D. Petersen finds that the only other name attributed to Medicine Water was Blocked Road, according to an interviews she held with Paul Goose, a Cheyenne, in 1960. (Personal communication, July 20, 1987) Donald Berthrong, in *The Southern Cheyennes* (pages 396 and 399), said that a Medicine Arrows and a Medicine Water were among several leaders who refused to surrender to the government in November, 1874, and who later left the area and went north toward Kansas.

made to remove the Pawnees to Indian Territory, the Kiowas, Comanches, and some Cheyennes had smoked the war pipe and began attacking the buffalo hunters they found destroying their life sustenance source. Adobe Walls, a trading settlement, was attacked by Grey Beard and Medicine Water and their men. These two leaders had accepted the Kiowa and Comanche call to battle, as had many of the young Cheyenne warriors who did not heed their chiefs' admonition to refrain from war. In 1874, Medicine Water became the most active of the Cheyennes in avenging the injustices against his people. He was accused of murdering some members of the German (Germain) family and holding others captive.[70] He was also charged with attacking and killing a survey party. This was in August. In May, a surveying party had fired on a band of friendly Cheyennes and wounded one of them, and Medicine Water's action seems to have been a response to this attack.[71]

If it were Medicine Water that the Pawnees and Williamson encountered, then the woman that Williamson described as Medicine Water's wife was Mochi, a woman warrior of the Cheyennes, who saw all the men in her family massacred at Sand Creek by Col. J. M. Chivington and his troops. She subsequently pledged and carried out revenge for this atrocity.[72] Later, in 1875, both Mochi and Medicine Water were arrested and taken to Fort Marion, Florida as U.S. prisoners with other southern plains Indian leaders.[73]

It is possible that the Pawnees and Williamson did encounter Medicine Arrow on their way to the agency. His son, Fox Tail, told Miles in mid-December that his father was some sixty miles northwest of the agency and would not come there because he was "fearful that the soldiers may get hold of his 'arrows'—in which lies the great secret of his 'medicine.'"[74] Great Bend, Kansas, from which point Williamson traveled south, is almost directly north and a little northwest of the Cheyenne agency. If Williamson were traveling in that general direction, the encounter could have occurred since it seems both parties were in the same area about the same time.

The main body of the Pawnees were on their way to this agency, and both Miles and the military officers held a council with the Cheyenne chiefs to inform them of this and to urge them to put aside the old feelings of hostility and revenge for past wrongs. According to Williamson, the Cheyennes were asked to accept the offer of friendship from the Pawnees when they arrived.[75]

This was not the first time that an attempt had occurred to reduce hostility between the tribes. In 1871, Agent Troth had permitted a party of Pawnees to travel into Indian Territory to visit the Cheyenne and Arapaho tribes to make peace if possible. Barclay White had not given approval for this journey and had forcefully informed the agent and the chiefs of his displeasure after it had been completed.[76]

Another attempt to make peace with their traditional enemies, the Cheyennes and Osages seemed to have occurred without government knowledge. Sometime in 1874, after the massacre at the hands of the Sioux in August 1873, Roan Chief (Roaming Chief) took fifteen warriors and went south toward the Osage reservation located north of the Arkansas River in north-central Indian Territory. Proceeding directly to the Osage Agency, the Pawnees sought council with the Osages for the purpose of making peace and to seek their assistance in going to the Cheyennes for the same purpose.

Cyprian Tayrien, a mixed-blood French-Osage clerk at Coffey's Trading Post witnessed and later reported the events in which he took part. He said the Osage chiefs hesitated because they did not know how the Cheyennes would react to their taking the peacemakers' role. Some Osages had taken part in the Custer massacre of Cheyennes on the Washita River some years before. They also heard that the Pawnee Scouts had fought against the Cheyennes in the past. For these reasons the only chief that volunteered to accept the Pawnee request was Ka-he-ga-ton-ga of the Hominy Creek Band. He had had some experience in dealing with the Cheyennes and apparently thought that the mission might be terminated satisfactorily.

After proper feasting and pipe ceremonies, the two groups prepared to depart. There were thirty-six Osage warriors, their chief, and the Pawnees. Also, it was decided to allow John Ferguson of the trading store and his assistant, Tayrien, to take a wagonload of trade goods with them. The party moved westward out of the Osage country into the Eagle Chief Creek area in present Major County, Oklahoma. The plan was to hunt buffalo for a few days, then turn south toward the Cheyenne Agency.

Suddenly, a group of some two hundred Cheyennes led by Chief Stone Calf arrived at the hunting site. They were angry at finding the Osages and Pawnees on what they considered their hunting grounds. The Osage chief, as spokesman for the trespassers, eloquently and persuasively induced the Cheyennes to consider the Pawnee peace proposal, which was agreed to after negotiations took place.[77]

Later Stone Calf advocated peace and surrender to the government and had brought the various Cheyenne bands into the agency in March 1874.[78] Thus, his commitment to cessation of Cheyenne warfare against their old enemy seems indicated. Curiously, Williamson does not mention a peace council between the Pawnees and the Cheyennes at the agency.

The Death of Pitaresaru

The advance party of forty chiefs, leaders, and their families left the Pawnee reservation in October, before the second and larger group led by John Williamson. Williamson had been instructed to tell them, should he encounter them on the way, that they were to travel expeditiously on to the Wichita Agency. Apparently the two parties did not meet one another and the first communication from the first group came in a letter that was sent from Fort Larned, Kansas, on November 12, 1874. It was directed to Jonathan Richards, the Wichita agent. It is a significant message for several reasons. The most important is that Sun Chief, son of Pitaresaru, tells that the head chief is dead.[*] It said,

> Please tell the Pawnee people that 40 lodges of Pawnees are coming to your agency are on the Arkansas travelling slow. Can't tell

[*] G. B. Grinnell knew Sun Chief, Pitaresaru's son, as he called him. Luther North said that a Pawnee at the time referred to Sun Chief as the chief, saying, he is now Pitaresaru (Grinnell, Nebraska Historical Society Archives, MS. 616). Some sources say that he was the nephew of Pitaresaru. If he were the son of Pitaresaru's sister, he would have as much or perhaps more right to assume the role of chief. Garland Blaine explained that a man's sister's child was truly of

how long it will take to make the journey. Pitaresaru, the Head
Chief of the Chowee Band is dead. His son is coming—look out
for us.

Sun Chief X his mark

Tell my brothers that we are coming with wives and children.

Good Chief X his mark

Also tell them that Tererecowwaw the oldest chief of the Pitahawirata is coming with his people.

Ter re cowwa X his mark

I am Skidi Chief. Ten Lodges with me.

Captain Chief X his mark
Lekelawedeshar[79]

One of the great Pawnee chiefs was dead. And after his death,
questions began about the mysterious death, when it occurred
and under what circumstances. There are several accounts, all of
which differ in some way. George Bird Grinnell, personally acquainted with the Pawnees, seems not to have an account from
them but from John Williamson that he obtained in later years.
He said that Pitaresaru left the agency to go to Columbus to get a
load of government freight. Some place between his village and
the town he accidentally shot himself in the leg with his own
pistol. "He was brought back to the agency seemingly not very
badly hurt and for a few days was seen about. This was in 1874?"
asked Grinnell.

W. W. Mannington of Monroe, Nebraska, made a coffin, and
Williamson buried the chief.* Later, Williamson said that several "professors" tried to have him show them where the grave

---

the maternal bloodline, while a man's wife's son might be or not be his own son.
The term used for a chief's sister's son was *piraresaru*, or "child chief." This
child had a greater right and chance to succeed his uncle. In Pawnee kinship
terminology, this child was called "son" by his maternal uncle (Garland J. and
Martha R. Blaine, unpublished notes).

* It would seem imperative that such a respected and important chief be given
the honor of traditional ceremony by his people. It seems that Williamson, an
outsider, should not have anything to do with his burial. To the author, this
seems to give some credence to the suspicions concerning the conditions surrounding his death.

Pitaresaru, Man Chief (meaning "Chief of Men") of the Chaui Band and head chief of the Pawnees. Born in 1823, he became Head Chief when he was twenty-nine. It was said that he made the welfare of the whole tribe the one purpose of his life. He attempted to withstand the pressures of the U.S. government to remove his people from Nebraska and, under mysterious circumstances, died as the result of a gunshot wound in 1874. Courtesy of Hastings Museum, Hastings, Nebraska.

was, but he refused, thinking that they wanted to get the remains for some purpose.

In another account, John B. Dunbar, who had lived among the Pawnees for many years, said that Pitaresaru, although he was not in favor of removal, decided to send his son, Sun Chief, to go to investigate the new country to which the Pawnees might be removed. Knowing of his great influence over his people, certain "agitators" for removal were accused of causing his death, although it was popularly believed he had accidentally shot himself with a pistol. "It is quite confidently asserted, also, that the shot was from another hand and with malicious intent." Gangrene developed, causing death. Immediately after this, the tribe was "hurried away to the Territory."[80] This would place his death in the fall of 1874, before the October or November departure of the two groups of Pawnees.

In speaking of Pitaresaru's many positive qualities, Dunbar said,

> To those not well acquainted with the tribe, his quiet and imperturbable demeanor sometimes carried the impression that he was deficient in force and decision. Wisely he preferred to influence his tribe usually by suggestion and persuasion, and so skillful was he in the application of these means that he oftentimes controlled without his presence or desires being felt; but when occasion required he could easily assume imperial attitude and authority. . . .
> In personal intercourse he was dignified but affable . . . and many anecdotes and bon-mots attributed to him are still in circulation in the tribe.[81]

Pitaresaru, or Man Chief, is still remembered a century later. His songs are sung and danced to at Pawnee events where war-dance songs and others are sung (personal observation by author). His songs resulted from his visions and experiences and were composed and sung by him in the sacred societies to which he belonged. Some are listed below:

I Am Exalted Among the People, composed when he was selected to be the head chief.

The Heavens Are Speaking. The words of this song say "I stood here, I stood there, the clouds are speaking. I say, 'You are the ruling power, I do not understand, I only know what I am told. You are the ruling power, you are now speaking. This power is yours, O Heavens.'" It was said that Pitaresaru would go out in the storm and stand here and there and listen to Tirawahut speak "through the clouds." He knew that the ruling power existed in the heavens and listened for his voice in the storm.

O Expanse of the Heavens. This translates to say, *I believe that in you, O Heavens, dwell the ruling powers.*

Power Is in the Heavens. This says, "My spirit rests in the belief that power is in the Heavens."

Our Hearts Are Set in the Heavens. This proclaims, "It is there that our hearts are set, [our spirits are found], in the expanse of the heavens."[82]

Stories about his death continued to be told. George E. Hyde heard that Pitaresaru, still bitterly opposed to his people leaving their ancestral lands, went with the group that John Williamson accompanied. On the first day of the march, as he forded the Loup River, he was shot in the leg and carried back to the agency. "Some said that his pistol had gone off accidentally, others that he had shot himself so that he might be buried in the land of his fathers. . . . It was even whispered that the whites had instigated the shooting because the chief continued his opposition to removal." After his death from the wound, he was buried in the Chawi cemetery on the hill south of the Loup.[83]

A version attributed to Maj. Frank North claimed that Pitaresaru was shot in the knee by the accidental firing of his pistol as he was crossing the Loup. He was with the group of Pawnees who left in the autumn of 1874. The wound was serious and the tribe decided to stop and camp while he recovered. Pitaresaru believed that this was a sign of misfortune for his tribe and that they would suffer much loss of life and "regret the move they were making away from their homeland." He also believed that he was to die, although doctors who were brought from Columbus said that the wound was not serious enough to cause death.[84]

In 1976, Garland J. Blaine, head chief of the Pawnees, gave a Pawnee account of Pitaresaru's death with the following story:

> They wanted the Pawnees to move to Indian Territory, but the Pawnee chief, Man Chief, Pitaresaru, said, "No, we are going to stay right here". Well, one morning they sent word for him to come across the river to the agent's building. So he started across the river and he was shot. Shot in the leg. He got away and dragged himself into the bushes. Whoever shot him did not come on down because he was afraid. He did not live very long after that. Gangrene set in and he died of blood poisoning. They are pretty sure it was some whiteman working at the agency. They planned it to get rid of his opposition. He was the Head Chief and when he said, no, that was it.[85]

The Pawnees have continued to believe that Pitaresaru's death was caused by a deliberate act by the whites. With the death of this powerful and respected leader, the people's sense of foreboding increased, as they found themselves journeying south toward an unpredictable future.

Before the advance party arrived at Fort Larned and sent the message of Pitaresaru's death, it had encountered a company of the U.S. Sixth Cavalry under Capt. D. Madden, who notified Maj. Gen. John Pope, commanding at Fort Leavenworth, that a party of 250 Pawnees were in the vicinity of Fort Hayes. Pope notified Enoch Hoag, superintendent of the Central Superintendency, of this fact and requested that they be sent back to their reservation.[86] Pope's concern was that the situation in Kansas was tense, with "hostile" Indians present and that the Pawnees added another factor to a possibly dangerous situation.

The Pawnees told Capt. D. Madden that they had permission from their agent and presumably showed the pass that Burgess had given them. They added that they planned to hunt buffalo and then go visit the Osages. This met with resistance because Pope said the Osages were still giving difficulty.[87] A message that they were in transit to a new home in Indian Territory under orders of the commissioner of Indian Affairs seemed to lessen the agitation about their presence.

Apparently, the party traveled from Fort Hayes to Fort Larned directly in the week that lapsed between the notification of their presence at the latter fort and the writing of the letter concerning the death of Pitaresaru written on November 12. Before leaving the fort, they had another letter written for them addressed to Supt. Barclay White. In it they announced their arrival and said that they had not been able to "draw" any food from any of the forts at which they had stopped, nor had they seen any buffalo on their way. They planned to cross the Arkansas River that evening on their way to the Wichita Agency. As evidence of their hunger, they added that White should make sure that there would be food for them at the Wichita Agency when they arrived.[88]

If the Indian office authorities had expected that food for the hungry Pawnees could be procured at posts along the route, then the fact that this assistance was not forthcoming indicates faulty communication and planning. It would seem that the military posts and Major General Pope's office would have been informed of their movement through the state so that the confrontation between the Pawnees and the military and the consequent telegrams, orders, and letters of explanation would not have been necessary.

Pawnee problems with the authorities in Kansas were not over. On December 7, Gov. Thomas A. Osborne sent a letter to Superintendent Hoag, complaining that over five hundred Pawnee Indians were in western Barber County, stealing and running off cattle that had been stampeded by a snow storm. About two hundred head had been recovered from them on the second day of December. He demanded that the whole group leave the state at once.[89]

The estimate of over five hundred people would indicate that this was Williamson's group. It will be recalled that the party encountered a great blizzard in that region and that the people were in desperate need of food. The number of cattle taken may well have been exaggerated as claims against Indians were often inflated, and the snow storm offered a good pretext to claim Indian depredation. It is possible that many of the cattle may have later been recovered, like the horse previously mentioned. Or persons other than the Pawnees may have "rustled" the cattle. Williamson claimed that cattle and horse thieves were present in Kansas at that time.[90]

The Pawnee "trail of tears," such as the Cherokees, before them, was oppressingly difficult. They carried not only all their possessions, but the burden of Pitaresaru's death and the terrible sadness of leaving their homeland. They had been unjustly accused of hay, horse, and cattle stealing, and faced an irate gun-carrying posse. In a starving condition, they had to accept rejected, substandard flour, and also buy beef from a man who claimed he had sold to starving Indians before. They had been ordered by military men to get back to their reservation in Nebraska and had been told to get out of Kansas by its governor. These were the *we-tuks* times.

Agent Burgess Travels to Indian Territory to Locate a Reservation

After the October 10 council meeting, Com. E. P. Smith was informed of the Pawnee decision, and he gave his approval of the resolution for Pawnee removal on the 14 in a letter to Barclay White.[91] He reiterated that the Pawnees be located east of the ninety-sixth meridian in Indian Territory, on lands that the Cherokees, in the treaty of July 19, 1866, had agreed could be used by the government for the future settlement of friendly Indian tribes. A map study of the region shows that three-fourths of the territory lay west of this north-south line and that east of it were the established homes and lands of the Cherokees, Creeks, Choctaws, and a few small tribal reservations in the far northeast corner. It had been stated that the Pawnees would be placed in an area not occupied by other tribes, but Smith's decision seemed to contradict that. Any location east of that line was from 150 to 250 miles from the Wichita Agency, again indicating that the Pawnee plan to live near their friends at that agency was not regarded seriously by the government.

Agent Burgess was instructed to travel south and undertake the necessary steps to locate a reservation. On November 11, he told the chiefs who remained on the reservation (the others having left to migrate south) that he would soon be leaving to search out a place for them and that George P. Howell would be in charge of the agency during his absence.[92] On November 23, he left the agency accompanied by his son, Henry Edwin, who was to act as interpreter, and by another individual called a "special assistant." He made a stop at Lawrence, Kansas, to talk with Supt. Enoch Hoag.[93] The Pawnees would be under his jurisdiction in Indian Territory, and Burgess would report to him and be under his authority.

From there, Burgess was directed to travel to Baxter Springs, Kansas, where the party took a hack to go to the Quapaw Agency, located in the far northeast corner of the territory. He arrived there on December 8 and conferred with Agent Hiram W. Jones. He was informed that this was a small reservation and that while it was suitable for a small tribe, such as the Quapaws, its limited amount of land certainly would not meet the needs of the Pawnees.[94] This agency contained the small reservations of the Quapaws, Senecas, Miamis, Wyandots, Peorias, Ottawas, and other remnants of once powerful eastern tribes. * The total area of their combined reservations was approximately the same size as the Pawnees' Nebraska reservation. With audacity, the government sought to place the Pawnees in the confines of this agency, which

---

* The U.S. government continued to settle or attempt to settle other tribes on these lands. Modocs from California and Oregon were brought there in 1874; and in the spring of 1875, Supt. Enoch Hoag wrote to the agent, informing him that the government wanted to relocate some three thousand hostile plains Indians that had recently surrendered to the military. He asked if there was a suitable location for them at the Quapaw Agency and, if "possibly the Quapaws might at some suitable time in the near future be induced to surrender their reservation to the Government for this purpose permanently for a suitable compensation," and if the Osages might be willing to adopt the Quapaws. (See E. Hoag to H. W. Jones, March 10, 1875. Oklahoma Historical Society, Archives and Manuscripts. Quapaw Agency—Removal from One Reservation to Another.) This time the agent answered more positively than he had to Agent Burgess. He said the Quapaws had a reservation of some sixty-thousand acres, a large part of which was unoccupied, and "a portion thereof might be obtained." Many of the Quapaws, he added, had said that they wished to remove and join the Osages, and if they did so, then their lands could be used to settle the southwestern Indian Territory agency Indians referred to by the superintendent. (See Jones to Hoag, March 13, 1875, Oklahoma Historical Society, Archives and Manuscripts. Quapaw Agency—Removal from One Reservation to Another.)

would have meant that tribes already located there would have to cede land to make a place for them, and the Pawnees would have been confined to a very small area.

If the agent had prior authority to turn down Burgess's inquiry, then why was he sent there to make such a request? Burgess spent only one day there and arrived the next day at the U.S. Consolidated Agency for the Cherokees, Creeks, Choctaws, Seminoles, and Chickasaws at Muskogee. There he had been instructed to talk to the leading men of the Cherokees about the Pawnees settling on their lands east of the ninety-sixth meridian and west of the MKT railroad line. He had been told, he said, that this land was "about what we want."[95]

By this time, the U.S. government had had enough vigorous dealings with the educated and savvy Cherokees that it should have known what the response to such a request would be. For such an encounter, Superintendent Hoag had arrived, and with Agents Ingalls and Burgess, was "at council of the Commissioners of these nations." Burgess addressed the Cherokees about his mission, and "they met the case in all frankness and courtesy, but all unite in being unwilling to part with any portion of their territory east of the 96th meridian to tribes not sufficiently advanced in civilization to abandon their tribal relations and to be incorporated with them in their general interests and municipal affairs," he reported.[96]

Principal Chief William Potter Ross, a Princeton University graduate, said the Cherokees were willing to sell land *west* of the ninety-sixth meridian to friendly tribes. It was suggested to Burgess that the tract lying in the forks of the Arkansas and Red Fork (Cimarron) rivers, south of the Osage reservation, might well serve the needs of the Pawnees. The Cherokee suggestion was based on the aforementioned treaty of July 19, 1866, with the United States, in which it had been agreed that the United States was authorized to settle "civilized" tribes *east* of the ninety-sixth meridian and to settle "friendly" Indians on unoccupied land *west* of that line.[97] Apparently, the latter rather than the former description fit the Cherokee estimation of the Pawnees.

After this pleasant and firm rejection of Commissioner Smith's plan to settle the Pawnees east of the ninety-sixth meridian, Burgess agreed to look at the land that was offered as a possible

William Potter Ross, chief of the Cherokees from 1866–67 and 1872–75. In 1874 he and the Cherokee council met with Pawnee Agent William Burgess and others to discuss establishment of a Pawnee reservation on Cherokee ceded lands. Courtesy Western History Collections, University of Oklahoma Library.

alternative and left Muskogee, traveling to Okmulgee, the Creek Nation's capital, thence to the Sac and Fox Agency further west, near the Deep Fork River, five miles south of the present town of Stroud, Oklahoma. Once there, following previous instructions, Burgess examined the country between the Canadian and Red Fork of the Arkansas. This was not the area suggested by the Cherokees, but it was the area directly west of the Sac and Fox reservation, which later became the Ioway and Kickapoo reservations.

These reservations were part of former Creek and Seminole lands that had been relinquished to the federal government after the Civil War as reparations in the 1866 treaties. These lands in Indian Territory had been assigned to these tribes in the 1830s in exchange for their homelands in the eastern and southern United States.

After examining this area, the party turned north and visited the area suggested by the Cherokees, south of the Osage reservation between the forks of the Arkansas and Cimarron rivers. Burgess inspected it and decided it was suitable for the Pawnees. Then they turned south and west and traveled to the Wichita Agency, arriving there early in January 1875.[98] There Burgess found that a small group of Pawnees had arrived, but the others had not.

The Pawnee agent had been directed to inspect land between the forks of the two rivers mentioned above, but he was not the only one interested in that area. At the same time that Burgess headed toward his council with the Cherokee leaders and Superintendent Hoag, Agent John D. Miles answered a letter from the commissioner of Indian Affairs. A map of Indian Territory had been enclosed, on which Miles was requested to draw the outlines of a "proposed location of the Cheyennes." Instead of that smaller scale map, Miles used a larger scale Barrett's Survey map of 1873 to delineate the boundaries of such a reservation. The southern boundary was the Red Fork or Cimarron River, with the agency to be placed north of that river on Big Turkey Creek, which flowed south into the river some miles north of the agency at Darlington. The eastern edge was at the juncture of the Arkansas and Cimarron, including the area inspected by Burgess. The northern edge was marked as the Arkansas River and the

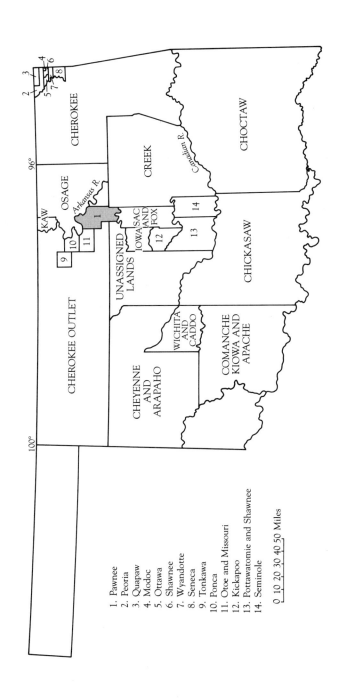

CHEROKEE OUTLET

CHEROKEE

KAW

OSAGE

Arkansas R.

CHEROKEE

96°

CREEK

Canadian R.

CHOCTAW

9

10

11

1

IOWA

SAC AND FOX

12

13

14

UNASSIGNED LANDS

CHICKASAW

CHEYENNE AND ARAPAHO

WICHITA AND CADDO

COMANCHE KIOWA AND APACHE

100°

1. Pawnee
2. Peoria
3. Quapaw
4. Modoc
5. Ottawa
6. Shawnee
7. Wyandotte
8. Seneca
9. Tonkawa
10. Ponca
11. Otoe and Missouri
12. Kickapoo
13. Pottawatomie and Shawnee
14. Seminole

0 10 20 30 40 50 Miles

2 3 4 5 6 7 8

Kansas border. All the land between those two rivers, a sizable section of the entire territory, was included. He sent his map to Enoch Hoag, who had just met with the Cherokees and Burgess. Well aware that this same area was already proposed by the Cherokees for the Pawnee reservation, and Burgess had his approval to inspect it, he wrote to the commissioner, not mentioning this but approving of Miles's plan and enclosing the map and Miles's long letter explaining that such a large area would enable the government to separate widely the different bands of Cheyennes, thus making them less able to congregate for hostile purposes. Hoag's approval was based on the tentative plan to have both the Arapahoes and Cheyennes share the same reservation in the future.[99]

Even as the Pawnees traveled the hard winter route from their Nebraska homeland, the decision of where they were to be settled was in doubt. The government played less than an honest role in allowing agents to seek the same land for the settlement of tribes that had little to say in the final decision.

✝✝✝
10
1875

The Pawnees Live on Three Reservations

When the people first saw the reservation in Indian Territory, they did not like the land and wanted to go back to Nebraska. The religion was born there and the people were buried there. They might have to come here, but someday they would go back.
— Garland J. Blaine, October 1, 1966

After Williamson left the Pawnees in the Great Bend area, they decided to go as planned to search for buffalo. Apparently, they traveled southwest into western Kansas and then into Indian Territory. They finally located some buffalo west of Camp Supply and hunted and processed them for meat and robes. Afterwards, they traveled southeast and arrived at the Wichita Agency on February 16, 1875, some three months after leaving Nebraska. By then their hunger was so great that by the time they arrived at the agency, they had consumed most of their meat and had traded their robes for needed supplies.[1] There were many emotional greetings as the 360 Pawnees who had been at the Wichita Agency for a year located their relatives and good friends among the new arrivals. Soon they were joined by the "advance" group containing chiefs and other leaders who had been designated to select the new reservation. Agent William Burgess estimated about 1,760 Pawnees were now gathered among the Wichitas.

Although Agent Jonathan Richards had been authorized to issue beef cattle weekly to them until they could go to their own reservation, this large number was a strain on the agency supplies. For this reason, no sooner had the tribe arrived than Burgess called a council, so that the October 8, 1874, council resolution to inspect the reservation he had selected for them could be implemented. Although their horses were jaded from the long journey, the agent urged that he and the selected group of forty, "or as many of them as can go," should depart to look at the new land as soon as possible.

Accompanied by the Pawnee group, his son, and John Williamson and A. L. Alexander, Burgess left on February 22, going by way of the Sac and Fox Agency. There he completed his camping outfit. Then the group proceeded to the new reservation on the other side of the Cimarron River.[2] The 150 to 200 mile journey took less than ten days. On March 3, 1875, the chiefs, the agent, and others held a council at the new reservation. The Pawnees had explored the land, and Burgess claimed they were well satisfied with it, although they declared it was a very great distance from their friends, the Wichitas.

Burgess now composed a letter to the commissioner of Indian Affairs from the chiefs formally accepting the location selected for the tribe by the agent. They requested that the commissioner grant them this land as their new home and that other agreements made in the October 8 council by the government be carried out. It was requested that the Pawnees at the Wichita and Nebraska agencies be brought to the new reservation at the earliest possible time. The agent was careful to add that the Pawnees requested necessary funds be appropriated to them so that their hunger could be alleviated and that the trappings of civilization, such as schools, houses, and farm equipment be acquired.[3]

In the old Pawnee confederacy, the Chawis, Pitahawiratas, and Kitkahahkis each took the position of the leading band in turn, and that band's head chief became the head chief of all three bands in major decision making with other tribes, the U.S. government, and intertribal activities. Just how long the length of this cycle was has not been determined. The Skidis, who had been separated from the main tribe for a long period of time, were not part of this leadership cycle.[4] At this time in history, the Chawi was the leading Band. Since its recent head chief, Pitaresaru, was dead, Sun Chief, his son or nephew, had become the traditional leader of the tribe. In Nebraska council documents signed by the chiefs and leaders, traditionally, the leading

band Chawi chiefs signed first, then the Pitahawirata or Kitkahahki, then the Skidi chiefs.

In the document signed at the new reservation, an unheard
breach of precedent occurred. The first signer was a Skidi, Comanche Chief, followed by a Kitkahahki chief, Lacharachihix
(Man Chief?), then a Pitahawirata chief, Terrerecox. No Chawi
chiefs signed, only Se-tid-ah-row-weet, and Ta-coo-wi-ta-coo,
designated as soldiers of that band. Following them were seven
other signers, four Kitkahahkis and three Skidis for a total of
twelve. For some reason, traditional rank order and balanced
representation were not observed in the signing.

At the October 8 council, Sun Chief's name and signature, an
X, was the first on the list of men who were to be reservation
selection members, but he was not in the group that went there
to inspect it. According to Burgess, at the Wichita Agency, the
original forty agreed to "deputize" a group to go with him, and
the whole tribe would abide by its decision. How this group was
selected is not given, but it does not seem to represent the tribal
power structure, being singularly lacking in Chawi and Pitahawirata chiefs. However, it is possible that illness or other causes
prevented the Chaui head chief and others from going to the
new reservation.

After the council and the petition signing, the Pawnees were
directed to return to the Wichita Agency. Burgess sent the Pawnee acceptance of the new reservation for official approval. It
was soon given.[5] Burgess crossed the Arkansas River to the Osage
reservation. There he received mail and instructions from the
Indian Office. He arranged with agent Isaac G. Gibson at the
Osage Agency to put out bids for men to break five hundred to
eight hundred acres of new reservation ground for crops to be
planted before the Pawnees arrived.[6] The pressing problem of
providing the Pawnees with food and other needs in this unculti-
vated land faced him.

Burgess returned to the Nebraska Pawnee Agency, and in May
he and Supt. Barclay White traveled to Indian Territory to plan
the new agency's location. It was decided to place it on Black
Bear Creek near a small waterfall. The practical Quaker eye en-
visioned that a suitable mill could be built there. Places for the
agent's house, offices, lumber mill, and employee's dwellings were

laid out.[7] Charles Chapin was a member of a party that Burgess hired in Nebraska to go to the new reservation to construct the needed buildings. He remembered that there were six or eight others, with George Scott selected as foreman. Taking wagons filled with supplies, they traveled to Arkansas City, Kansas. From there they traveled southward and eventually came to the agency site.[8]

While the agency buildings were going up, plans were made for the Pawnees at the Wichita Agency to come to the new reservation. In May, John Williamson received instructions to go there and return guiding the Pawnees. Agent Richardson was notified of the plans and his assistance sought in supplying them with whatever food he could spare for the journey. If any tribal members were too ill or infirm, Burgess asked that they might be allowed to stay with their Wichita friends until such time as they could travel.

Apparently, the journey was to be made afoot and on horseback, since Burgess suggested that wagons would slow progress when rivers and creeks had to be crossed.[9] It is also possible that there were no wagons available or that Burgess did not want to go through the long drawn-out government-required process of acquiring them. So once again, the people shouldered their belongings, or loaded them on their horses, and traveled to what for many was an unwanted destination.

In May, Burgess requested approval of Robert F. Catterson, Oak Park, Illinois, to serve as subagent at the new reservation. Burgess needed to take care of Pawnee affairs and urgent business in Nebraska.[10] Beginning with the early months of 1875, Pawnee financial affairs were in straitened circumstances. A special bill requesting the sale of the Nebraska reservation and an advance of funds to be used to aid the tribe and construct the new agency had been recommended for passage. But in the last crowded days of the recent congressional session, it was not called up for a vote. Therefore, there were no urgently needed funds available for the coming fiscal year.

In March, Commissioner of Indian Affairs E. P. Smith informed the secretary of the Interior that an emergency existed for the Pawnees. He cited their two-year crop and hunt failures, "leaving these Indians with but a small annuity fund of about ten dollars per capita with which to be maintained for a whole year." [11] He said the Pawnees were without means to "procure subsistence," or to prepare their homes, or to return to Nebraska, or to live there if they should return.

So serious was the situation that the commissioner finally requested that presidential assistance be sought in giving the Indian Office authority to obtain the funds so badly needed. It was estimated that $150,000 would be adequate and that the Pawnee Nebraska lands were worth three to four times that amount. [12]

There was an unusually quick response to this request. On March 12, Acting Secretary of the Interior B. R. Cowan informed Commissioner Smith that approval had been given for procurement of the necessary funds, until funds could be obtained through the regular congressional appropriation. The commissioner was instructed to proceed to remedy the Pawnee situation by seeking those suppliers in the open market who would furnish needed food and other items without a contract and would wait for payment until such a time as Congress would appropriate money to reimburse their costs. [13]

Some three weeks later, Commissioner Smith replied that he had received a bid for cattle and flour to be supplied to the Pawnees. However, he added, it was difficult at that distance to see that what was "expedient and right in the matter" was carried out. He recommended that Board of Indian Commissioners representatives be asked to go to Indian Territory to oversee the selection and obtaining of supplies and to investigate the aforementioned cattle and flour offer, as well as any others that might have been received for consideration. * [14]

Involvement of the Board of Indian Commissioners resulted partially from stipulations found in the Deficiency Act passed by Congress the previous year. It provided that no funds appropriated by Congress for payments of deficiencies in the Indian Service could be made until any obligation for payment could be ex-

---

* The Board of Indian Commissioners was created by Act of Congress on April 10, 1869 (U.S. Statutes, 40). The act authorized the U.S. president to select an independent committee of philanthropic and intelligent men who would serve without compensation. Among other duties, their responsibilities included working on an equal basis with the secretary of the Interior to oversee the disbursement of Indian appropriation monies.

amined by the secretary of the Interior and the Board of Indian Commissioners.[15] Under the 1870 Indian Appropriations Act, this body was authorized to inspect vouchers and goods purchased for Indians to prevent shoddy, substandard annuity goods from being foisted upon the Indians with a resulting handsome profit for the supplier. If the board's approval was not given, it recommended that payment be withheld. This was part of an effort, beginning with the Grant administration, to reduce the fraud that was rampant in the Indian Service at that time.[16]

Secretary of the Interior Columbus Delano again reminded the commissioner that it "was to be distinctly understood that, under the authority herein conferred, no obligation will be assumed by the Government, nor any responsibility, nor by implication, is any promise of payment to be inferred from it."[17] This provision resulted from an 1871 law that stated that no contract or purchase could be made without a previous appropriation for that purpose. Indian agents were expected to send estimates of Indian and agency needs for the coming fiscal year so that the amount could be approved or modified and included in the appropriation requests made by the Indian Office to Congress. Since no Pawnee appropriation had been passed in Congress this year, it was hoped that parties could be found who in the interest of humanity would be willing to "rely upon the justice of a Christian Government for payment."

The secretary continued that if it were impractical for the superintendent and agents involved to handle the matter, then, as Smith had suggested, the Board of Indian Commissioners should be asked to lend support. B. Rush Roberts was suggested as a likely person to consult on the matter.[18] As a member of the Society of Friends, he had visited the Pawnee Nebraska reservation on several occasions on Friends Committee inspection tours.

The Indian Office knew that it would be exceedingly difficult to supply the Pawnees with food and other necessities, or build the new agency, without suppliers having government contracts for payment in hand. Very few business men were willing to take a chance on selling to the government with only the hope that Congress would appropriate enough money for them to be paid in the future. Without an approved binding contract to assure payment, even the most sympathetic seller would hesitate.

Knowledge that the appropriation bill and the provision approving the Pawnee land sale had not come before Congress was probably known by suppliers who had dealt with the Pawnees before.

For this reason, the problem that Smith described as "the embarrassing position" in which his office found itself was handed over to the Board of Indian Commissioners. He wrote a long letter to F. H. Smith, secretary of the Board of Indian Commissioners, explaining the situation to him and seeking assistance. He said it was necessary to purchase enough supplies to last the Pawnees until July 1, 1876. These were to include beef cattle, flour, corn, sugar, coffee, clothing materials, farming equipment, construction materials, a sawmill, wagons, and work oxen. If possible, the commissioners were to see to the procurement of a work force to build temporary housing for the employees and Indians and, of course, see that a sawmill was put into operation. In addition to all this, the commissioners were to go to the Nebraska agency and talk to the Pawnees remaining there and decide when the most feasible time was for them to go to their new reservation. This had to be done to decide how many supplies to purchase. Fewer goods would be needed if the Pawnees could be convinced to stay until the following spring when they would be able to raise their own food (if drought or grasshoppers did not cause devastation). On the other hand, if they moved before then, in the fall, after harvest of the present crop, they would have to leave in time to be able to assist the Indian Territory Pawnees in putting out crops in Indian Territory the following spring.[19]

Next came consideration of the proposed reservation sale. John H. Funk, of the Mennonite church group in Elkhart, Indiana, had expressed interest in purchasing the entire 50,000 acres. The commissioners were to discuss this matter with him on their way to Nebraska. If the entire parcel could be sold to the Mennonites, then much time and effort would be saved, and funds would become available sooner.[20]

Commissioner Smith estimated that the lands were worth at least $300,000. He said that sale of the reservation would "remove many difficulties to procuring a future appropriation, because the amount to be appropriated will be sure to be reimbursed by the sale of Indian lands, instead of being a donation to the Indians."[21] This latter expression was erroneous because the Pawnees had received unfair or no compensation for land ceded to the United States and largely occupied by settlers by this time. So any funds received could not be considered a donation.

Board members F. H. Smith and B. Rush Roberts promptly began their task. Less than a week later, on April 14, they were in Chicago and talked to the Mennonite representative, Mr. Funk. The outcome was that he planned to meet with other men of the order and endeavor to form a joint-stock company to raise capital for purchasing the land for exclusive church member use. This would include members emigrating from other countries.[22]

From Chicago, the two men traveled to the Pawnee Nebraska Agency to discuss the approximate time for the Pawnees remaining there to emigrate to their new reservation. The chiefs and leaders strongly urged that the people be allowed to go as soon as possible. The commissioners learned that "several hundred acres of wheat had been sown," and curiously, in spite of the fact that the majority of the tribe was already in Indian Territory, "several thousand acres" of the Nebraska reservation were in the process of being cultivated. It will be recalled that in the previous year, the Pawnees agreed to set aside the majority of their annuity funds to plow new lands. It would seem that, at this late date, it had not been done for the Pawnees but for future users. This seems especially true since the tribe had never needed such a large amount, and when the chiefs agreed to this expenditure, government plans were already afoot for tribal removal.

The commissioners pointed out to the chiefs that no preparations were yet made for caring for school children, the infirm, and the aged at the new reservation. For that and several other reasons, they could not be allowed to leave now. The earliest time would be in the fall after their crops were harvested.

One strong argument given by the chiefs for moving as soon as possible was the continuing Sioux attacks. With so few able-bodied men there, they were at the mercy of the marauders. Regardless, the commissioners decided that the Pawnees must stay where they were until the crops were harvested. A terse notation in the council journal stated that the chiefs agreed to remain on the reservation until fall.[23]

It was probably kept in mind by Smith and Roberts that food

supplies resulting from the hoped-for harvest would decrease the amount of food that would have to be purchased and supplied for the balance of the tribe. From the Pawnee point of view, working in the fields meant the food supply would be enhanced, but at the cost of losing lives to the Throat Cutters.

Supt. Barclay White had been invited by the two men to accompany them when they visited the agency, but he had been visiting another agency and could not go. When they returned to his Omaha office, they told him of their visit and stressed the Pawnee need for military protection from the Sioux. The commissioners also brought up the problem of the tremendous amount of timber stolen from the reservation, estimated at from one to two hundred wagonloads each day.

The commissioners requested that White ask for a military force to be stationed near the agency to prevent this theft and to protect the people from the Sioux. Considering the history of Sioux invasion and attack and the fact that there were only children, old, and infirm persons, and a few others, unable to defend themselves, it seems difficult to understand why protection was not sought and given long before the commissioners forced the issue. Apparently with this insistence, Maj. Gen. George Crook dispatched a small force to the agency from Omaha Barracks.[24] Nevertheless, in August the Sioux stealthily approached the Skidi village through a nearby cornfield and killed Eagle Chief's wife. Burgess reported, "Captain Wheaton's company was stationed within sight, within a few hundred yards of the point of attack. It was not only inadequate for protection, but of no practical benefit whatever against Indians." And again, a week later, a party of Indians, or fourteen men "dressed like Sioux," attacked and killed Charlie Fighting Bear, herding horses near the village, only forty rods from the carpenter's house.[25]

From Omaha, the commissioners traveled to Saint Louis, where they met Agent Burgess, who just returned from the East. Their plans now turned to obtaining the much-needed Pawnee supplies. In Chicago, they had met a former commissioner, C. G. Hammond, who informed them that no businessmen in that city would deal with them on the terms they had to offer. Only with "sufficient consideration" would any deal be made without a contract and with only the hope that Congress would eventually appropriate money. Another former commissioner, J. V. Farwell, also was discouraging in his assessment of their success. Saint Louis businessman, Robert Campbell, also a businessman and former commissioner, was eager to be of assistance, until he learned of the conditions that the Indian Office imposed. He said it was futile unless they could find men who would speculate for a liberal profit margin.[26]

And it was true, they could find no business that would deal with them. Later, some offers made to supply flour, beef, and other supplies were so exorbitant that the commissioners refused them. Admitting that further efforts were futile to obtain the needed food and supplies for the Pawnees, they returned to Washington. They informed Commissioner Smith it was impossible to do what had been assigned them and asked to be relieved of the duty. At this, Smith earnestly appealed to them, saying that there was no other way to provide for the Pawnees and asking if they would continue their efforts. They agreed, and from time to time, were able to obtain needed supplies, probably at handsome profits for the suppliers, whose reluctance to do business at this time under any other terms is understandable.

In February, Burgess filled out a standard printed annuity goods request form used by the Office of Indian Affairs, dated February 1, 1875. On this form, items were divided into classes, with a standard 1874 price for each item. Of the items listed, Burgess requested the following: 100 scarlet woolen blankets; 50 indigo blue blankets; 120 yards each of blue and scarlet cloth; 80 woolen shawls; 5 pounds of linen thread; 40 dozen spools of cotton thread; 2,000 yards of standard calico prints; 400 yards each of indigo blue drilling, bed ticking, brown sheeting, and duck material; 100 yards each of red and blue flannel; 200 yards each of blue denim and hickory shirting; 5 dozen cotton handkerchiefs; 4 dozen each of men's wool socks and women's wool hose; 40 red flannel shirts; 20 gray flannel shirts; 50 hickory shirts; 25 calico shirts; 10 pounds of assorted yarn; 10 suits of officers' clothing (for agency Indian police); 60 sack coats for men in assorted sizes; 150 pants of assorted sizes; and 100 men's wool hats, assorted sizes. Items other than clothing were 5 dozen best cast steel axes, 4 dozen tin plates, 5 dozen tinned-iron tablespoons, 10 dozen tinned-iron teaspoons, 5 dozen six-inch butcher knives, 5 dozen good quality knives and forks, 3 dozen pocketknives, 2 dozen hatchets, 2 dozen cast steel shears, and needles of assorted sizes.

The total price of all items was $3,072.98.[27] These items were supposedly requested and approved by the chiefs and were to be handed out during the annual annuity goods distribution. The few pictures known of Pawnees at this time do not indicate a wide use of some of the clothing items listed. Burgess requested no children's clothing, and no footwear for either adults or children, although the government's form listed them as available for purchase. It is assumed that moccasins were worn by those who still had the animal skins to make them.

While the Indian commissioners tried to obtain Pawnee supplies, Pawnees in Nebraska and at the Wichita Agency tried to alleviate the uncertainty of their future food supply by planting their traditional crops.[28] When the larger group reached the new reservation via the Wichita Agency, they found that land had been broken, as planned by Burgess, and they proceeded to plant crops, unafraid of Sioux attack for the first time in many years. At least in that respect, stress had been reduced. They had brought their own seeds with them from Nebraska, especially the seeds of Mother Corn.[29] It was necessary from time to time to replace the sacred ears in the Sacred Bundles, and these ears grew from seeds of corn saved for this purpose. Since all seeds originally had been given them by Tirawahut, only seeds from Nebraska should be planted, cared for and harvested in the traditional way. In Nebraska, the remaining tribal members planted crops, alert for enemy attack. Even though soldiers were stationed at the agency, a successful Sioux raid did occur, and two of the tribe were killed by the Throat Cutters.[30]

Since the tribe was divided, it was necessary to hold councils with chiefs in both Indian Territory and Nebraska. On April 6, 1875, the chiefs in Nebraska approved the resolution that congressional appropriations made for salaries of employees provided by treaty stipulations be diverted to the "benefit of the Pawnees at large" as designated by the agent and superintendent.[31] Nine signatory names were listed, beginning with Eagle Chief and Lone Chief of the Skidi Band. In a July 5 council, the Nebraska chiefs requested the sum of $3,000.00 be paid to them and to the leading soldiers as salaries "while they faithfully serve in the performance of the duties respectively assigned." The same two chiefs' names were at the top of the list of eleven leaders.

The resolution was also passed in Indian Territory on April 15th by twelve men in council. In this instance, the Pitahawirata chief, "Ter-re-kow-wa" (Terrecowah), and Good Chief's names led the list. It was also requested that $450.00 be set aside to pay the men who had accompanied the agent to inspect the new reservation. There must have been a need, for a request for $1,000 was sought to build a hospital and purchase supplies for it. However, it was asked that the sum be restored to their annuity when the Nebraska land was sold.

This resolution was sent to the Pawnee reservation in Nebraska, where the chiefs there also agreed on July 27 to the hospital building proposal and to pay the men who had inspected and approved of the new reservation.[32] On August 18, the Nebraska chiefs agreed that funds for the Pawnee Manual Labor School be diverted for the construction of a school on the new reservation.[33] At this time, 140 Pawnee pupils were said to attend the Nebraska school. The majority of the tribe's children were in Indian Territory with their families.

In September, the time for removal of the remaining Nebraska Pawnees was at hand, and Burgess made preparations for it. It was estimated that twelve wagons and teams would be needed, and accordingly bids were opened for supplying these items through advertisements in local papers. The bids were to be submitted by October 1, and Studebaker Bros. Manufacturing Company of Saint Joseph, Missouri, was awarded the wagon contract, with a bid of $78.75 per wagon.[34]

There were many details for Burgess to take care of before leaving the agency. One was to hire someone to manage the government property and buildings; another was to appoint E. L. Burgess, his wife, as village matron at the new reservation, and Julia A. Nichols and Marianna Burgess to continue as teachers there and to care for the children during removal. A son had accompanied him as an assistant on the search for the new reservation, and another son, Charles, is noted as a witness to tribal council minutes during the last months in Nebraska.[35] In all, five members of the Burgess family became involved in influencing and controlling Pawnee life.

Wanted!
HORSES,
Wagons and Harness
FOR THE PAWNEE INDIANS.

Sealed Proposals will be received at the office of the Superintendent Indian Affairs Omaha, Nebraska, until noon of Friday Oct. 1st A. D., 1875, for the delivery at Columbus, Platte county, Nebraska, October, 10th 1875, of the following articles, required for the Indian service.

Twenty-three (23) American Horses, from four (4) to eight [8] years old, well broken to harness, sound and kind, and weighing not less than one thousand (1000) pounds each. Also, twelve (12) two horse Wagons, three inch axletree, with neck yoke and double tree, brake, cover and spring seat. Also, twelve [12] sets double harness without breeching.

Bidders will give full description of the articles offered.

Said proposals will be opened at the above named office, No. Eighteenth St., south of Howard St., Omaha, Neb., at noon Friday, October 1st, A. D. 1875.

Bidders are invited to be present at the opening of the bids.

The Government reserves the right to reject any and all bids, interests of the public service requires such rejection.

Sept. 20,'75. **BARCLAY WHITE, Supt. Indian Aff's.**

Advertisement for bids to supply wagons, horses, and harness for the final removal of Pawnees remaining on the Nebraska reservation in 1875. Courtesy of National Archives (Pawnee Agency microfilm RG 75 M234 R 661-0370).

The Pawnees on the new reservation sought permission to go on a hunt, and it was given by Supt. Barclay White, with the stipulation that the children not go and that two white men accompany the group to supervise them. A compelling reason for allowing a hunt was that the "tribe is now subsisted at a heavy expense and in a sickly condition, [and] I believe a hunt at this time would be advantageous to the tribe." [36] The tribe had been in a constant state of hunger and malnourishment for several years and the "sickly condition," resulting partially from lack of food, motivated White's allowing them to go.

Even while Pawnees still lived on their Nebraska reservation in 1875, the agent received numerous requests from as far away as Brooklyn, New York, eagerly wanting to know when Pawnee land would be available for sale and use. [37]

The Last to Leave

Dry leaves scuttled across the agency schoolyard and along the Loup River banks when the last of the Pawnees to live on the Nebraska reservation began their trek southward. There were about 370 altogether. It was hoped that some good would come from leaving their homes: there would be the happy sight of seeing relatives again, the fear of Sioux attack would be gone, there might be more game to hunt, Tirawahut might give the blessing of good hunting and crops and a better way of living in the new place. Who was not to hope?

At the end of November 1875, Burgess and his family arrived at the new agency. Several employees and Pawnees had accompanied him, twenty-six persons in all. En route they had passed the others moving more slowly. He estimated there were approximately four hundred who would arrive in about ten days. [38]

According to an account obtained from Pawnees in the 1920s, the Pawnees left in November, and the government provided twenty-four wagons to carry those who had no means of transportation. Others went in buggies or had pack ponies to carry their belongings. This time a herd of cattle was driven with them so that fresh meat might be provided, and other food supplies were issued weekly.

When all were ready to begin their journey, the line of wagons and horses was said to be two miles long. The distance traveled each day was between ten and twelve miles. The route chosen crossed the Loup and the Platte rivers, then followed along the Big Blue River in Kansas toward present Manhattan. There they stopped and held "a big war dance." Moving slowly, the group continued by Junction City, Winfield, and Arkansas City. From there, they crossed Walnut Creek just above its mouth east of the town. Moving onward, they forded Salt Creek near the Kaw Agency. They entered the Osage reservation, and when they arrived at Fairfax, the leaders climbed the hill, on which the water tower was later built and looked across the Arkansas toward the new land. They crossed the wide river at a ford called old Government Crossing, about five miles below the present town of Ralston. Once on the other side, they were on the Pawnee reservation and continued on to the agency on Black Bear Creek.[39]

A first-hand account by one who had watched the Pawnees passing his family's farm in Kansas was given to Garland J. Blaine. In 1942, he became friends with a Mr. Sochek (spelled as the name was pronounced). They worked together, and one day the old man asked Garland what tribe he was.

I answered Pawnee. "Pawnee!" he said, "why I saw Pawnees come through Kansas, three groups—during a few years period." He said he bet he saw my grandparents in one of the groups. "Those Indians came through some riding, some walking. We had a good well on our farm and they would camp a few hundred yards from our well, and they would talk to my father, make signs, and point at the well. My father would make an Indian sign for alright, which was the right hand palm down, fingers extended straight out and the right arm horizontal chest high near the heart—with a swift motion forward about six inches. This meant good or alright. After that the Pawnees would get all the water they wanted."

He remembered the Pawnees coming. A way off in the distance, you could see the dust rise, and it would keep a certain density, a certain variation. We knew it was a large column of people. He would run to tell his father, who would say,"Yes, I have seen it. It's probably Indians hunting or going south." Pretty soon they appeared. They came by about ten o'clock in the morning, in small groups, probably families, and there would be very little intervals between groups. And sometimes the group would be four or five abreast, sometimes two, sometimes a single person, like a boy on a horse. They went by until evening, and then they started trailing off to mostly people afoot. Just about dark, they would still be going by, and there might be an old man and an old lady, or an old lady and a young boy, or an old man and a young boy with their dog. Yes, for many hours they went by. Sometimes they stopped or sometimes they bypassed—maybe they had something already cooked and they'd just keep walking. Or they would eat and get up and move on. Until way after the sun went down they would still be walking by. All during the day there seemed to be younger warriors who seemed to be walking along guarding. There weren't alot of them but the column was dotted with them here and there. He remembered then, that the Pawnees were not in a straight line, that scouts were well ahead and he heard that they were on the watch for buffalo. They moved more or less zig-zag in front of the group. "I suppose they did not know what their supply of food would be when they got down there," Mr. Sochek said. * [40]

Some Pawnees in later years recalled the events of their leaving Nebraska and the journey south. Stacy Howell recalled in 1983 that his aunt was very young when she came to Indian Territory. Her father tied her on a horse so she could not fall off as she rode. She said they would send the scouts out ahead to find a good camping place. Sometimes they would stay more than one day at a place, particularly if they spotted buffalo. The soldiers who accompanied them would go off and shoot buffalo and tell the Pawnees where they fell, and the people would go off and butcher them and bring the meat back. They saved the hides and later sold them to traders. Mr. Howell could not recall the route that was followed. [41]

* Whether the above migration was the one in the fall of 1875 or an earlier one is not certain. It may have been the Williamson-led group, because the 1875 smaller group in wagons would be seen to pass by the Sochek farm in a shorter time. The inference of buffalo hunting would be more applicable to an earlier group, who were not forced to follow roads as were the group with wagons, who had few young men, and had children comprising about one-third of the group.

Garland J. Blaine heard his grandmother talk about the journey. She came as a young girl, as did Stacy Howell's aunt. Her future husband, a Pitahawirata Band member, also came as a young man. He later was named Wichita because one of his relatives married a Wichita while the Pawnees were staying with that tribe and lived among that tribe for a time.

In the 1930s or early 1940s, Effie Blaine was asked to testify or tell about the journey as background information for a claim that the Pawnees had against the government. This is what she said happened:

They would get all the old people together and take them to the Court house in Pawnee, and tell them that they could not lie, and to tell all they could remember about their coming from Nebraska. So these people [attorneys] would ask questions, and the interpreter would say, "This man wants to know this." The people would answer. So at one time after the people had left, the lawyer and the interpreter, James Sun Eagle, told my grandmother, "Aunt, we like, the lawyers like your testimony, but there wasn't too much of it. Some of the people who were younger than you, well, the lawyers liked their answers better. We thought since you were older, you would give more testimony.

And my Grandmother said, "What do you mean? You said that we could not lie. We had to tell what we saw and did—no adding, no taking away. He said, they asked if you walked and you said, no. If you got a drink of water at the spring, and you said, no. You said you saw springs and you saw people getting water. You said you saw people walking, but you didn't walk. They asked you, if you, during this time, if you recalled being around a camp fire, and you said, yes. And you remembered rows of campfires against a darkening sky. But you said you didn't help cook or you didn't help build the fire. You didn't cook, but you ate. Some of the men said they remembered taking the horses out and hobbling them, and sitting and watching the horses, and picking up dried wood so they could build a fire, and helping around with the cooking such as keeping wood nearby so that the ladies could cook. And they remembered getting water, everything like that.

She said, my father was a chief and a warrior. Of course, I remember these things, but I didn't do them. We had people with us under my father's protection. If I wanted a drink of water, they went and got the water for me. I didn't walk because my father had many horses and I had a horse to ride. I didn't build a fire because it was the job of the people under my father's protection. And those small boys, of course they had to build the fire. It was their job. And of course they had to walk, their fathers weren't warriors. They were under the protection of a warrior. And their wives, children, they had to walk, unless my father wanted to give a man a horse, and said, go get us some fresh meat. Here is a horse. I want you to keep it as long as you look after it real well. If you do, you may keep it. But any time you abuse this horse, or do not take care of it, so that it gets sick, then I will have to take it away from you. . . .

These other people who said they did those things, of course they didn't lie. And I didn't lie either. But they had to do those things, and I did not. My father's name then was Leading with the Bear, and he brought his people in the Pitahawirata tribe [akitaru] down from Nebraska to the Wichitas.[42]

Later she told her grandson that she was in the first group that left Nebraska. They would march all day and in the evening after they set up camp, the old people who were walking would just be catching up. Her father's group were the "first" camp and camped separately from the others.[43]

A Kitkahahki Band member recalled his grandmother's description of the removal from Nebraska. She said they were told that they were going to have to leave their homes and move here. They did not even know where it was they were going. They did not want to leave, but they had to go anyway. When they were on their way, at night they could hear shots. She claimed soldiers were shooting. People would disappear, and they never did know what happened to them. They wanted to get rid of us, he concluded.[44]

Phillip Jim, whose grandmother came from Nebraska and is buried near Lone Chimney, Oklahoma, recalled that he had been told a story by a Chaui, who had heard it from Mean or Mad Bull, who took part in the episode told here:

One of the groups of Pawnees that came to Indian Territory strayed off, lost their way. They went toward the southwest and finally came to a place where the Wichitas live. Scouts had been sent out and they were the ones that saw a big camp with many tipis. It was near the place where Willie Campbell [a Wichita] lives near Anadarko. Right in the middle of the encampment was a big lodge. The little group of scouts wanted to go over to the camp, but Mad Bull, said, no, they will slaughter us. Let me go by myself. They finally consented and gave him a pipe. They were many miles away from their main camp. It was further back. The leader of the scouts told the others to follow Mad Bull, but to stay out of sight. Mad Bull came nearer the big camp and stayed hidden until it was dark.

Then he got up and headed for the lodge in the middle of the camp. No dogs barked at him. He carried the pipe. And he had his bows and arrows and a knife, too. He got close and could hear voices inside the lodge. Quickly, he raised the flap and stepped inside. The startled men inside said, "Wuh." They didn't know who he was. He made signs and said, "I came from over there. I bring this pipe on behalf of my people, the Pawnee. We want to stop war and fighting between our people." Several voices said, "No, no, no. Leave here. We do not make peace with the Pawnee." But he said, "I bring the pipe and I want to smoke it with you in the name of my people." He saw some Comanches, some Kiowas, and others.

He went to the first man seated by the entrance and he offered him the pipe. The man refused. Mad Bull said, "This is the sacred pipe, you smoke it." The man refused again, so Mad Bull thrust it into his mouth. He went around the circle forcing each to take the pipe. When he got to the headman, he offered him the pipe and he accepted. He said, "You are sincere or you would not force us to smoke. Go back to your people and tell them to come here. There will be food and we will eat together."

Mad Bull went out and returned to the scouts. They all rode back to the main group and talked to the chief. He saw the pipe Mad Bull had taken into the lodge. It had blood on it where he had forced the men to smoke it. He agreed to go to the enemy camp and the rest of the tribe would follow. The head chief went unarmed, but his warriors carried their weapons. When they arrived at the enemy camp they went straight to the lodge. Here they were invited in, and signs were made for them to sit down. The headman said, "We will now be friends and make war no more." The Pawnees were invited to say that was what they wanted. They answered they were coming from their old home to live here and they wanted to be friends with their former enemies. When they finished smoking the pipe, they ate. Then the headman told the Pawnee leaders to tell their people to come and be friends with the people in the tribes there. This they did.[45]

After telling this story, Phillip Jim said that once, when he was down at Anadarko, he asked a Kiowa he knew about this story, and he said it was true, that the Kiowas had the same story.[*]

In all, several groups of Pawnees left their homes in Nebraska to come to Indian Territory. The first groups were of various numbers, with some small ones consisting of an individual or two, who may have left the reservation without permission and may never have been recognized as having made the journey. The only group that did not go first to the Wichita Agency was the last one that departed the Nebraska reservation in late 1875. According to Effie Blaine and others, not all the Pawnees left Nebraska. Some women who had married local white men stayed, some men who were working for white men stayed, and some orphans who were living with white families stayed at their request. Then, there were the few men who secretly remained to seek revenge against the Cut Throats for family members' deaths.[46]

Before the last group arrived at their new agency, B. Rush Roberts and F. H. Smith visited the agency and described what they saw:

> On arriving in front of the agency buildings, more than a mile from them, our eyes rested upon one of the most beautiful scenes we had witnessed in our whole journey. In the foreground were about twenty men, Indians and whites, with their teams and mowing-machines, busily engaged in cutting, raking, and stacking hay. In the distance the long row of new buildings, many of which were occupied, extending in a straight line on one side of the avenue for over a half mile in length, and the surrounding country for miles away dotted with the white tents of the Indians in their several villages. . . .[47]

The Pawnees did not just arrive and set up housekeeping in the tents described above. When the larger group containing the

---

[*] In *Pawnee Hero Stories and Folk Tales*, George B. Grinnell collected several tales in which a brave Pawnee entered a lodge of the enemy but not under the circumstances given by Phillip Jim.

majority of the chiefs arrived from the Wichita Agency, Effie Blaine, whose father was among them, described the ritual that took place.

> The chiefs of each band picked out an old man and said to him, "You are to officially announce to the people that this is where we chiefs have decided that we will live." So the day came when it was to take place. In the council chiefs got up and talked. Outside the people came. The old man then went out of the council toward the east, lifted his arms and blessed the chiefs with his palms turned upward, then turned downward over their heads, shoulders, arms, thighs, until he touched Mother Earth. Then he blessed himself. Then he lifted his arms again and prayed to Tirawahut and asked him to give the people health and happiness, but he knew, he said, that with this happiness also came death. And at the end he proclaimed, "I have picked out this place in the name of the chiefs of this tribe. I have picked out this place where we will see life come, and at the same time death will come. But this is where we will live."
>
> At the same time he stomped on the ground very hard several times. The reason he did this was to show that we believe that when we pick out a place we will know happiness, this is where we will know death and sorrow. We know that after we have picked out a place that we who select it will not live very long. That is why the chiefs picked out this old man to make the proclamation. They had said to him, "You have seen happiness. You have seen sorrow. You have lived a good life. You have had a lot of descendents. We know you will have no fear in your heart to pick out for us a place to live." And this he did.[48]

The chiefs, who had not wanted to come here, knew only too well that they had not selected this place but that their agent and the government had done so. But they believed that, in order to have Tirawahut's blessing in this new land, the above ritual must be observed as it had been for centuries in their homeland whenever a new site for a village was selected. *

The new home or reservation was described in the official rec-

---

* Following this tradition, John White of the Field Museum in Chicago, considerately invited Garland J. Blaine to dedicate the new mudlodge built there in the 1970s. Speaking in Pawnee, he and other Pawnees went through the ritual he had learned from his grandparents.

ords as "commencing at a point in the middle of the main channel of the Cimarron River, where the 97th meridian of west lon-
gitude crosses the same; thence north on said meridian to the
middle of the main channel of the Arkansas River; thence down
the middle of the main channel of the Arkansas River to the
mouth of the Cimarron River; thence up the main channel of
said Cimarron River to the place of the beginning." This area
was said to contain about 391,000 acres.[49] The actual number
was 230,014.04 acres from the Cherokee Outlet and 53,005.94
acres from Creek lands ceded in 1866, or a total of 283,019.98
acres.* The new Pawnee reservation was established by Congress
in an Act of April 10, 1876.[50]

The removal to Indian Territory did not solve all Pawnee
problems or make life easier. The different climate and environment, endemic diseases, and continuing food shortages contributed to a high death rate in the next quarter century.

Wichita Blaine told his grandson how difficult life was then:

> When we first moved here we had little to eat. We'd get a bag
> of flour and make fry bread day after day. Sometimes I would go
> out and bring home a deer, but we got little of it. I had to give
> some to my aunts, the two old sisters, who had had the same hus-
> band, but he was dead. There were other old men and women I
> knew without food who I would carry some of the meat to.
>
> After awhile the deer were gone and we had to hunt prairie
> chickens and that's what we ate for awhile. Then they were gone.
>
> One time I decided to go down toward the Cimarron. There
> was a white man who had lots of cattle. When it was dark, I took

---

* The Cherokee Outlet was a strip of land, approximately sixty miles wide,
extending from the ninety-sixth to the one-hundredth meridian of west longi-
tude in Indian Territory. It lay directly south of the Kansas border. It was
granted to the Cherokees in the Treaty of May 6, 1828, so that the tribe would
have "free and unmolested" access and use. In the July 19, 1866, treaty with the
Cherokees, the United States was authorized to settle "civilized" Indians on
any unoccupied Cherokee lands east of the ninety-sixth meridian, and "friendly"
Indians on unoccupied lands west of this meridian. Eventually, the Pawnee,
Ponca, Otoe, Missouria, Kaw, Tonkawa and other tribes were removed from
their homelands and placed on reservations in the Cherokee Outlet west of the
aforementioned meridian.

Pawnee family in tipi on their reservation in Indian Territory a few years after removal of the tribe from Nebraska. Note the bleak landscape and the sparse furnishings. Courtesy of Archives and Manuscripts Division of the Oklahoma Historical Society.

one of the cattle out and drove it toward a creek. There I hit it over the head and killed it. I then took a branch and went up and brushed up the grass so they could not see where the trail was. Then I butchered the cow in the dark. Every sound, I would stop and look around. I hurried and hoped the creek water would carry away the blood. I had a good horse and loaded all the parts on him and followed the creek for a while, then turned west. First, I threw off the hooves. After awhile I threw off the head, and then farther on the gut portions. I then turned north toward home, getting there before the sun rose. We sprinkled the hide with pepper. We couldn't spread it outside then, but waited until the next night and scraped it, so we could make what we needed from it.

We sure had a lot of good meat! We cut and dried some down near the creek where no one would see it.

Garland when young, once asked, "Grandpa, did you steal any more cows?" Grandpa said,

"I did not *steal* any cows. I went and would have stood up and not run, and would have shot anyone who stopped me. That's not stealing. I was ready to die if I had to—but my family had to eat." [51]

Such conditions took their toll. By the end of the century less than seven hundred tribal members were living. When Garland J. Blaine was born in 1915 and given a child-name, Kuruks awaki, Little Spotted Bear, the Pawnee language was still spoken by everyone. The remaining Sacred Bundles hung on west walls of the few mudlodges or in small, newly constructed government frame houses. In the winter, families gathered and camped together in tipis for a few weeks and shared what they had. They told stories, performed the sacred dances, mourned their dead, and remembered life as it had been before reservation days in Nebraska. They still spoke of Nebraska as "home."

Abbreviations

Bureau of American Ethnology Annual Report	BAE AR
Commissioner of Indian Affairs Annual Report	CIA AR
Kansas State Historical Society	KSHS
National Archives, Record Group, Microcopy, Roll	NA RG M R
Nebraska State Historical Society	NSHS
Office of Indian Affairs	OIA
Oklahoma Historical Society, Archives and Manuscripts	OHSAM

Notes

Chapter 1

1. Addison E. Sheldon, "Land Systems and Land Policies in Nebraska," *Publications of the Nebraska State Historical Society,* vol. 20 (1936), p. 10.

2. Charles Little and James B. Chase to Ulysses S. Grant, June 15, 1869, NA, Northern Superintendency, RG 75 M234 R600.

3. Sheldon, "Land Systems and Land Policies," p. 11.

4. Samuel Janney to Ely Parker, January 8, 1871, NA, Northern Superintendency, RG75 M234 R600.

5. Sheldon, "Land Systems and Land Policies," p. 12.

6. Weston A. Goodspeed, ed., *The Province and the States,* vol. 5 (Madison: Western Historical Association, 1904), p. 246.

7. Barclay White to F. A. Walker, July 6, 1872, NA, Northern Superintendency, RG75 M234 R600.

8. Goodspeed, *Province and the States,* p. 244. Barclay White to E. P. Smith, August 19, 1873; Barclay White to R. W. Furnas, August 26, 1873, NA, Northern Superintendency, RG75 M234 R600.

9. R. W. Furnas to Barclay White, August 23, 1873, NA, Northern Superintendency, RG75 M234 R600.

10. Goodspeed, *Province and the States,* p. 247.

11. Barclay White to E. P. Smith, April 28, 1874, NA, Northern Superintendency, RG75 M234 R600.

12. P. W. Hitchcock to E. P. Smith, March 28, 1874, NA, Northern Superintendency, RG75 M234 R600.

13. B. Rush Roberts to E. P. Smith, January 28, 1875, NA, Northern Superintendency, RG75 M234 R600.

14. Jacob Troth to Samuel Janney, May 31, 1870, NA, Pawnee Agency, RG75 M234 R661.

15. Garland J. and Martha R. Blaine, unpublished notes.

16. Samuel Janney to Ely Parker, June 23 and June 30, 1870, NA, Pawnee Agency, RG75 M234 R661.

17. William Burgess to Barclay White, February 1, 1874, Pawnee vol. 2, OHSAM.

18. William Burgess to John Bratt & Co., April 3, 1874, Pawnee vol. 2, OHSAM.

19. William Stolley, "The Pawnees," in History of the First Settlement of Hall County, Nebraska, Chapter X, Nebraska History, (Special Issue, April 1946), pp. 61–704.

20. Bayard H. Paine, Pioneers, Indians and Buffaloes (Curtis, Nebraska: Curtis Enterprise, 1935), p. 134.

21. Barclay White to F. A. Walker, November 20, 1872, NA, Pawnee Agency, RG75 M234 R661.

22. Blaine, unpublished notes.

23. Jacob Troth to Samuel Janney, June 30 and July 24, 1870, NA, Pawnee Agency, RG75 M234 R661.

24. Barclay White, "The Barclay White Journals," vol. II, Swarthmore College, Library, p. 142.

25. Blaine, unpublished notes.

26. Jacob Troth to Barclay White, November 9, 1872, Pawnee vol. 1, OHSAM.

27. Barclay White to F. A. Walker, November 11, 1872, NA, Pawnee Agency, RG75 M234 R661.

28. White, "Journals," vol. I, pp. 340–42.

29. Jacob Troth to Barclay White, December 24, 1872; Barclay White to F. A. Walker, December 26, 1872, NA, Pawnee Agency, RG75 M234 R661.

30. White, "Journals," I, pp. 344–45.

31. Pawnee, vol. 2, OHSAM, p. 28.

32. Samuel Janney to Ely Parker, January 30, 1875. NA, Northern Superintendency, RG75 M234 R600.

33. Wilhelm Dinesen, "A Dane's View of Frontier Culture: Notes on a Stay in the United States, 1872–1874," Nebraska History, vol. 55(2) (1974), pp. 265–85.

34. William Burgess to Barclay White, February 18, 1873, Pawnee vol. 1, OHSAM.

35. Jacob Troth to Samuel Janney, August 8, 1870, NA, Pawnee Agency, RG75 M234 R661.

36. Pawnee Council Volume, November 1, 1871, OHSAM.

37. Ibid., January 22, 1872, OHSAM.

38. Ibid., June 14, 1873, OHSAM.

39. Ibid., September 12, 1873 and May 5, 1872. Pawnee vol. 2, April 30, 1874, p. 152, OHSAM.

40. James R. Riding-In, "Pawnee Removal," Master's thesis, University of California, Los Angeles, 1985.

41. Goodspeed, *Province and the States*, pp. 231–32.

42. Riding-In, "Pawnee Removal," pp. 83–84.

43. Ibid., pp. 83, 86.

44. Samuel Janney to Ely Parker, January 11, 1870, NA, Pawnee Agency, RG75 M234 R661.

45. Samuel Janney to Ely Parker, December 9, 1869, NA, Pawnee Agency, RG75 M234 R661.

46. Samuel Janney to Ely Parker, January 1, 1870, NA, Pawnee Agency, RG75 M234 R661.

47. Samuel Janney to Ely Parker, January 27, 1870, NA, Pawnee Agency, RG75 M234 R661.

48. Jacob Troth to Samuel Janney, November, 1869, NA, Pawnee Agency, RG75 M234 R661.

49. Samuel Janney to Ely Parker, Proceedings of Trial, January 1, January 11, January 25, 1870, NA, Pawnee Agency, RG75 M234 R661.

50. Samuel Janney to Ely Parker, February 10, 1870, NA, Pawnee Agency, RG75 M234 R661.

51. Samuel Janney to Ely Parker, March 26, 1870, NA, Pawnee Agency, RG75 M234 R661.

52. Samuel Janney to Ely Parker, May 5, 1870, NA, Pawnee Agency, RG75 M234 R661.

53. Samuel Janney to Ely Parker, May 5, 1871, NA, Pawnee Agency, RG75 M234 R661.

54. Samuel Janney to Ely Parker, October 3, 1870, NA, Pawnee Agency, RG75 M234 R661.

55. Samuel Janney to Ely Parker, November 30, 1871, NA, Pawnee Agency, RG75 M234 R661.

56. Samuel Janney to Ely Parker, May 5, 1871, NA, Pawnee Agency, RG75 M234 R661.

57. Samuel Janney to Ely Parker, June 13, 1871, NA, Pawnee Agency, RG75 M234 R661.

58. *Omaha Tribune and Republican*, June 13, 1871, NA, Pawnee Agency, RG75 M234 R661.

59. Elvira Platt, "Some Experiences as a Teacher among the Pawnees," Collections of the Kansas State Historical Society, vol. XIV (1915–18), p. 793.

60. Barclay White to F. A. Walker, January 5, 1872, NA, Pawnee Agency, RG75 M234 R661. White, "Journals," vol. I, pp. 302–303.

61. Donald F. Danker, *Man of the Plains: Recollections of Luther North* (Lincoln: University of Nebraska, 1961), pp. 129–30.

62. White, "Journals," vol. I, pp. 302–303.

63. Blaine, unpublished notes.

64. White, "Journals," II, p. 22.

65. Paine, *Pioneers, Indians and Buffaloes*, 65.

66. Barclay White, Report to Commissioner of Indian Affairs, March 28, 1874; July 10, 1874, NA, Northern Superintendency, RG75 M234 R600.

67. Pawnee Council Volume, June 1, 1871, OHSAM. E. Platt, "Experiences as Teacher among Pawnees."

Chapter 2

1. George A. Dorsey, *The Pawnee: Mythology*, Part I, (Washington, D.C.: Carnegie Institute, 1906), p. 90.

2. Gene Weltfish, *Caddoan Texts: Pawnee South Bands Dialect*, Publications of the American Society of Ethnology, vol. 17 (New York: G. E. Stechert, 1937), p. 86.

3. Pawnee Council Volume, June 8, 1872, OHSAM, p. 53.

4. Waldo R. Wedel, *Prehistoric Man on the Great Plains*, (Norman: University of Oklahoma Press, 1970), p. 88.

5. Waldo R. Wedel, "Some Reflections on Plains Caddoan Origins," *Nebraska History*, vol. 60 (2) (1979), p. 272.

6. Roger T. Grange, "An Archeological View of Pawnee Origins," *Nebraska History*, vol. 60 (2) (1979), pp. 139–41. Wedel, *Prehistoric Man*, pp. 109–10.

7. Roger T. Grange, "Archeological View," 141–42.

8. John B. Dunbar, "The Pawnee Indians, Their Habits and Customs," *Magazine of American History*, vol. 5 (5) (1880), p. 322.

9. Luther H. North, Ms. 449, January 3, 1930, Archives, NSHS.

10. Blaine, unpublished notes.

11. Rev. John Dunbar, "Letters Concerning the Presbyterian Mission in the Pawnee Country near Bellevue, Nebraska, 1831–1849," Collections of the Kansas State Historical Society, vol. 14, (1918), p. 653.

12. Wedel, *Pawnee Archeology*, p. 60.

13. Waldo R. Wedel, *An Introduction to Pawnee Archeology*, BAE, Bulletin 112 (1936), p. 57.

14. John Williamson, MS 2710, Series 2, Archives, NSHS, p. 23.

15. John B. Dunbar, "The Pawnees, Their History and Mythology," *Magazine of American History*, vol. 4 (4) (1880), p. 276.

16. Rev. John Dunbar, "The Presbyterian Mission among the Pawnees," p. 329. Williamson, ms. 2710, p. 22.

17. White, "Journals," II, pp. 312–13.

18. Blaine, unpublished notes.

19. Ibid.

20. White, "Journals," II, pp. 312–13.

21. Blaine, unpublished notes.

22. White, "Journals," III, p. 328.

23. Blaine, unpublished notes.

24. Francis P. Prucha, ed., *Documents of the United States Indian Policy*, (Lincoln: University of Nebraska Press, 1975), p. 21.

25. Charles J. Kappler, comp., *Indian Affairs: Laws and Treaties*, vol. 2, Treaties, (Washington: 1904), p. 42.

26. Prucha, *Documents*, p. 33.

27. Francis P. Prucha, *The Great White Father: The United States Government*

and the American Indians, vol. II, (Lincoln: University of Nebraska Press, 1984), p. 149.

28. Kappler, *Indian Affairs,* pp. 416–17.

29. Ibid., pp. 764–765.

30. Prucha, *Documents,* p. 78.

31. *Annual Reports,* Commissioner of Indian Affairs, Government Printing Office, Washington, D.C., 1871.

32. Pawnee Council Volume, September 7, 1871, OHSAM.

33. Ibid., September 25, 1871.

34. Ibid., April 8, 1872.

35. Ibid., May 20, 1872; June 11, 1872.

36. Ibid., May 20, 1872.

37. William Burgess to Barclay White, March 16, 1874, Pawnee vol. 2, OHSAM.

38. Ibid.

39. White, "Journals," vol. I, p. 393. William Burgess to Barclay White, July 29, 1874, Pawnee vol. 2, p. 219, OHSAM.

40. Pawnee Council Volume, March 18, 1874, OHSAM, p. 89.

41. Ibid., April 4, 1874, p. 90.

42. Ibid., August 17, 1874, p. 93.

43. Brian Dippie, *The Vanishing American: White Attitudes and U.S. Indian Policy,* (Middletown: Wesleyan University Press, 1982), p. 108.

44. H. B. Parkes, "The Agrarian Counterattack," in *Political Parties in American History,* vol. 2, Felice A. Bonadio, ed. Morten Borden, gen. ed. (New York: G. P. Putnam's Sons, 1974), p. 900.

Chapter 3

1. George A. Dorsey, *The Pawnee Mythology,* p. 488.

2. Ibid., 526.

3. George B. Grinnell, *Pawnee Hero Stories and Folk Tales with Notes on the Origin, Customs and Character of the Pawnee People,* p. 86; Weltfish, *Caddoan Texts,* p. 244; Dorsey, *The Pawnee Mythology,* p. 480.

4. Garland J. Blaine, unpublished family songs, album 1.

5. Frances Densmore, *Pawnee Music,* BAE, Bulletin 93 (Washington, D.C.: Government Printing Office, 1929), p. 41.

6. E. A. Hoebel, *Man in the Primitive World,* second ed. (New York: McGraw Hill, 1958), p. 566.

7. Blaine, unpublished notes.

8. Ibid.

9. Ibid.

10. Ibid.

11. Ibid.

12. Ibid.

13. Dunbar, "The Pawnee Indians," p. 329.

14. Blaine, unpublished notes.

15. Ibid.
16. Ibid.
17. Ibid.
18. Jacob Troth to Agent of the Comanches, January 22, 1870, Kiowa Agency-Depredations, OHSAM.
19. Maj. Gen. J. M. Schofield to Lt.Gen. P. H. Sheridan, Jan. 7, 1870; Gen. P. H. Sheridan to Gen. C. C. Augur, Jan. 19, 1870, NA, Pawnee Agency, RG75 M234 R661.
20. Samuel Janney to Ely Parker, Jan. 21, 1870, NA, Pawnee Agency, RG75 M234 R661.
21. Jacob Troth to Samuel Janney, Jan 29, 1870, NA, Pawnee Agency, RG75 M234 R661.
22. Gen. C. C. Augur to Maj. Gen. George L. Hartsuff, Feb. 1, 1870, NA, Pawnee Agency, RG75 M234 R661.
23. Gen. J. M. Schofield to Gen. George L. Hartsuff, February 4, 1870, NA, Pawnee Agency, RG75 M234 R661.
24. Samuel Janney to Ely Parker, April 22, 1870, NA, Pawnee Agency, RG75 M234 R661.
25. Ibid., June 3, 1870.
26. Danker, *Man of the Plains*, pp. 138–40.
27. Jacob Troth to Maj. Gen. J. J. Reynolds, Oct. [?] 1872, Pawnee vol. 1, OHSAM.
28. Jacob Troth to Barclay White, Nov. 9, 1872, Pawnee vol. 1, OHSAM.
29. Jacob Troth to Maj. Gen. J. J. Reynolds, October [?], 1872; Jacob Troth to Barclay White, Nov. 11, 1872, Pawnee vol. 1, OHSAM.
30. Jacob Troth to Barclay White, December 9, 1872, Pawnee vol. 1, OHSAM.
31. Jacob Troth to Barclay White, January 20, 1873, Pawnee vol. 1; Pawnee Council Volume, January 13, 1873, OHSAM.
32. Pawnee Council Volume, January 24, 1873, OHSAM.
33. William Burgess to Barclay White, February 2, 1873, Pawnee vol. 1, OHSAM.
34. Pawnee Council Volume, March 20, 1873, OHSAM.
35. Ibid., May 10, 1873, OHSAM.

Chapter 4

1. Pawnee Council Volume, OHSAM, p. 18.
2. James R. Murie, *The Ceremonies of the Pawnee*, Part II, South Bands, *Smithsonian Institution Contributions to Anthropology*, no. 27. Douglas R. Parks, ed. (Washington, D.C.: Government Printing Office, 1979), p. 429.
3. Dorsey, *The Pawnee*, p. 109. Dorsey, *Traditions of the Skidi Pawnee*, Memoirs of the American Folk Lore Society, vol. 8, Boston: Houghton Mifflin: London, D. Nutt. Reprinted, New York, Kraus, 1969), p. 283.
4. Gene Weltfish, *The Lost Universe: With a Closing Chapter on "The Universe Regained"* (New York and London: Basic Books. Reprinted as *The Lost*

Universe: Pawnee Life and Culture [Lincoln: University of Nebraska Press, 1977]), p. 231.

5. Garland J. and Martha R. Blaine, Pawnee Music Collection, album 1, record 2, side 2, song 5.

6. Ibid., record 5, side 1, song 1.

7. Blaine, unpublished notes.

8. Ibid.

9. Blaine, Pawnee Music Collection, album 1, record 6, side 1, song 1.

10. Weltfish, *Lost Universe*, pp. 98–99.

11. Dorsey, *The Pawnee*, Number 93.

12. Dorsey, *Traditions of the Skidi Pawnees*, p. 344.

13. Ibid., Tradition Number 97.

14. Dunbar, "Letters Concerning the Presbyterian Mission," p. 749.

15. Sir Charles Augustus Murray, *Travels in North America During the Years 1834, 1835, and 1836*, (London: R. Bentley; New York: Harper and Brothers; reprinted, New York: Da Capo, 1974), p. 321.

16. Blaine, unpublished notes.

17. Murray, *Travels in North America*, 282–83, 353.

18. Blaine, unpublished notes.

19. Ibid. Also, Martha R. Blaine, "The Pawnee-Wichita Visitation Cycle: Historical Manifestations of an Ancient Friendship," *Pathways to Plains Prehistory:* Anthropological Perspectives of Plains Natives and Their Pasts, Don G. Wyckoff and Jack L. Hofmann, eds. Oklahoma Anthropological Society, Memoir 3, The Cross Timbers Heritage Association, Contributions 1. Cross Timbers Press, Duncan, Oklahoma, 1982, pp. 113–34.

20. Blaine, unpublished notes.

21. Ibid.

22. Ibid.

23. Ibid.

24. Ibid.

25. Ibid.

26. Murray, *Travels in North America*, pp. 370–71.

27. Weltfish, *Caddoan Texts*, pp. 217–18. Weltfish, *Lost Universe*, p. 97.

28. Blaine, unpublished notes.

29. Ibid.

30. Ibid.

31. Murray, *Travels in North America*, pp. 353–56, 378.

32. Garland J. Blaine and Martha R. Blaine, "*Paresu arirake:* The Hunters that Were Massacred," *Nebraska History*, vol. 58 (3) (1977), pp. 342–58.

33. Murray, *Travels in North America*, p. 329.

34. Blaine, unpublished notes.

35. Ibid.

36. Dunbar, "The Pawnee Indians," p. 330.

37. Murray, *Travels in North America*, p. 353.

38. Ibid.

39. Commissioner of Indian Affairs, *Annual Report*, 1872.

40. Kappler, *Indian Affairs, Treaties*, p. 416.

41. Pawnee Council Volume, OHSAM, p. 3. Barclay White to E. P. Smith, June 17, 1873, NA, Northern Superintendency, RG75 M234 R600.

42. Pawnee Council Volume, OHSAM, p. 18.

43. Pawnee, vol. 1, OHSAM, p. 411.

44. Pawnee Council Volume, OHSAM, p. 91.

45. Pawnee vol. 1, OHSAM, pp. 209–11.

46. R. W. Frazer, Forts of the West: *Military Forts & Presidios & Posts Commonly Called Forts West of the Mississippi to 1898* (Norman: University of Oklahoma Press,1977), p. xiv.

47. Blaine, unpublished notes.

48. Samuel Janney to Ely Parker, June 3, 1870, NA, Northern Superintendency, RG75 M234 R600.

49. Ibid., July 7, 1870.

50. Pawnee Council Volume, November 1, 1871, OHSAM.

51. Ibid.

52. Jacob Troth to General E. Ord, July 11, 1872, Pawnee vol. 1, pp. 56–7 OHSAM.

53. Commissioner of Indian Affairs, *Annual Report*, 1872, p. 223. Barclay White to Indian Commissioner, September 19, 1872, NA, Pawnee Agency, RG75 M234 R661.

54. Jacob Troth to Gen. E. Ord, October 17, 1872, Pawnee vol. 1, OHSAM.

55. Jacob Troth to Barclay White, January 20, 1873 and January 23, 1873, Pawnee vol. 1, OHSAM.

56. Pawnee Council Volume, January 13, 1873, OHSAM.

57. William Burgess to Barclay White, January 21, 1873, Pawnee vol. I, OHSAM.

58. William Burgess to Col. J. J. Reynolds, March 8, 1873, Pawnee vol. I, OHSAM.

59. Blaine, "*Paresu arirake*," pp. 342–58.

60. Paul Riley, "The Battle of Massacre Canyon," *Nebraska History*, vol.54 (2) (1973), p. 239.

61. Blaine, unpublished notes.

62. Report of Major General W. S. Hancock, Headquarters, Department of Dakota, October 1872, p. 41, in *Report of the Secretary of War*, Forty-second Congress, Third Session, HR Ex. Doc. 1, Part 2 (Washington, Government Printing Office, 1872).

63. Ibid., p. 56, Report of Major General John Pope, September 28, 1872, Headquarters, Department of the Missouri.

64. Kappler, *Indian Affairs: Treaties*, pp. 490, 525.

65. Ibid., p. 1,002.

66. Brig. Gen. E. O. C. Ord, Headquarters, Department of the Platte, September 30, 1872, *Report of the Secretary of War*, 1873, p. 52. Indian Office Circular, June 12, 1869, NA, RG75 LS vol. 90, pp. 352–53.

67. Barclay White to F. A. Walker, July 10, 1872, NA, Northern Superintendency, RG75 M234 R600.

68. Jacob Troth to Barclay White, November 9, 1872, Pawnee vol. I, OHSAM.

69. Barclay White to F. A. Walker, December 26, 1872, NA, Pawnee Agency, RG75 M234 R661.

70. William Burgess To Whom It May Concern, July 10, 1874, Pawnee vol. 2, OHSAM.

71. Pawnee Council Volume, OHSAM, p. 42.

72. Pawnee Council Volume, June 9, July 7, July 8 and September 7, 1871; January 22, 1872, OHSAM.

73. Blaine, "*Paresu arirake,*" pp. 342–58.

74. Pawnee Council Volume, October 19, 1872, OHSAM.

75. William Burgess To Whom It May Concern, July 10, 1874, Pawnee vol. 2, OHSAM.

Chapter 5

1. Edwin T. Denig, *Five Indian Tribes of the Upper Missouri: Sioux, Arickaras, Assiniboines, Crees and Crows* (Norman: University of Oklahoma Press, 1961), pp. xv–xxiv.

2. Ibid., pp. 17–18.

3. Ibid., p. 38.

4. Dunbar, "Letters Concerning the Presbyterian Mission," p. 656.

5. Ibid., p. 663.

6. Ibid.

7. Percival G. Lowe, *Five Years a Dragoon ('49 to '54), and Other Adventures on the Great Plains,* (Kansas City, Missouri: F. Hudson Publishing Company. Reprinted, Don Russell, ed., Norman: University of Oklahoma Press, 1965), p. 241.

8. Preston Holder, *The Hoe and the Horse on the Plains: A Study of Cultural Development Among North American Indians* (Lincoln: University of Nebraska Press, 1970), pp. 100, 124, 131.

9. George E. Hyde, *The Pawnee Indians,* (Denver: University of Denver Press. Reprinted, Lincoln: University of Nebraska Press, 1973), p. 364.

10. J. W. Powell, "Indian Linguistic Families of America North of Mexico," BAE, *Seventh Annual Report, 1885–86* (Washington, D.C.: Government Printing Office, 1891), p. 116.

11. Blaine, unpublished notes.

12. Ibid.

13. Gottlieb F. Oehler and David Z. Smith, *Description of a Journey and Visit to the Pawnee Indians* (Fairfield, Washington: Ye Galleon Press, 1974), p. 20.

14. Blaine, unpublished notes.

15. Ibid.

16. Blaine, Pawnee Music Collection.

17. Ibid.

18. Blaine, unpublished notes.

19. Ibid.

20. Ibid.
21. Ibid.
22. Ibid.
23. Ibid.
24. Ibid.
25. Ibid.
26. George P. Belden, *The White Chief: or Twelve Years Among the Wild Indians of the Plains,* Gen. James S. Brisbin, ed. (Cincinnati and New York: C. F. Vent. Reprinted in facsimile, Athens, Ohio: Ohio University Press, 1974), pp. 76–77.
27. Blaine, unpublished notes.
28. Ibid.
29. Col. Richard Dodge, *Our Wild Indians: Thirty Years Personal Experience Among the Red Men of the Great West* (Hartford: A. D. Worthington. Chicago: A. G. Nettleton. Reprinted as *Thirty-three Years Among Our Wild Indians,* Freeport, New York: Books for Libraries Press, 1970), pp. 456–58.
30. Blaine, unpublished notes.
31. Ibid.
32. Ibid.
33. Kappler, *Indian Affairs: Treaties,* vol. 2, page 765.
34. Blaine, unpublished notes.
35. Pawnee Council Volume, OHSAM.
36. Kappler, *Indian Affairs: Treaties,* p. 906.
37. Ibid., p. 998.
38. Blaine, unpublished notes.
39. Jacob Troth to Samuel Janney, May 21, 1870, NA, Pawnee Agency, RG75 M234 R661.
40. Jacob Troth to Samuel Janney, June 11, 1870, NA, Pawnee Agency, RG75 M234 R661.
41. Luther North, MS 449, NSHS Archives.
42. Agent Poole, Whetstone Agency to S. Janney, June 28, 1870, NA, Pawnee Agency, RG74 M234 R661.
43. Samuel Janney to Ely Parker, June 22, 1870, NA, Pawnee Agency, RG75 M234 R661.
44. Samuel Janney to Ely Parker, June 30, 1870, NA, Pawnee Agency, RG75 M234 R661.
45. J. Troth to S. Janney, October 6, 1870; S. Janney to Ely Parker, October 12, 1870, NA, Pawnee Agency, RG75 M234 R661.
46. S. Janney to E. Parker, October [n.d.], 1870, NA, Pawnee Agency, RG75 M234 R661.
47. Ibid.
48. Samuel Janney to Ely Parker, December 3, 1870, NA, Northern Superintendency, RG74 M234 R600.
49. Samuel Janney to Ely Parker, December 27, 1870, NA, Pawnee Agency, RG75 M234 R661.
50. Ibid.

51. Samuel Janney to Ely Parker, January 13, 1871, NA, Pawnee Agency, RG75 M234 R661.

52. Samuel Janney to Ely Parker, February 2, 1871, NA, Pawnee Agency, RG75 M234 R661.

53. Pawnee Council Volume, OHSAM, p. 5.

54. Ibid., pp. 6–8.

55. Ibid., p. 8.

56. Ibid., p. 10.

57. Ibid., p. 16.

58. Ibid.

59. Samuel Janney to Ely Parker, April 4, 1871, NA, Pawnee Agency, RG75 M234 R661. Pawnee Council Volume, OHSAM, p. 18.

60. Samuel Janney to Ely Parker, June 8, 1871, NA, Pawnee Agency, RG75 M234 R661.

61. Samuel Janney to Ely Parker, June 5, 1871, NA, Pawnee Agency, RG75 M234 R661.

62. Ibid.

63. Barcley White to H. R. Clum, October 27, 1871, NA, Pawnee Agency, RG75 M234 R661.

64. Maj. N. B. Sweitzer, Second Cavalry, to Gen. George D. Ruggles, June 12, 1872, NA, Pawnee Agency, RG75 M234 R661.

65. George B. Grinnell, *Two Great Scouts and Their Pawnee Battalion: The Experiences of Frank J. North and Luther H. North, Pioneers in the Great West, 1865–1882, and Their Defence of the Building of the Union Pacific Railroad* (Cleveland: Arthur H. Clark. Reprinted, Lincoln: University of Nebraska Press, 1973), p. 233.

66. Ibid.

67. Report of Maj. Gen. W. S. Hancock to the Secretary of War, October 3, 1872, HR Ex. Doc., Third Session, Forty-Second Congress (Washington, D.C.: Government Printing Office, 1873), p. 40.

68. J. Troth to Barclay White, June 18, 1872, Pawnee vol. 1, OHSAM.

69. J. Troth to L. G. Webster, July 11, 1872, Pawnee vol. 1, OHSAM.

70. Pawnee Council Volume, September 16, 1872, OHSAM.

71. Jacob Troth, September 24, 1872, Commissioner of Indian Affairs, *Annual Report,* 1872, p. 223.

72. Jacob Troth to J. B. Omohundro, October 12, 1872, Pawnee vol. 1, OHSAM.

73. Jacob Troth to B. White, December 9 and December 13, 1872, Pawnee vol. 1, OHSAM.

74. Barclay White to F. A. Walker, December 12, 1872, NA, Pawnee Agency, RG75 M234 R661.

75. Ibid., December 12, 1872.

76. William Burgess to Barclay White, January 21, 1873, Pawnee vol. 1, OHSAM.

77. William Burgess to Barclay White, February 2 and February 20, 1873, NA, Northern Superintendency, RG75 M234 R600.

78. William Burgess to J. G. Gassman, Yankton Agency, March 28, 1873, Pawnee vol. 1, OHSAM.

79. Telegrams from Gen. E. O. C. Ord to Gen. Philip Sheridan, July 7, 1873; Gen. Philip Sheridan to Gen. William D. Whipple, Asst. Adj. Gen.; July 24, 1873, NA, Pawnee Agency, RG75 M234 R662.

80. Blaine, *Paresu arirake*, p. 344.

81. Ibid. (excerpts, with permission of Nebraska State Historical Society).

82. William Burgess to Barclay White, February 16, 1874, Pawnee vol. 2, OHSAM.

83. Prucha, *The Great White Father*, pp. 499–500.

84. Pawnee Council Volume, February 12, 1874, OHSAM.

85. William Burgess to J. G. Gassman, May 29, 1874, Pawnee vol. 2, OHSAM.

86. Frederick W. Hodge, *Handbook of American Indians North of Mexico*, BAE, Bulletin 30, vol. II, (Washington, D.C.: Smithsonian Institution, 1912), p. 989.

87. William Burgess to Barclay White, July 3, 1874, Pawnee vol. 2, OHSAM.

88. Pass from William Burgess, "To Military Officers and others it May Concern," July 22, 1874, Pawnee vol. 2, OHSAM.

89. William Burgess to Barclay White, July 3, 1874, Pawnee vol. 2, OHSAM.

90. Ibid.

91. Pawnee Council Volume, February 12, 1874, OHSAM.

92. White, "Journals," vol. II, p. 137.

Chapter 6

1. Paul C. Phillips and J. V. Smurr, *The Fur Trade*, vol. 1 (Norman: University of Oklahoma Press, 1967), pp. 17, 19.

2. Benjamin Hallowell, Franklin Haines, John H. Dudley, and Joseph Howell, "Quaker Report on Indian Agencies" (Reprint of Society of Friends Delegation Report, 1869), *Nebraska History*, vol. 45 (2) (Summer 1973), pp. 150–212.

3. Ibid., p. 184.

4. Kappler, *Indian Affairs, Treaties*, p. 765.

5. Ibid., p. 766.

6. Commissioner of Indian Affairs, *Annual Report*, 1845, 1869, 1872.

7. Blaine, unpublished notes.

8. Commissioner of Indian Affairs, *Annual Report*, 1867, p. 273.

9. Barclay White to Commissioner of Indian Affairs, February 22, 1873, NA, Pawnee Agency, RG75 M234 R662.

10. Pawnee Council Volume, OHSAM, p. 46.

11. Barclay White to Commissioner of Indian Affairs, December 24, 1872, NA, Pawnee Agency, RG75 M234 R661. William Burgess to Barclay White, January 20, 1873, Pawnee vol. 1, OHSAM.

12. William Burgess to Barclay White, March 15, 1873, Pawnee vol. 2, OHSAM.

13. Pawnee Council Volume, March 20, 1873, OHSAM.

14. Blaine, unpublished notes.

15. Alice C. Fletcher, *The Hako: A Pawnee Ceremony*, BAE, Twenty-second Annual Report, Part 2 (Washington, D.C.: Smithsonian Institution, 1904), pp. 1–372.

16. Dunbar, "The Pawnee Indians," p. 261.

17. Ibid., p. 261.

18. Russell L. Barsh and James Y. Henderson, *The Road: Indian Tribes and Political Liberty* (Berkeley: University of California Press, 1980), p. 63.

19. Prucha, *Documents*, p. 140.

20. Martha Royce Blaine, *The Ioway Indians* (Norman: University of Oklahoma Press, 1979), pp. 259–60.

21. Ibid., pp. 239–42.

22. Martha Royce Blaine, "The Pawnee-Wichita Visitation Cycle: Historical Manifestations of an Ancient Friendship," in *Pathways to Plains Prehistory: Anthropological Perspectives of Plains Natives and their Pasts*, Don G. Wyckoff and Jack L. Hofman, eds., Memoir 3, Contributions 1, Oklahoma Anthropological Society and Cross Timbers Heritage Association, 1982, pp. 113–34.

23. Pawnee Council Volume, March 18, 1873, OHSAM.

24. Ibid., June 1, 1871.

25. Pawnee vol. 2, March 16, 1874, OHSAM, p. 121.

26. Pawnee Council Volume, OHSAM, p. 87.

27. Ibid., p. 89a.

28. Ibid., p. 90.

29. Ibid., p. 20.

30. Commissioner of Indian Affairs, *Annual Report*, 1872, p. 223.

31. Pawnee Council Volume, OHSAM, pp. 25–26.

32. Proceedings of a Convention of Agents of the Northern Superintendency, August 20, 1870, NA, Pawnee Agency, RG75 M234 R600.

33. Pawnee Council Volume, OHSAM, p. 12.

34. Ibid., p. 13.

35. Ibid.

36. Samuel Janney to Ely Parker, May 5, 1871, NA, Pawnee Agency, RG75 M234 R661.

37. Pawnee Council Volume, OHSAM, p. 19.

38. Ibid.

39. Ibid., p. 20.

40. Ibid.

41. Jacob M. Troth, Report No. 10, Commissioner of Indian Affairs, *Annual Report*, 1872, p. 223.

42. Pawnee Council Volume, OHSAM, p. 28.

43. Ibid., p. 29.

44. Commissioner of Indian Affairs, *Annual Report*, 1871, p. 453.

45. Jacob Troth to Barclay White, September 13, 1872, Pawnee vol. 1, OHSAM.

46. Pawnee Council Volume, March 3, 1871, OHSAM.

47. Ibid., November 1, 1871, p. 41.

48. Samuel Allis, "Forty Years among the Indians and on the Eastern Borders of Nebraska," Transactions and Reports of the Nebraska Historical Society, First Series, Vol. 2, 1887, p. 153.

49. Platt, "Some Experiences as a Teacher among the Pawnees," Collections of the Kansas State Historical Society, vol. XIV, pp. 741, 786.

50. George E. Hyde, Pawnee Indians, p. 256.

51. Ibid., p. 289.

52. Blaine, unpublished notes.

53. Platt, "Some Experiences as a Teacher among the Pawnees," p. 794.

54. Garland J. Blaine—talks with his Grandfather, Wichita Blaine—unpublished notes.

55. Blaine, unpublished notes.

56. Hyde, Pawnee Indians, p. 294.

57. Commissioner of Indian Affairs, Annual Report, 1867.

58. Blaine, unpublished notes.

59. Commissioner of Indian Affairs, Annual Report, 1869, 1870, 1872.

60. Blaine, unpublished notes.

61. Elvira Platt, School Report, Commissioner of Indian Affairs, Annual Report, 1871, p. 454.

62. Commissioner of Indian Affairs, Annual Report, 1870, p. 451.

63. Jacob Troth to Barclay White, August 29, 1872, Pawnee vol. 1, OHSAM.

64. Jacob Troth, "Agent's Report of Employees," First Quarter, 1870, NA, Pawnee Agency, RG75 M234 R661.

65. Jacob Troth to Samuel Janney, April 29, 1871, NA, Pawnee Agency, RG75 M234 R661.

66. William Burgess, Annual Report, in Commissioner of Indian Affairs, Annual Report, 1873, p. 194.

67. Ibid.

68. Ibid.

69. Dunbar, "The Pawnee Indians," pp. 333–38. George B. Grinnell, Pawnee Hero Stories, p. 374.

70. Blaine, unpublished notes.

71. Ibid.

72. Ibid.

73. Ibid.

74. Ibid.

75. Ibid.

76. M. R. Gilmore, Uses of Plants by the Indians of the Missouri River Region, (Reprint, Lincoln: University of Nebraska Press, 1977), pp. 12–13, 17–18, 74, 78, 81.

77. Samuel Janney to Ely Parker, May 30, 1870 and March 29, 1870, NA, Pawnee Agency, RG75 M234 R661.

78. Pawnee Council Volume, July 8, 1871, OHSAM.

79. Ibid., February 2, 1874.

80. Ibid., April 20, 1871.

81. Pawnee vol. 2, OHSAM, p. 92.

82. Grinnell, *Pawnee Hero Stories*, p. 374.

83. Wilhelm A. Dinesen, "A Dane's View of Frontier Culture: Notes on a Stay in the United States, 1872–1874," *Nebraska History,* vol. 55 (2) (1974), 284–5.

Chapter 7

1. Kappler, *Indian Affairs, Treaties*, p. 29.

2. Prucha, *The Great White Father*, p. 170.

3. Prucha, *Documents* p, 32.

4. Ibid., p. 66.

5. Grant Foreman, *The Five Civilized Tribes*, (Norman: University of Oklahoma Press, reprint, 1971), p. 423.

6. Prucha, *Documents*, p. 97.

7. Ibid., p. 88.

8. Ibid., p. 70.

9. Blaine, *The Ioway Indians*, pp. 215–16.

10. Kappler, *Indian Affairs*, p. 764.

11. Pawnee Council Volume, OHSAM, pp. 81–82.

12. Barclay White to Commissioner of Indian Affairs, December 22, 1875, NA, Northern Superintendency, RG75 M234 R600.

13. White, "Journals," vol. I, pp. 286ff.

14. Holder, *The Hoe and the Horse*, p. 63.

15. Samuel Janney to Ely Parker, October 29, 1870, NA, Pawnee Agency, RG75 M234 R661.

16. White, "Journals," pp. 297ff.

17. Ibid.

18. Pawnee Council Volume, OHSAM, pp. 46, 59.

19. Ibid., pp. 50–51.

20. Ibid., pp. 61–62.

21. Ibid., p. 63.

22. Ibid.

23. Ibid., p. 71.

24. Ibid., p. 72.

25. Ibid., p. 25.

26. Samuel Janney to Ely Parker, July 10, 1871, NA, Pawnee Agency, RG75 M234 R662.

27. William J. Eccles, *The Canadian Frontier, 1534–1760*, (Albuquerque: University of New Mexico Press, 1974), pp. 124–25.

28. Frank R. Secoy, *Changing Military Patterns on the Great Plains, Monographs of the American Ethnological Society*, vol. XXI, (Locust Valley, New York: J. J. Augustin Publisher, 1953), p. 28.

29. Pawnee Council Volume, November 14, 1870, OHSAM.

30. Ibid., July 7, 1871.

31. Ibid., July 8, 1871.

32. Ibid., September 25, 1871.
33. Ibid., August 17, 1874.
34. Ibid., February 2, 1874.
35. Ibid., March 3, 1874.
36. Wilcomb E. Washburn, *The American Indian and the United States*, vol. I, *American Indian Commissioners' Reports*, Report of Edward P. Smith, Nov. 1, 1874, in Edward P. Smith, November 1, 1874, pp. 194–95.
37. Ibid.
38. White, "Journals," vol. II, pp. 308–309.

Chapter 8

1. Kappler, *Indian Affairs, Treaties*, pp. 156–59.
2. Charles C. Royce, comp., "Schedule of Indian Land Cessions in the United States," in *Eighteenth Annual Report of the Bureau of American Ethnology, 1896–97*, Part 2, Washington: Smithsonian Institution, Government Printing Office, 1899), p. 751. Addison E. Sheldon, "Land Systems and Land Policies in Nebraska," in *Publications of the Nebraska State Historical Society*, vol. XXII (1936), p. 19.
3. Kappler, *Indian Affairs*, p. 571.
4. Francis P. Prucha, *Guide to Military Posts of the United States*, (Madison: State Historical Society of Wisconsin, reprint, 1966), p. 82.
5. Royce, "Indian Land Cessions," p. 819; A. E. Sheldon, "Land Systems," p. 19.
6. Pawnee Council Volume, April 3, 1871, OHSAM.
7. S. W. Green and George H. Thummell to William Burgess, October 10, 1871; William Burgess to C. Delano, October 10, 1871, NA, RG75 M234 R661.
8. Pawnee Council Volume, OHSAM, p. 44.
9. John L. Champe and Franklin Fenega, "Notes on the Pawnee," in *American Indian Ethnohistory Series: Plains Indians, Pawnee and Kansas (KAW) Indians*, David Agee Horr, ed., (New York: Garland, 1974), pp. 77–79.
10. Pawnee Council Volume, OHSAM, p. 44.
11. William Burgess to Edward Parker, May 25, 1872, Pawnee, vol. I, OHSAM, p. 13.
12. Commissioner of Indian Affairs, *Annual Report*, 1875, p. 30.
13. Kappler, *Indian Affairs, Laws*, vol. 1, p. 139.
14. Ibid.
15. Pawnee Council Volume, June 11 and June 14, 1872, OHSAM, pp. 56, 58.
16. Jacob Troth to Barclay White, July 9, 1872, Pawnee vol. 1, OHSAM, p. 45.
17. Jacob Troth to Barclay White, July 18, 1872, Pawnee vol. 1, OHSAM, p. 64. Jacob Troth to Barclay White, July 18, 1872, NA, Pawnee Agency, RG75 M234 R661.
18. Ibid.
19. Barclay White to F. A. Walker, July 20, 1872, NA, Pawnee Agency, RG75 M234 R661. Pawnee Council Volume, OHSAM, p. 70.

20. Contract, October 9, 1872, NA, Pawnee Agency, RG75 M234 R661.

21. Secretary of the Interior to the Commissioner of Indian Affairs, July 31, 1872, NA, Pawnee Agency, RG75 M234 R661.

22. Barclay White to E. P. Smith, June 11, 1873, NA, Pawnee Agency, RG75 M234 R661.

23. Commissioner of Indian Affairs, *Annual Report*, 1873, p. 20.

24. William G. Thummell to E.P. Smith, November 7, 1873, NA, Pawnee Agency, RG75 M234 R661.

25. Pawnee Council Volume, OHSAM, p. 96.

26. Commissioner of Indian Affairs, *Annual Report*, 1874, p. 24.

27. Sheldon, "Land Systems," p. 12.

28. Charles C. Royce, "Cherokee Nation of Indians: A Narrative of Their Official Relations with the Colonial and Federal Government," *Fifth Annual Report of the Bureau of American Ethnology*, (Washington: Smithsonian Institution, Government Printing Office, 1887), pp. 360–61.

29. Kappler, *Indian Affairs, Laws*, pp. 159–61.

30. Ibid.

31. Ibid.

32. Sheldon, "Land Systems," pp. 206, 332.

33. Blaine, unpublished notes.

34. Frances Densmore, "It is Mine, This Country Wide" by Wichita Blaine in *Pawnee Music*, Bulletin 93, BAE (Washington, D.C., Government Printing Office, 1929), p. 58.

Chapter 9

1. Commissioner of Indian Affairs, *Annual Report*, 1849, p. 49.

2. Commissioner of Indian Affairs, *Annual Report*, 1875, p. 218.

3. Pawnee Council Volume, OHSAM, pp. 83, 84.

4. Alfred Sorrenson, "Life of Major Frank North, The Famous Pawnee Scout." Transcript in Oklahoma Historical Society Library.

5. Pawnee Council Volume, OHSAM, p. 87.

6. Jonathan Richards to E. P. Smith, February 5, 1874, NA, Pawnee Agency, RG74 M234 R663.

7. Ibid.

8. Ibid.

9. William Burgess to Barclay White, February 16, 1874, Pawnee vol. 2, OHSAM, p. 82.

10. Ibid.

11. Pawnee Council Volume, OHSAM, p. 89.

12. William Burgess to Barclay White, May 12, 1874, Pawnee vol. 2, OHSAM, p. 168.

13. Pawnee Chiefs to the Commissioner of Indian Affairs, May 20, 1974, NA, Pawnee Agency, RG75 M234 R663.

14. Dunbar, "Letters Concerning the Presbyterian Mission," pp. 668, 733, 763, 773.

15. Ibid.

16. Pawnee Council Volume, OHSAM, p. 91.

17. Ibid., p. 92.

18. John Williamson, "The Story of the Pawnee's Removal South," John Williamson Collection, Series 2, MS 2710, Archives, NSHS, pp. 1–3.

19. B. F. Spooner on Behalf of Pawnees, August 21, 1874, NA, Pawnee Agency, RG75 M234 R663.

20. E. G. Platt to Samuel Janney, June 5, 1871, NA, Pawnee Agency, RG75 M234 R661. Peter Dufy, Lester Platt, and others to Commissioner of Indian Affairs, August 20, 1872, NA, Pawnee Agency, RG75 M234 R661.

21. Lester Platt to E. P. Smith, September 7, 1874, NA, Pawnee Agency, RG75 M234 R663.

22. Dinesen, "A Dane's View," p. 279.

23. Petition of the Pawnee Chiefs to the Honorable Commissioner and Congressional Committee of Indian Affairs, Washington, D.C., September 7, 1874, NA, Pawnee Agency, RG75 M234 R663.

24. Williamson, "Pawnee's Removal South," p. 2.

25. Barclay White to B. Rush Roberts, October 16, 1874, Sixth Annual Report, Board of Indian Commissioners, 1875, p. 57.

26. Pawnee Council Volume, OHSAM, p. 94.

27. Ibid.

28. Williamson, "Pawnee's Removal South," p. 3.

29. Ibid.

30. William Burgess to Barclay White, September 8, 1874, Pawnee vol. 2, OHSAM, p. 235.

31. William Burgess to Commissioner of Indian Affairs, September 15, 1874, NA, OIA, Pawnee W, 1524–1874 in Berlin B. Chapman, "The Establishment of the Pawnee Reservation," Berlin B. Chapman Collection, OHSAM, p. 8.

32. William Burgess to Barclay White, September 11, 1874, Pawnee vol. 2, OHSAM, p. 240.

33. Ibid., p. 255.

34. Commissioner of Indian Affairs to Barclay White, September 22, 1874, NA, OIA, Large Letterbook 120, 196–98.

35. Chapman, "Establishment of the Pawnee Reservation," pp. 8–9.

36. White, "Journals," Volume II, pp. 28–29.

37. Sixth Annual Report, Board of Indian Commissioners, 1874, p. 55.

38. William Burgess, Annual Report, Commissioner of Indian Affairs, Annual Report, 1875, p. 321.

39. Blaine, unpublished notes.

40. William Burgess, Annual Report, Commissioner of Indian Affairs, Annual Report, p. 321.

41. Pawnee Council Volume, OHSAM, pp. 96–101.

42. Sixth Annual Report, Board of Indian Commissioners, 1874, p. 55.

43. To Whom It May Concern from William Burgess, October 8, 1874, Pawnee, vol. 2, OHSAM, p. 256.

44. Ibid., 259.

45. William Burgess to Jonathan Richards, October 8, 1874, Pawnee vol. 2, OHSAM.

46. Terrecowah to Commissioner of Indian Affairs, written by Lester Platt, October 10, 1874, NA, Pawnee Agency, RG75 M234 R663.

47. Pawnee Chiefs to Commissioner of Indian Affairs, written by Lester Platt, October 10, 1874, NA, Pawnee Agency, RG75 M234 R663.

48. William Burgess to Commissioner of Indian Affairs, October 16, 1874, NA, Pawnee Agency, RG75 M234 R662.

49. Ibid., October 21, 1874.

50. William Burgess to Barclay White, October 23, 1874, NA, Pawnee Agency, RG75 M234 R663.

51. William Burgess to J. W. Williamson and A. L. Alexander, October 30, 1874, Pawnee vol. 2, OHSAM, pp. 269–71.

52. Williamson, "Pawnee's Removal South."

53. Ibid., typed copy, p. 4.

54. Ibid., handwritten copy, p. 44.

55. Ibid., typed copy, p. 7.

56. Ibid., handwritten copy, pp. 45–46.

57. Ibid., p. 47.

58. Ibid.

59. Ibid., p. 49.

60. Ibid., p. 51.

61. Ibid., p. 52.

62. Ibid., p. 56.

63. Ibid., pp. 56–57.

64. Ibid., p. 58.

65. Ibid., p. 56.

66. George B. Grinnell, *The Cheyenne Indians: Their History and Ways of Life* Vol. 2, (Lincoln: University of Nebraska Press, 1972), pp. 5, 6, 102, 113, 153–54, 158, 163. Grinnell, *Two Great Scouts*, pp. 145, 261ff.

67. Williamson, "Pawnee's Removal South," p. 62.

68. Ibid., p. 65.

69. Peter J. Powell, *Sweet Medicine: The Continuing Role of the Sacred Arrows, the Sun Dance and the Sacred Buffalo Hat in Northern Cheyenne History*, Vol. I, (Norman: University of Oklahoma Press, 1969), pp. 84–86.

70. Karen D. Petersen, *Plains Indian Art*, (Norman: University of Oklahoma Press, 1971), p. 107. Powell, *Sweet Medicine*, p. 86.

71. Powell, *Sweet Medicine*, 84–85.

72. Mari Sandoz, *Cheyenne Autumn*, (New York: Avon, 1969), pp. 85–86.

73. Sandoz, *Cheyenne Autumn*, pp. 85–86. P. H. Oestreicher, "On the White Man's Road? Acculturation and the Ft. Marion Prisoners," Ph.D. diss. (Michigan State University, 1981), p. 266.

74. John D. Miles to Commissioner of Indian Affairs, December 22, 1874, NA, Upper Arkansas Agency, RG75 M882 R716.

75. Williamson, "Pawnee's Removal South," p. 66.

76. Barclay White to H. R. Clum, October 13, 1871, NA, Pawnee Agency, RG75 M234 R661.

77. Cyprian Tayrien, interview, 1912, in *Oklahoma: A History of the State and Its People* vol. I, by J. B. Thoburn and Muriel Wright (New York: Lewis Historical Publications Company, Inc., 1929), pp. 402–404.

78. Powell, *Sweet Medicine*, p. 85.

79. Kiowa Agency—File: Permits and Passes, November 12, 1874, OHSAM.

80. John B. Dunbar, "Pitaresaru—Chief of the Pawnees," *Magazine of American History*, Volume 5 (5) (1880), p. 344.

81. Ibid., p. 345.

82. Densmore, *Pawnee Music*, pp. 86–91.

83. George E. Hyde, *Pawnee Indians*, p. 321.

84. Sorrenson, "Life of Major Frank North," pp. 125–26.

85. Blaine, unpublished notes.

86. Gen. John Pope to Enoch Hoag, November 6, 1874; telegram from Cyrus Beede to Commissioner of Indian Affairs, November 7, 1874; Barclay White to Commissioner of Indian Affairs, November 7, 1874, NA, Pawnee Agency, RG75 M234 R663.

87. Ibid.

88. Good Chief, Sun Chief, Terrecowah, Captain Chief, and Joseph Esau to Barclay White, November 12, 1874, NA, Pawnee Agency, RG75 M234 R663.

89. T. A. Osborne to Enoch Hoag, December 7, 1874, NA, Pawnee Agency, RG75 M234 R663.

90. Williamson, "Pawnee's Removal South," p. 7.

91. Chapman, "Establishment of the Pawnee Reservation," p. 12.

92. Pawnee Council Volume, November 11, 1874, OHSAM.

93. "Establishment of the Pawnee Reservation," p. 13.

94. William Burgess to E. P. Smith, December 8, 1874, NA, Pawnee Agency, RG75 M234 R663.

95. Ibid.

96. William Burgess to Barclay White, December 12, 1874, NA, Pawnee Agency, RG75 M234 R663.

97. Royce, "Indian Land Cessions," p. 840.

98. William Burgess, Annual Report, 1875, Commissioner of Indian Affairs, *Annual Report*, p. 321. Jonathan Richards, CIA AR, 1875, p. 288.

99. John D. Miles to E. P. Smith, December 10, 1874; Enoch Hoag to E. P. Smith, December 16, 1874, NA, Upper Arkansas Agency, RG75 M234 R882.

Chapter 10

1. William Burgess to E. P. Smith, February 19, 1875, NA, Pawnee Agency, RG75 M234 R663.

2. Ibid.

3. To the Commissioner of Indian Affairs from the Chiefs and Headmen of the Pawnee Tribe of Indians, March 3, 1875, NA, Pawnee Agency, RG75 M234 R663.

4. Blaine, unpublished notes.

5. William Burgess, Annual Report, September 1, 1875, Commissioner of Indian Affairs, *Annual Report*, 1875, p. 321.

6. E. P. Smith to Isaac G. Gibson, March 31, 1875, NA, Pawnee Agency, RG75 M234 R663.

7. White, "Journal," vol. II, p. 40. William Burgess, Annual report, September 1, 1875, CIA AR, 321.

8. Charles Chapin, "Removal of Pawnee and Peace with their Neighbors—A Memoir of Charles Chapin," Nebraska History, vol. 26 (January-March 1945), p. 43.

9. William Burgess to Jonathan Richards, May 18, 1875, Kiowa Agency—Foreign Relations, OHSAM.

10. William Burgess to E. P. Smith, May 20, 1875, NA, Pawnee Agency, RG75 M234 R663.

11. E. P. Smith to the Secretary of the Interior, Forty-fourth Cong., First Ses., Ex. Doc. No. 80, March 6, 1875, p. 4.

12. Ibid.

13. Ibid., B. R. Cowen to E. P. Smith, March 12, 1875.

14. Ibid., p. 5. W. P. Smith to the Secretary of the Interior, April 2, 1875.

15. Paul Stuart, *The Indian Office: Growth and Development of an American Institution, 1865–1900*. Robert Berkhofer, ed., *Studies in American History and Culture*, No. 12 (Ann Arbor: University of Michigan Microfilm Press, 1980), p. 63.

16. Ibid., p. 62.

17. C. Delano to E. P. Smith, Forty-fourth Cong., First Ses. Ex. Doc. No. 80, April 5, 1875, p. 5.

18. Ibid.

19. Ibid., E. P. Smith to F. H. Smith, April 9, 1875.

20. Ibid.

21. Ibid.

22. Ibid., excerpt from *Annual Report*, Board of Indian Commissioners, 1874, p. 7.

23. Pawnee Council Volume, April 18, 1875, OHSAM, p. 102.

24. F. H. Smith to E. P. Smith, December 9, 1875, "Report to the Board of Indian Commissioners on the Removal of the Pawnees to Indian Territory," in Forty-fourth Cong., First Ses., Ex. Doc. No. 80, pp. 7–8.

25. Barclay White to F. H. Smith, September 3, 1875, Forty-fourth Cong., First Ses., (HR) Report No. 241, p. 8.

26. F. H. Smith to E. P. Smith, Op. cit.

27. William Burgess to Office of Indian Affairs, Department of the Interior, February 1, 1875, Estimate of Annuity Goods Required for the Year Ending June 30, 1876, NA, Pawnee Agency, RG75 M234 R663.

28. Jonathan Richards, Annual Report, Commissioner of Indian Affairs, *Annual Report*, 1875, p. 288.

29. M. R. Gilmore, *Uses of Plants by the Indians of the Missouri River Region*, (Reprint, Lincoln: University of Nebraska Press, 1977), p. 8.

30. Commissioner of Indian Affairs, *Annual Report*, 1875, p. 313.

31. Pawnee Council Volume, OHSAM, p. 94.

32. Ibid., pp. 103–105.

33. Resolution, August 18, 1875, NA, Pawnee Agency, RG75 M234 R663.

34. Bids submitted to William Burgess, September, 1875, NA, Pawnee Agency, RG75 M234 R663.

35. William Burgess to E. P. Smith, September 17 and October 1, 1875, NA, Pawnee Agency, RG75 M234 R663.

36. William Burgess to Barclay White, October 13, 1875; Barclay White to William Burgess, October 18, 1875, NA, Pawnee Agency, RG75 M234 R663.

37. Contract bids, various dates, 1875, NA, Pawnee Agency, RG75 M234 R663-0373ff.

38. William Burgess to Jonathan Richards, December 1, 1875, Kiowa—Foreign Relations, OHSAM.

39. Guy R. Moore, "The Pawnees: A Report for the Oklahoma Historical Society," February 5, 1924, Oklahoma Historical Society Library, pp. 14–15.

40. Blaine, unpublished notes.

41. Stacy Howell interview with Martha R. Blaine, June 11, 1983.

42. Author's interview with Garland J. Blaine, July 5, 1965.

43. Blaine, unpublished notes.

44. William T. and Rachel Eaves interview with Martha R. Blaine, October 20, 1982.

45. Phillip Jim interview with Garland J. Blaine, June 26, 1976.

46. Blaine, unpublished notes.

47. Report, Forty-fourth Cong., First Ses., 1876, HR, Ex. Doc. 80, p. 9.

48. Blaine, unpublished notes.

49. Commissioner of Indian Affairs, *Annual Report,* 1875, p. 30.

50. Chapman, "The Establishment of the Pawnee Reservation," p. 20. Kappler, *Indian Affairs,* p. 159. Vol. I, LAWS.

51. Blaine, unpublished notes.

Bibliography and Suggested Readings

Manuscript Collections

Garland J. and Martha R. Blaine Collection. Unpublished Notes and Pawnee Music., in possession of author. Oklahoma City, Oklahoma.
Nebraska State Historical Society. Archives and Manuscripts Division. Luther H. North Collection, ms 449. John Williamson Collection, Series 2, ms 2710.
Oklahoma State Historical Society. Archives and Manuscripts Division. Berlin B. Chapman Collection. "Establishment of the Pawnee Reservation."
Oklahoma State Historical Society, Library Division. Guy R. Moore. "The Pawnees, A Report for the Oklahoma Historical Society." February 5, 1924.
Swarthmore College, Library. Barclay White. "The Barclay White Journals," vols. I, II, III.

Dissertations and Papers

Baker, T. Lindsay. "The Buffalo Trade on the Southern Great Plains, 1830–1870." Symposium: "We Always Had Plenty: Native Americans and the Bison." Oklahoma City, Oklahoma: Center of the American Indian, April 21, 1989.
Flores, Dan. "Tribal Migrations and the Bison Herds." Symposium: "We Always Had Plenty: Native Americans and the Bison." Oklahoma City, Oklahoma: Center of the American Indian, April 21, 1989.
Oestreicher, P. H. "On the White Man's Road? Acculturation and the Ft. Marion Prisoners." Ph.D. diss., Michigan State University, East Lansing, 1981.

Riding-In, James. "Pawnee Removal," Master's thesis, University of California, Los Angeles, 1985.

Federal and State Documents

Board of Indian Commissioners, *Annual Report*. Washington, D.C.: 1874.

Annual Reports of the Commissioners, Indian Affairs. Washington, D.C., Government Printing Office, 1845, 1867, 1869, 1871, 1872, 1873, 1874, 1875.

U.S. Congress. Documents and records. 42 Cong., 3 sess., HR Ex. Doc. 1, Part 2, 1872. *Report of the Secretary of War*. 44 Cong., 1 sess., HR Report No. 241, 1876. *Pawnee Indians*. HR Ex. Doc. No. 80, 1876. *Pawnee Indians in Nebraska*.

Indian Claims Commission. *The Pawnee Tribe of Oklahoma v. United States*. Findings, July 14, 1950; June 17, 1957; June 14, 1960; January 31, 1961.

Kappler, Charles J., comp., *Indian Affairs: Laws and Treaties*. Vol. I, *Laws*. Vol. II, *Treaties*. Washington: 1904.

Organic Acts for the Territories of the United States. Compiled from the *Statutes at Large of the United States*. 56 Cong., 1 sess., Sen. Doc. 148. Washington: Government Printing Office, 1900.

U.S. Statutes at Large. Vol. 18. Sec. 3, p. 449. Indian Appropriations Act, March 3, 1875.

National Archives (NA)

Indian Office Circular. June 12, 1869. Ely Parker to Superintendents and Agents. Office of Indian Affairs, Vol. 90.

Commissioner of Indian Affairs, Office of Indian Affairs (OIA), Letters Sent, Large Letterbook 120.

Northern Superintendency, NA RG75 M234 R600.

Pawnee Agency, NA RG75 M234 R661, R662, R663.

Upper Arkansas Agency, NA RG75 M234 R882.

See Oklahoma Historical Society. Archives and Manuscripts Division (OHSAM). Satellite branch of National Archives Federal Records Center, Fort Worth, for federal records listed below:

Pawnee Council Volume.

Pawnee vols. 1 and 2 (letterpress).

Kiowa Agency—Depredations file.

Kiowa Agency—Foreign Relations file.

Kiowa Agency—Permits and Passes file.

Books, Articles, Memoirs, and Other Printed Sources

Allis, Samuel. "Forty Years Among the Indians and on the Eastern Borders of Nebraska," Transactions and Reports of the Nebraska Historical Society, first series, vol. 2. 1887.

———. "A Presbyterian Mission in Pawnee Country." Collections of the Kansas State Historical Society, vol. XIV. 1915–18.

Anderson, Gary C. "Early Dakota Migration and Intertribal War: A Revision." The Western Historical Quarterly, vol. XI (1) (January 1980).

Barreis, Charles and James E. Porter, eds. American Bottom Archeology: A Summary of the FA-1 270 Project Contribution to the Culture History of the Mississippi River Valley. Urbana: University of Illinois Press, 1984.

Barsh, Russell L. and James Y. Henderson. The Road: Indian Tribes and Political Liberty. Berkeley: University of California Press, 1980.

Belden, George P. The White Chief: Or Twelve Years Among the Wild Indians of the Plains, Gen. James S. Brisbin, ed. Cincinnati and New York: C. F. Vent. Reprinted in facsimile. Athens, Ohio: Ohio University Press, 1974.

Berthrong, Donald J. The Southern Cheyennes. Norman: University of Oklahoma Press, 1975.

Blaine, Garland James and Martha Royce Blaine, "Paresu arirake: The Hunters that Were Massacred." Nebraska History, vol. 58 (3), 1977.

Blaine, Martha Royce, The Ioway Indians. Norman: University of Oklahoma Press, 1979.

———. "The Pawnee-Wichita Visitation Cycle: Historical Manifestations of an Ancient Friendship." In Pathways to Plains Prehistory: Anthropological Perspectives of Plains Natives and Their Pasts. Don G. Wyckoff and Jack L. Hofmann, eds. Oklahoma Anthropological Society, Memoir 3. The Cross Timbers Heritage Association. Contribution 1. Cross Timbers Press, Duncan, Oklahoma. 1982.

———. "The Pawnee Sacred Bundles: Their Present Uses and Significance." Papers in Anthropology, vol. 24, no. 2. Norman: University of Oklahoma Press, Fall 1984.

———. "On to the Reservation: The Nebraska Indians and United States Indian Policy." First Voices. Nebraskaland Magazine, Vol. 62 (1) (Lincoln: 1984).

Champe, John L. and Franklin Fenega, "Notes on the Pawnee." In Plains Indians: Pawnee and Kansas (KAW) Indians, ed. David Agee Horr, ed. American Indian Ethnohistory Series. New York: Garland, 1974.

Chamberlain, Von Del. When Stars Came Down to Earth: Cosmology of the Skidi Pawnee Indians of North America. Ballena Press Anthropological Papers No. 26. Los Altos, California and College Park, Maryland: A Ballena Press/Center for Archaeoastronomy Cooperative Publication, 1982.

Chapin, Charles. "Removal of Pawnee and Peace with their Neighbors—A Memoir of Charles Chapin." Nebraska History, Vol. 26 (January-March 1945).

Danker, Donald F. Man of the Plains: Recollections of Luther North, 1856–1882. Lincoln: University of Nebraska Press, 1961.

Denig, Edwin T. Five Indian Tribes of the Upper Missouri: Sioux, Arickaras, Assiniboines, Crees and Crows. Norman: University of Oklahoma Press, 1961.

Densmore, Frances. Pawnee Music. Bureau of American Ethnology, Bulletin 93. Washington, D.C.: Government Printing Office, 1929.

Dinesen, Wilhelm A. "A Dane's View of Frontier Culture: Notes on a Stay in the United States, 1872–1874." *Nebraska History*, vol. 55 (2) (1974).

Dippie, Brian. *The Vanishing American: White Attitudes and U.S. Indian Policy.* Middletown: Wesleyan University Press, 1982.

Dodge, Col. Richard. *Our Wild Indians: Thirty Years Personal Experience Among the Red Men of the Great West.* Hartford: A. D. Worthington. Chicago: A. G. Nettleton. Reprinted as *Thirty-three Years Among Our Wild Indians,* Freeport, New York: Books for Libraries Press, 1970.

Dorsey, George A. *The Pawnee: Mythology,* Part I. Washington, D.C.: Carnegie Institute, 1906.

———. *Traditions of the Skidi Pawnee.* Memoirs of the American Folk Lore Society, vol. 8. Boston: Houghton Mifflin, Co. London: D. Nutt. Reprinted, Millwood, New York: Kraus Reprints. 1969.

Driver, Harold. *Indians of North America.* Rev. ed. Chicago: University of Chicago Press. 1969.

Dunbar, John B. "Pitalesharu—Chief of the Pawnees." *Magazine of American History*, vol. 5 (5) (1880).

———. "The Pawnees: Their History and Mythology." *Magazine of American History*, vol. 4 (4) (1880).

———. "The Pawnee Indians: Their Habits and Customs." *Magazine of American History*, vol. 5 (5) (1880).

Dunbar, Rev. John. "The Presbyterian Mission among the Pawnees in Nebraska, 1834 to 1836," *Collections of the Kansas State Historical Society*, vol. 11 (1910).

———. "Letters Concerning the Presbyterian Mission in the Pawnee Country near Bellevue, Nebraska, 1831–1849," *Collections of the Kansas State Historical Society*, vol. 14 (1918).

Eccles, William J. *The Canadian Frontier, 1534–1760.* Albuquerque: University of New Mexico Press, 1974.

Eggan, Fred, ed. *Social Anthropology of North American Tribes.* Chicago: University of Chicago Press, 1972.

Ewers, John. *The Horse in the Blackfoot Culture. Classics in Smithsonian Anthropology Series,* no. 3. Washington, D.C.: Smithsonian Press, 1980.

Fletcher, Alice C. *The Hako: A Pawnee Ceremony.* Bureau of American Ethnology. *Twenty-Second Annual Report,* Part 2. Washington, D.C.: Smithsonian Institution, 1904.

Foreman, Grant. *The Five Civilized Tribes.* Reprinted, Norman: University of Oklahoma Press, 1971.

Frazer, R. W. *Forts of the West: Military Forts & Presidios & Posts Commonly Called Forts West of the Mississippi to 1898.* Norman: University of Oklahoma Press, 1977.

Ganoe, William A. *The History of the United States Army.* Rev. ed. Ashton, Maryland: Eric Lundberg Reprint, 1964.

Gilmore, M. R. *Uses of Plants by the Indians of the Missouri River Region.* Reprint, Lincoln: University of Nebraska Press, 1977.

Goodspeed, Weston A., ed. *The Province and the States.* Vol. 5, *Iowa, Nebraska, Wyoming.* Madison: Western Historical Association, 1904.

Grange, Roger T. "An Archeological View of Pawnee Origins." *Nebraska History*, vol. 60 (2) (1979).

Grinnell, George B. *The Cheyenne Indians: Their History and Ways of Life*. Vols. 1, 2. Lincoln: University of Nebraska Press, 1972.

———. *Two Great Scouts and Their Pawnee Batallion: The Experiences of Frank J. North and Luther H. North, Pioneers in the Great West, 1865–1882, and Their Defence of the Building of the Union Pacific Railroad*. Cleveland: Arthur H. Clark. Reprinted, Lincoln: University of Nebraska Press, 1973.

———. *Pawnee Hero Stories and Folk Tales with Notes on the Origin, Customs and Character of the Pawnee People*. New York: Forest and Stream Publishing Company. Reprinted, New York: Charles Scribner's Sons. 1893. Lincoln: University of Nebraska Press, 1961.

Hallowell, Benjamin, Franklin Haines, John H. Dudley, and Joseph Howell. "Quaker Report on Indian Agencies." (Reprint of Society of Friends Delegation Report, 1869). *Nebraska History*, vol. 45 (2) (Summer 1973).

Hodge, Frederick W. *Handbook of American Indians North of Mexico*. U.S. Bureau of American Ethnology, Bulletin 30, Vols. 1 and 2. Washington, D.C.: Smithsonian Institution, 1912.

Hoebel, E. A. *Man in the Primitive World*. 2nd ed. New York: McGraw Hill, 1958.

Holder, Preston. *The Hoe and the Horse on the Plains: A Study of Cultural Development Among North American Indians*. Lincoln: University of Nebraska Press, 1970.

Hyde, George E. *Pawnee Indians*. Denver: University of Denver Press. Reprinted, Lincoln: University of Nebraska Press, 1973.

Lowe, Percival G. *Five Years a Dragoon ('49 to '54) and Other Adventures on the Great Plains*. Kansas City, Missouri: F. Hudson Publishing Company, Reprinted, Don Russell, ed. Norman: University of Oklahoma Press, 1965.

McHugh, Tom. *In the Time of the Buffalo*. Lincoln: University of Nebraska Press, 1979.

Milner, Clyde A., II. *With Good Intentions: Quaker Work among the Pawnees, Otos, and Omahas in the 1870s*. Lincoln: University of Nebraska Press, 1982.

Mooney, James. *Calendar History of the Kiowa Indians*. Washington, D.C.: Smithsonian Institution Press, 1979.

Murie, James R. *The Ceremonies of the Pawnee*. Vols. 1 and 2. *Smithsonian Institution Contributions to Anthropology*, no. 27. Douglas R. Parks, ed. Washington, D.C.: Government Printing Office, 1979.

———. "Pawnee Indian Societies." Anthropological Papers of the American Museum of Natural History, vol. 11, part 7, 1914. New York, N.Y.

Murray, Sir Charles Augustus. *Travels in North America During the Years 1834, 1835, and 1836. Including a Summer Residence with the Pawnee Tribe of Indians, in the Remote Prairies of the Missouri, and a Visit to Cuba and the Azore Islands*. London: R. Bentley; New York: Harper and Brothers. Reprinted, New York: Da Capo, 1974.

Oehler, Gottlieb F. and David Z. Smith. *Description of a Journey and Visit to the Pawnee Indians, Who Live on the Platte River, a Tributary to the Missouri, Seventy Miles from Its Mouth, . . . April 22–May 18, 1851, to Which Is Added a*

Description of the Manners and Customs of the Pawnee Indians, by Dr. D. Z. Smith. New York: [No Publisher]. Reprinted from the *Moravian Church Miscellany*, 1851–1852. New ed. Fairfield, Washington: Ye Galleon Press, 1974.

Oliver, Symmes C. "Ecology and Cultural Continuity as Contributing Factors in the Social Organization of the Plains Indians." *University of California Publications in American Archaeology and Ethnology*, vol. 48, no. 1. Berkeley and Los Angeles: Univ. of California Press, 1962.

Paine, Bayard H. *Pioneers, Indians and Buffaloes*. Curtis, Nebraska: Curtis Enterprise, 1935.

Parkes, H. B. "The Agrarian Counterattack." *Political Parties in American History*. Vols. 1–3. Vol. 2: 1828–1890. Felice A. Bonadio, ed. Morten Borden, gen. ed. New York: G. P. Putnam's Sons, 1974.

Petersen, Karen D. *Plains Indian Art*. Norman: University of Oklahoma Press, 1971.

Phillips, Paul C., and J. V. Smurr. *The Fur Trade*. Vols. 1 and 2. Norman: University of Oklahoma Press, 1967.

Platt, Elvira. "Some Experiences as a Teacher among the Pawnee," Collections of the Kansas State Historical Society, vol. XIV, 1915–1918.

Powell, J. W. "Indian Linguistic Families of America North of Mexico." *Seventh Annual Report of the Bureau of American Ethnology, 1885–1886*. Washington: Smithsonian Institution, Government Printing Office, 1891.

Powell, Peter J. *Sweet Medicine: The Continuing Role of the Sacred Arrows, the Sun Dance and the Sacred Buffalo Hat in Northern Cheyenne History*. Vols. 1 and 2. Norman: University of Oklahoma Press, 1969.

Prucha, Francis P. *Documents of United States Indian Policy*. Lincoln: University of Nebraska Press, 1975.

———. *The Great White Father: The United States Government and the American Indians*. Vols. I and II. Lincoln: University of Nebraska Press, 1984.

———. *Guide to Military Posts of the United States*. Reprinted, Madison: State Historical Society of Wisconsin, 1966.

Richardson, James D., ed. *A Compilation of Messages and Papers of the Presidents, 1789–1902*. Vols. 1-10. Washington, D.C.: Bureau of National Literature and Art, 1907.

Riley, Paul. "The Battle of Massacre Canyon." *Nebraska History*, vol. 54 (2) (1973).

Royce, Charles C. "Cherokee Nation of Indians, A Narrative of Their Official Relations with the Colonial and Federal Government." *Fifth Annual Report of the Bureau of American Ethnology, 1883–1884*. Washington: Smithsonian Institution, Government Printing Office, 1887.

———, comp. "Schedule of Indian Land Cessions in the United States," *Eighteenth Annual Report of the Bureau of American Ethnology, 1896–97* Part 2, Washington: Smithsonian Institution, Government Printing Office, 1899.

Sandoz, Mari. *Cheyenne Autumn*. New York: Avon, 1969.

Secoy, Frank R. *Changing Military Patterns on the Great Plains. Monographs of the American Ethnological Society*, vol. XXI. Locust Valley, New York: J. J. Augustin, 1953.

Sheldon, Addison E. "Land Systems and Land Policies in Nebraska." Publications of the Nebraska State Historical Society, vol. XXII (1936).

Sorrenson, Alfred. "Life of Major Frank North, The Famous Pawnee Scout." "Copied from the Columbus Times, Columbus Nebraska in which it ran as a serial, weekly, beginning with May 9, 1896 and ending January 30, 1897." Transcript in Oklahoma Historical Society Library.

Stolley, William. "The Pawnees." In History of the First Settlement of Hall County, Nebraska. Chapter X: Nebraska History, (Special Issue, April 1946).

Stuart, Paul. The Indian Office: Growth and Development of an American Institution, 1865–1900. Robert Berkhofer, ed. Studies in American History and Culture, no. 12. Ann Arbor: University of Michigan Microfilm Press, 1980.

Tatum, Lawrie. Our Red Brothers and the Peace Policy of President Ulysses S. Grant. John C. Winston Co., 1899. Reprinted, Lincoln: University of Nebraska Press, 1970.

Cyprian, Tayrien. Interview, 1912. In Oklahoma: A History of the State and Its People, by J. B. Thoburn and Muriel Wright. Vol. 1. New York: Lewis Historical Publications Company, Inc., 1929.

Washburn, Wilcomb E. The American Indian and the United States. Vols. 1–4. Vol. 1. American Indian Commissioner's Reports. New York: Greenwood Publishers, 1973.

Wedel, Waldo R. An Introduction to Pawnee Archeology, U.S. Bureau of American Ethnology, Bulletin 112. Washington, D.C.: Smithsonian Institution, Government Printing Office, 1936.

———. "Some Reflections on Plains Caddoan Origins" Nebraska History, vol. 60 (2) (1979).

———. Prehistoric Man on the Great Plains. Norman: University of Oklahoma Press, 1970.

Weltfish, Gene. Caddoan Texts: Pawnee South Bands Dialect. Publications of the American Society of Ethnology, vol. 17. New York: G. E. Stechert, 1937.

———. The Lost Universe, with a Closing Chapter on "The Universe Regained." New York and London: Basic Books. Reprinted as The Lost Universe: Pawnee Life and Culture. Lincoln: University of Nebraska Press, 1977.

White, Richard. The Roots of Dependency: Subsistence, Environment and Social Change among the Choctaws, Pawnees, and Navajos. Lincoln: University of Nebraska Press, 1983.

———. "The Winning of the West: The Expansion of the Western Sioux in the Eighteenth and Nineteenth Centuries." The Journal of American History, vol. LXV (2) (September 1978).

Will, George and George E. Hyde. Corn Among the Indians of the Upper Missouri. Lincoln: Reprinted, University of Nebraska Press, 1964.

Wishart, David J. "The Dispossession of the Pawnee." Annals of the Association of American Geographers, vol. 69, no. 3 (September 1979).

Zweiner, Dan. "Gardens of the Iowa, Garden Varieties" and "A Native American Seed Catalogue." Des Moines: Iowa Natural Heritage Foundation, 1982.

Index

Acculturation: of Indians by government; 41 ff.; of Pawnees and agriculture, resistance to, 42–43; hunting patterns, 44; chiefs' attitude toward, 46; purpose of, 143

Adobe Walls (trading settlement): 253

Agencies: Whetstone Agency, 119, 121, 127, 128; Spotted Tail Agency, 120; Santee Agency, 122, 125, 126, 128, 131; Wichita Agency, 217, 255, 262, 266, 271, 288; council of, regarding Pawnee removal to, 217–18; schools of, 218; tribes of unsettled, 221; Pawnees to travel to and desire to live at, 237; Cheyenne and Arapaho Agency, on Pawnee removal route, 248; location of, 251, 255; "Advance Party" to, 261; Quapaw Agency, 263, 266; U.S. Consolidated Agency (Five Civilized Tribes), 264; Sac and Fox Agency, 266, 270; Pawnees arrive at, 269; Osage Agency, 271; to remove from, 272; Pawnees plant crops at, 279; Kaw Agency, 283

Agriculture: South American, 48; European, 408

Alexander, A. L. (Pawnee Agency employee): 237, 270

Alights on the Cloud (Cheyenne): 249

Allis, Samuel (Pawnee missionary): on Sioux warfare, 99 n.; early Pawnee school of, 164

Allotment of land in severalty to Indians: Act of 1886, 43; reasons for, 43; proposed for Pawnees, 43, 45; effects of Sioux attacks on, 44; Pawnees pressured to accept, 45; suggested by Quakers, 146; government reasons for, 158–59; impracticability of, 159; Pawnee chiefs resist, 160–62; allotment for Santee Sioux, Omahas, and Winnebagos, 160–62; Pawnees view of, 162–63

American Bottoms, archeological site: 32 n.

Anadarko, Okla.: 287

Animals: sacred animals, kinship names for, 69; anthropomorphism, 69; hunted, 73, 76; bears revered, 74

Annuity: definition of, 181; early Indian experiences with, 181; government ideas for uses of, 181–85; Indians loss

$27.95